VICTORIA WOOD

VICTORIA WOOD

Neil Brandwood

This paperback edition published in Great Britain in 2006 by
Virgin Books Ltd
Thames Wharf Studios
Rainville Road
London W6 9HA

First published in 2002 by Virgin Books Ltd

ISBN (10) 075351124X
(13) 9780753511244

Typeset by Phoenix Photosetting, Chatham, Kent

Printed and bound in Great Britain by Mackays of Chatham

ACKNOWLEDGEMENTS

Thanks to the following:

Sarah Lester.

Anne and Peter Brandwood, Susan, Jeanette, Dave, Mark, Lee, Alex, Nicola, Laura, Claire and Jack.

Bill Allen, Michele Bowker, Brian Carr, Saiqa Chaudhari, Victor and Natalia Cherepanov, Rich Connor, Mike Crutchley, Tony Devine, John Ellaby, John England, Trudy Hamilton, Paul Heaton, Sarah Hesketh, Ellen Kirby, Jo Langdon, Sue and Rebecca Lester, Sheila McNulty, Jackie and Tony Menzies, Tony "The Tiger" Parkinson, Dany Robson, Reshma Rumsey, Jen Smith, Tracy Stott, Andrew Swinton, Phil Thorp, David Walsh, Maxine Wolstenholme, Jane Judd and Claire Kingston.

'I have enough ambitions to live five lives.'

Victoria Wood

PROLOGUE

THE chubby little girl is full of anticipation as she climbs into her father's car for the one-and-a-half mile drive down the rutted track for the rendezvous at the bottom of Castle Hill Road. Passing Gypsy Brook and Hercules Farm on the right and Harwood Fields and the disused quarry on the left, she can barely contain her excitement at the thought of what is to come.

Back at the house her birthday buffet is laid out for the party. Games have been prepared and the candles stand on her cake ready to be lit, blown and wished upon.

It is not simply her birthday that makes it such a special occasion; for the first time her classmates will be coming to *her* home. Its remoteness usually discourages visitors.

Just before reaching the church the girl's father turns right at Gallows Hill. The car continues on its journey to Jericho, a name inspired by the 'Cities of Judgement' sermon given by the Methodist evangelist John Wesley on one of his visits.

When they reach the designated pick-up point the little girl's joy evaporates. Only one classmate stands there – Graham Howarth. She is crestfallen; the other children must have better things to do with their Saturday.

'Happy birthday,' says Graham, as he gets into the car.

The girl smiles bravely, but the agony and humiliation are prolonged by her well-meaning father who decides to drive to the home of Dennis Ford, one of the absent party guests. Mrs Ford says he is out playing somewhere.

The car begins the slow climb back through the bleak landscape to Birtle Edge House.

MORE than thirty years later the little girl – now a woman – makes her way up the same road. This time she is in the driving seat and knows that millions of people will share her journey.

She steers the Land Rover Discovery past a recently planted wood next to the church, little guessing the congregation had considered naming it in her honour.

She is accompanied by a film crew. They are shooting a documentary on her – Britain's best-loved comedienne. She has sold out more shows at the Royal Albert Hall than any other solo performer, an experience she described as 'instant gratification, like having two-and-a-half thousand friends round, and you're the funniest one in the room'. She has been voted the person most people would like as their next-door neighbour, and it was rumoured that the most famous woman in the world, Diana, Princess of Wales, wanted her as a friend.

For the past twelve years her birthday has been listed in *The Times*.

CHAPTER 1

*'I believe we all have a certain time in our lives that we're good at. I
wasn't good at being a child.'*

Victoria Wood

WHEN Helen Wood gave birth to her fourth and final child in 1953 the
relief she felt at the baby's safe delivery may well have been tinged with
disappointment. It was another girl.

Helen and Stanley Wood's first child, a boy whom they named
Christopher, had been born almost a generation earlier, in 1940.
Penelope arrived on 2 August 1945, and Rosalind followed almost five
years to the day later, on 4 August 1950.

The two slim, dainty and dark-haired Wood girls had already forged
a strong bond and developed a closeness that left the newcomer to the
family in an unenviable position. Three was a crowd; another sister was
not required and lacked the novelty that a baby brother would have
brought.

The birth of Victoria Wood on 19 May was dutifully announced in
the *Bury Times* four days later, more as a matter of routine than of pride.
It was the done thing, and Victoria's siblings had previously been
introduced in the same terse few lines. The fact that Helen had yet
another baby was certainly no cause for celebration, and Victoria grew
up suspecting her mother wanted a career instead of her.

Victoria was the only baby born in the upstairs delivery room of
Holyrood Maternity Home that day. The building stood on Bury Old
Road in Prestwich, a small town five miles north of Manchester, whose
most notable claim was that it had one of the largest mental asylums in
Europe. The Woods' other children had been born in less comfortable
circumstances, but Stanley's dedication to the world of insurance meant
he could afford the £10 a week for Helen's stay in the private home
during her final pregnancy.

Mother and baby returned home ten days after the birth on the day
that Britain's new queen was crowned. The coincidence influenced

Helen and Stanley's choice of a regal name for their daughter, and it was a decision that newspaper and magazine subeditors have delighted in ever since. The reign of 'Comedy Queen Victoria', who is often described as 'amused' or 'victorious', serves as alternative headline fodder whenever the 'Wood' wordplay dries up.

The name was highly appropriate. Marie Lloyd, the risqué star of music hall who was known for her saucy songs and is regarded as the very first British comedienne, was actually called Matilda Alice Victoria Wood. Years later, Stanley's daughter would joke in her own stage show: 'They call me Vic because I'm blue and I bring tears to your eyes.' It was a line worthy of her namesake and predecessor.

Marie Lloyd would no doubt have had fun with the name Ramsbottom. It is a word that has an irresistibly humorous ring to it and it is easy to understand why Victoria, never one to waste a comic opportunity, sometimes gives the impression that she lived in this picturesque village within the borough of Bury in Lancashire. In actual fact the first and only home Victoria knew in Bury was more than four miles away at number 98 Tottington Road. Stanley had bought the house on 22 January 1952 for £1,600. The end of a block of four spacious terraced houses set back from the road, it had the advantage of being just ten minutes' walk from Bury town centre while being elevated above its industrial and commercial heart.

Victoria stresses she is 'definitely middle class'. It is a social stratum she knows intimately, having imbibed suburban mores from birth. Be it in song, sketch or stage show, the world of the middle classes dominates Victoria's work. She delights in and derides the culture of hostess trolleys, champagne-coloured bathroom suites and shopping trips to Benetton, and her audiences lap up the mockery.

In 1953 Stanley's financial circumstances reflected the growing prosperity of the country as a whole. As well as the comfortable house on Tottington Road he was able to afford his first car, an Austin Ruby. It has to be said, however, that the car was more a work necessity than a family luxury: Manufacturers Life of Canada had offices in Manchester but Stanley, who worked as an insurance underwriter, spent most of his time visiting clients at their homes and businesses.

Victoria escaped being working class by just seven years. When her parents first arrived in Bury in 1946 with Chris and Penny, life did not look promising. Having previously lodged with relatives in Manchester they decided to strike out on their own, and rented two rooms in a shared house on Walshaw Road.

'Without wishing to sound like a Hovis advert, it was very hard,' recalls Chris Foote Wood. 'We didn't suffer in any way. We were always dry, warm and fed, but it was very spartan.'

The weekly treat came on Saturdays, when a box of sweets would be taken down from on top of a cupboard and they would each select one. Sometimes Stanley would buy a Mars Bar during their Sunday walks and divide it into four on their return home.

Helen found it easier to cope with the conditions than her husband as she had experienced the hardship of growing up in Bradford, a poor area of Manchester. Her family, the Mapes, lived in a small terrace on Gibbon Street, which was where Helen, or Ellen Colleen as she was christened, was born on 14 October 1919. Her boiler fireman father, John, fought in France in the First World War but returned to Britain after being gassed. According to Chris Foote Wood, he was incapacitated, but not enough to stop him having a large family.

Both John and Ada Mape were of Irish descent, and Chris believes the Irish influence has contributed to his sister's talent.

'I'm convinced in my own mind that the Irish blood is a factor in Victoria's success. There's the dourness and stability of my father's Lancashire side of the family and the entertainment from the Irish side.'

It is to Victoria's credit that she has never used the struggles of her relatives to add background colour to her public persona. Lesser entertainers and professional Northerners might have been tempted to treat their interviewers to moist-eyed reminiscences about their exaggerated humble origins, but the fiercely private Victoria has no truck with that. Quite the opposite in fact.

In the song 'Northerners' she sent up the clichés of Northern hardship by adopting the role of an unsuccessful singer who cannily swaps her skin-tight suits for shawls and boots and becomes a wealthy star by pretending to be Northern. Accompanied by washboard, she traded on every stereotypical image of grimness imaginable, from back street abortion and the outside privy, to headscarves and mushy peas.

Victoria stripped away the sentimentality even further in the sketch 'Service Wash' in which she played a Northern pensioner reminiscing fondly about the good old days when rugs were made by stitching mice onto sacking and you could hardly hear yourself coughing up blood for the sound of clogs.

When *Observer* journalist Richard Brooks made the mistake of asking whether Victoria had ever holidayed in the working-class Mecca of Blackpool as a child, her loathing of being seen as a lowly Lancashire lass revealed itself. Stung by the assumption of stereotype, she rounded on him. 'What do you take me for?' she barked. 'We used to go to Vienna.' The journalist expressed disbelief but it was true: Stanley drove the family across Europe with a Sprite Musketeer four-berth caravan in tow.

'He just had this idea that I was from the North and would come in with clogs and a shawl and a tin bath,' Victoria later complained of Brooks.

Even before she was born, the Woods were already upwardly mobile. In August 1947 they swapped their overcrowded lodgings on Walshaw Road for a comfortable semi of their own in Ramsey Grove. The purchase was made possible by Stanley supplementing his income with a variety of odd jobs. 'I don't want to go into detail, but he was very enterprising,' says his son. Helen too, was doing her bit by taking part-time work as a telephonist and market researcher.

A modest boost to the Wood-family income came in their first year at the new house, when Stanley's 168-page naval thriller, *Death on a Smokeboat*, written under the butch nom de plume of Ross Graham, was published by Hurst and Blackett.

The novel was just one of the many works he would publish over the years. Although Stanley left school early for a job in a flour mill, an incomplete education did not seem to have disadvantaged him in matters literary. Indeed, the ever-resourceful Stanley would later use his experiences at the mill as the basis for a play. He had sold his first play at the age of sixteen and was a keen theatregoer from a young age. This was largely due to the many trips he made with his mother, Eleanor, to Manchester's Palace Theatre, Hippodrome, Theatre Royal and Miss Horniman's Gaiety Theatre.

His father, John, had won the Croix de Guerre in the First World War, but at the outbreak of the Second Stanley, initially at least, reached for his pen rather than a gun. In *Mrs Clutterbuck Over Europe* he described how an indomitable, no-nonsense, Northern matron put Hitler in his place.

Published by Samuel French in 1939, the broad-humoured comic verse was written in Lancashire dialect. It told the tale of the comically overweight Mary Anne Eliza Jane Clutterbuck and her attempts to obtain a gas mask that would fit over her five chins. Her search took her from her home town of Tubtwistle to Whitehall and then to Hitler's private den. As she steamrolled through bureaucracy she was constantly insulted about her weight (at one point she is advised to apply for a specially produced animal gas mask for herself, marking the envelope OUTSIZE PONY) and frustrated (there is a note on 10 Downing Street saying SPRING CLEANING. BACK NEXT WEEK). Eventually she confronted Hitler behind closed doors. After the meeting she tottered out, secure in the knowledge that her street would never be bombed, but remained tight-lipped about what took place. The only way to get something done quickly and well, she concluded, was to do it 'thesel'.

The writing would continue throughout most of Stanley's life. Besides the satirical lyrics he would set to popular tunes of the day for the company's annual do, he also wrote everything from radio comedy scripts for Wilfred Pickles to plays, novels and a radio programme about the sinking of the Mary Rose. Radio was one of his favourite media but, for some inexplicable reason, he rationed broadcasts.

'The radio was quite restricted in our household, surprisingly,' remembers Chris Foote Wood. 'I don't know why. It was a case of under the bedclothes.' He says there was always a market for Stanley's work and regrets that his father could not bring himself to abandon insurance to become a full-time writer. 'I'm sure he could have been a great success but he was a family man mainly. He always thought his first duty was to hold down a regular job and look after his family. It was the psychology of the time.'

Stanley's selfless side also emerged in his public-spiritedness. 'He was a big organiser, a Mr Fix-It. He had fingers in every pie,' says Chris. 'He used to organise all sorts of events, shows and charity dos. For several years after the war he booked the Derby Hotel for a week before Christmas for a toy fair. He had contacts, God knows how. He got toy manufacturers to come along and sell their toys. It was an amazing thing.'

Besides his theatrical, literary and community interests, Stanley was also an enthusiastic musician and played the piano semi-professionally in a dance band in Manchester.

Like Stanley, Ellen, who preferred to be known as 'Helen', had seen her education end prematurely when she left school at fourteen without any qualifications. The two of them had a mutual interest in Liberal politics, but it was at a Young Communist rally in Manchester where they first met.

Stanley was born on 1 July 1912, at 38 Lightoaks Road, a pleasant terraced house with a neat front garden on a tree-lined street in Pendleton, Salford. His father was a post office clerk and his mother also worked for the post office for a period. When Stanley was fifteen they moved to a larger house at 21 Belgrave Road in nearby Chorlton-cum-Hardy.

There was no doubt that Helen Mape was definitely marrying 'up' when she wed Stanley on 11 July 1940 at Manchester Register Office, even though her father had by then become a mill foreman and the family were living at the more upmarket 358 Lower Broughton Road in Salford. On paper nothing could have seemed more respectable. Stanley was an insurance claims inspector and his bride was working as a clerk for a raincoat manufacturing firm. It bore all the hallmarks of an unremarkable wedding, except that Helen was already four months' pregnant.

One can only guess the effect the discovery had on the young couple. The law and the health risks meant abortion was not an option, even if it had been desired. At 27 Stanley, who was still living with his parents, may have been ready for marriage, but Helen, whose ambitious streak would become apparent in time, did not necessarily share his enthusiasm.

By the time the baby was born on 15 December 1940, in St Mary's Hospital, Prestbury, Stanley and Helen had found accommodation at 8 Heathbank Road, Cheadle Hulme. It was not home for long, as

Stanley's war obligations took the family south to Plymouth. He became a sublieutenant in the Royal Naval Volunteer Reserve and they took up residence at 1 Townsend Villas.

Chris remembers his father telling him that he captained a destroyer, but there were no exaggerated heroics. Occasionally it would stumble across a German ship in the Channel when it was foggy and fire a few shots, but that was about as dramatic as it got.

The surprise and panic caused by Helen's first pregnancy had understandably made the couple cautious about being caught out again. Money was tight and the upheavals caused by the war meant circumstances were not ideal for another baby. This could explain the five-year gap between Chris's birth and Penny's arrival at the Alexandra Home in Devonport, Plymouth, in August 1945. Although Stanley's occupation was stated as 'sublieutenant' on Penny's birth certificate, he insisted that 'author' was added in parentheses; writing evidently held more attraction than battle or insurance and the war allowed for some indulgence and a temporary escape from the workaday world.

The Wood's first daughter was born at a more stable time than her brother. The war in Europe was over, and it was quickly followed by the Japanese surrender. Hostilities may have ceased but Stanley, who had gone on to become a divisional officer at the Royal Naval Barracks at Devonport, had to wait until he was demobbed in June 1946 before he could return to his Northern roots.

Had the family decided to stay at Townsend Villas and settle in the South it is doubtful the public would have ever heard the name Victoria Wood. Victoria herself is certain that she would not have become what she is today had she not been born and raised in Lancashire. 'I think there's something special about coming from the North West. Most of our good comedians come from the North West,' she has said. 'I think there's something special about the way people talk and the attitude people have. People are very ironic there which they tend not to be in other parts of the country. I just think it's given me a lot.'

The return to Lancashire meant a return to the world of insurance for Stanley. For some, it may have seemed a drab comedown, but Stanley, who would go on to specialise in insuring pharmaceutical chemists, derived a great deal of satisfaction from his work.

'Why they settled in Bury, I honestly don't know,' says Chris Foote Wood. Bury is a typical East Lancashire cotton town with the motto *Industry Overcomes All Things*. It has the dubious honour of being Home of the Black Pudding.

The town was a coincidentally apt place for someone fresh from naval service. It was the home town of Robert Whitehead, inventor of the torpedo and who, incidentally, was the great-grandfather of the famous von Trapp children. But the town's most famous son is Sir Robert Peel, creator of the Metropolitan Police. A tower was erected on the bleak Holcombe Hill in his honour and a statue of the former prime minister stands proudly in the town centre, unfortunately gesturing to the men's public toilets.

The Woods' decision to settle in the town was most probably due to Bury Liberal Association appointing Stanley as the Liberal agent for the borough. As the agent for Bury and Radcliffe in the 1950 General Election, Stanley would need to draw on all his skills at salesmanship to persuade the electorate to share his political passion. The candidate was the Oxford-educated history master at Bury Grammar School, Colin Hindley. For once, Stanley's persuasive charms would desert him. The Conservative candidate won with 26,485 votes, Labour polled 25,705 and Hindley received a meagre 5,662 votes – the smallest Liberal vote in Bury since 1942. Seemingly, the Bury public were more convinced by Stanley's insurance policies than his political ones.

His reaction to the humiliating result was splashed across the front page of the *Bury Times* under the headline: LIBERALS DETERMINED TO MAKE A FIGHTING COMEBACK. 'Although it has been said it was a thoughtful election,' he said, 'I feel we were up against a sort of cup final-cum-football pools mentality with the majority of the voters seeing it as a two-party fight.' Stanley believed it was inevitable that in the future there would be a fairer system of distributing seats so that millions of votes would not be wasted. But his mood was buoyant and he claimed Bury's Liberals would become more active and confirmed in their beliefs. Their attitude, he said, was: 'When are we going to have another fight?'

He was being somewhat over-optimistic. When the next General Election was held in October 1951, confidence was so low that, for the first time in twenty years, Bury Liberals did not even have a candidate. Perhaps bruised by defeat, Stanley never stood in any elections himself. But his Liberal sympathies influenced the young Chris, who used to help him deliver campaign leaflets.

Victoria's main memory of living at 98 Tottington Road is of sitting in bed, reading. But even at such a tender age a yearning for celebrity had already begun, and she had a feeling inside that one day she would be on stage. 'I remember sitting in our garden on Tottington Road thinking "I want to be famous". I can remember that from before I was five. It's very, very clear to me,' she said.

'I don't know whether it's partly being the youngest of four and feeling sort of a bit anonymous and wanting to make my mark and feeling that I couldn't really compete with the rest of my family – and so I had to do something different, I had to find another way through. It might be that.' Her idea of fame meant being somebody of significance. 'I didn't feel important and I wanted to.'

In some families the youngest child is pampered, but that was not the case with the Woods. Victoria felt she was one of those people who was just there. Penny and Rosalind were quite happy without her company, Stanley's spare time was taken up with writing, and Helen's attention was focused on Chris. He had a severe bout of tuberculosis when young, and spent months in bed.

'All I have ever wanted to do is make people laugh, probably to make people like me,' said Victoria.

Occasionally there would be opportunities to make a mark as a youngster. Entertainment had been a part of Stanley's childhood and it was a tradition he handed down. Chris remembers having to dance, sing, recite or play the piano whenever he visited his paternal grandparents, and Victoria was also encouraged to perform.

She recalled: 'When I was very, very little I pulled faces a lot – it was what I could do, what I was good at. They used to say, "Go in the kitchen and make up a face." I used to go out, come back with a new expression and be very amusing to people.'

Those front room performances might have been the only concerts Victoria ever gave if one Sunday afternoon outing had ended differently.

'I remember Victoria straying onto our land once,' says Joan Wood (no relation) who lived four doors away at the other end of the Tottington Road terrace. 'She was lost or misplaced. She was only a little girl when she wandered into the rough at the bottom where there were trees and rhododendrons. It was a rough patch leading down to the water. One afternoon there was a ring at the bell. It was the two elder ones and they asked could they go through to have a look because they'd lost Victoria.'

Joan's husband, Neville, accompanied Chris and Penny down the steps and they found Victoria in the undergrowth.

'He picked her up and twisted his knee coming back up the steps. He always joked that it was because of Victoria Wood that he had to have a cartilage operation. The cartilage used to come out but he could manoeuvre it back,' she recalls fondly.

Joan was the only woman in the terrace who had anything in common with Helen: both women were roughly the same age and both had to contend with small children (Joan gave birth just a year before Victoria was born). But despite such apparent similarities, there was little closeness.

'I didn't have a lot to do with her. There was no popping into each other's houses or exchanging Christmas cards. I used to see her pushing the pram down the road and we'd stop and talk about the children, but that was about it.'

More often than not Helen would be making her way to the embroidery shop at the bottom of the road. Needlework was a hobby of hers and she was a staunch member of the Costume Society, travelling all over the country to attend shows, events and exhibitions.

One of Victoria's most outstanding talents is the ability to create finely drawn comic characters who remain believable in their absurdity. Explaining their origins, she said: 'They're not invented characters. They do exist. Maybe I remember them from my very early childhood when we lived in a street.' Her immediate next-door neighbour on Tottington Road could have been the template for the crouched and senile Mrs Overall of Victoria's celebrated soap opera, *Acorn Antiques*. Joan Wood has vivid memories of the occupant of number 96. 'A very, very old lady called Mary Park lived there on her own. She was a little bent old thing with a bun. She'd been seen distressed on the doorstep. She should never have been there on her own. Her family had owned an antiques shop on Bolton Street.'

The fourth occupants of the row were two spinsters. Miss Gladys Craighill was the manageress of a leather stall in Bury indoor market, and Miss Mary Wolstenholme managed a gown shop in Bolton Street.

Mrs Wood herself is vaguely recognisable in some of Victoria's characters. 'They live in a beautiful cottage just outside Cambridge,' she says of her textile artist son Michael ('He's got a piece in Brisbane Cathedral') and his wife. 'They've no children; they have rabbits.'

It was a lonely life at Tottington Road for Victoria, who does not remember having any friends or visitors. Prior to beginning Elton County Primary School she believed she was the only child in Bury, and on her very first day at school she embraced a male classmate because, according to her, she had never seen a little boy before. So isolated had she been that she had little understanding of how to behave – even claiming all lost school property as her own.

No sooner had Victoria started at the school than the Woods decided to move house. A change of school at such an early age would have been an unsettling experience for most small children, but the location of Victoria's new home would have a more profound effect on her. Ironically, the girl who grew up to be voted the ideal neighbour, had no neighbours. Initially damaging, but ultimately forming her, the isolation ruled out any hope of a normal childhood.

'I come from a pretty ordinary place,' claims Victoria, but it would have been difficult for the Woods to find a more extraordinary home than Birtle Edge House. Perched high on the moors above Bury, in its lofty position it commands a tremendous view over the Pennines and across to Manchester. But the remote location also means the house is frequently enveloped by fog. In the winter it is not unusual for it to be cut off by snow for up to two weeks at a time, and when it rains the narrow road becomes a stream.

'Northern country. Bits of moors, bits of barns, bits of factories . . . It wasn't pretty country, *at all* . . . but it was space, it had space', is how she remembers it. The town's elders had viewed the site more positively when they decided to build Birtle Edge House half-a-century earlier.

They deemed its 'bracing heights' perfect for the new Bury Children's Holiday Home, which would provide beneficial breaks and 'delightful holidays' in the country for the town's most poverty-stricken youngsters. The Home, which was later used as an observation post during the Second World War and to house Polish war refugees, was the gift of local businessman Cuthbert Cartwright Grundy, and was officially opened on 1 August 1908. It was a great civic occasion and assembled guests witnessed Warth Prize Band lead a procession of fifty poor children from Bury Ragged School.

'We do not pretend to have solved any great social problem, but we earnestly trust that some boy or girl who shall come here will carry away with them some thought of beauty and order, given them by some wild flower, or by a bird's sweet song, which will help them to grow to noble manhood or pure womanhood, and enable them to fill useful places in the life and work of our town,' said Mr H. Crabtree, the secretary of the Home, in his opening day speech. When the Woods moved in exactly fifty years later one of the first things they did was rip out the overgrown rhododendrons.

The idea of a large, sprawling house on the hillside may sound idyllic, but the building cannot escape its past. Even today, when the sunshine is glinting off the white walls, and Red Admirals flutter around those rhododendron bushes which survived Helen's hands, there is an air of institutionalised austerity about the place.

'Underfed and delicate children will be better for coming to this home, breathing the air of these hills and having good, nourishing food,' Mr Crabtree had said in 1908. The Wood children, by comparison, lived more frugally according to Joan Lloyd, who often saw Helen doing her shopping at Holt's, the corner shop at the bottom of Castle Hill Road. 'She always used to buy a quarter of ham or tongue or corned beef for all of them; I don't know how they didn't starve,' she recalls. Victoria herself says the meals Helen prepared, of which Spam curry was a speciality, were 'horrendous'.

The framed portrait of Cuthbert Grundy was not the only thing the Woods inherited when they became the new owners of Birtle Edge House. Inadequate plumbing and the absence of electricity was the legacy of the building's past. Electricity was quickly installed, but up until 1986, when a bore hole was finally made, Stanley Wood had to walk half a mile to pump the household water supply into a holding tank.

As Bury Children's Holiday Home, the entrance to the building was across a quadrangle. It boasted a veranda where Sunday services were held in the summer, a large entrance hall, a dining room that seated thirty, two dormitories with enough room for twenty-eight beds, a huge kitchen, a scullery and a pantry.

Helen Wood immediately set about dividing the house with hardboard walls. One of the dormitories was converted into three bedrooms for the girls, Stanley had an office and Helen had her own name-plated room which she used for sewing. The locks installed on all the internal doors for security summed up the distinctly individual lives.

'We lived in a very strange way. We all lived in separate rooms,' said Victoria. 'We weren't the most demonstrative of families. In fact, the idea was to be on your own as much as you could. We used to get our meals and retreat to our rooms.' The living room was rarely used, its neon lights making it look, as Victoria says, 'like Death Row'.

There were no friends or neighbours calling in, and no family get-togethers. Helen did not believe in festivities, leaving Stanley to carve the Christmas turkey. She was against even relatives visiting and as a result Victoria never knew her aunts and uncles, and remembers only her paternal grandmother. A rented television did provide a welcome focus, but Helen always insisted on sending it back in the summer because she thought it was wrong to watch it then. The field-sized garden would have been ideal for pony or dog, but there were to be no surrogate friends to keep the lonely Victoria company. 'We've never been a family to keep pets,' says Chris Foote Wood.

As Chris had left home in 1958 to study engineering at Durham University, there was no time for any real relationship to be forged between him and Victoria. The age gap, and the fact that he already had a child of his own by the age of 23 added to the situation and, although still in touch, they remain relatively distant.

'When you're a child thirteen years is a lifetime. I was five when he went away to university and I didn't have much to do with him after that,' said Victoria. With her sisters it was different. They were there but Victoria was made to feel like an unwelcome outsider.

'They were *horrible*. *All* sisters are horrible. Well, mine were. Very bossy, and they treated me like a nuisance. They were very proficient at giving "young Victoria" a good quashing, telling-off and bossing-about.'

Whatever she wanted to do, they found very babyish, although they did indulge in childish sadism, using Victoria as the butt of their teasing. 'I was cruelly sat on, sat on and tormented for many years, and made to eat putty.'

Unfortunately, Victoria's relationship with her parents, particularly Helen, did not make up for the rather strained state of affairs she had with her siblings.

'Indomitable' and 'scary' are the words she uses to typify her mother. They were qualities that did not endear Helen to those living in the Birtle area. Joan Lloyd's memories of her as being a rather difficult and cold woman are typical of the few people who actually came into contact with her. 'She was very aloof and snobby. You never got past first base with her. She wasn't popular at all. She wouldn't even look at you.' Her memories of Stanley are more favourable and she remembers him as 'a bit of a toff, a pleasant, well-spoken man who always gave you a smile'.

Helen's flintiness did not mellow with age and years later, when she was the sole inhabitant of Birtle Edge House, she was still giving short shrift to outsiders. One unfortunate woman made the mistake of telephoning to see if she was OK after a particularly deep fall of snow. 'I am perfectly capable of looking after myself,' declared Helen loftily, before slamming the receiver down.

Distant if not dysfunctional, is probably the best way of describing life at Birtle Edge House. The closest Victoria came to acknowledging the parental ambivalence came in 1996 when she was the subject of *The South Bank Show*. In one telling segment Melvyn Bragg probed her about the effects of Helen and Stanley's disinterest. She responded with a rueful smile, a jutting chin and a sigh as she warily chose her words. 'That's just the way it was and I didn't expect anything different really.

That's what we were used to: that we all lived in a very separate way.' Tactfully, she avoided coming out and saying her parents did not care what she did, and instead said: 'There was encouragement in the sense that you could do what you wanted, which was a bit scary in a sense.'

As to Helen's reaction after viewing the documentary? 'She just said how nice the garden looked,' says Pam Wheeldon who, with her husband, bought Birtle Edge House in the mid-1990s when Helen moved to Skipton.

The parental indifference must have hurt and Victoria dealt with it by withdrawing. There were no attempts at gaining Helen's or Stanley's approval or attention. 'I'm glad to be doing something they like, but I always did what I wanted to do . . . I didn't do it for them,' she once said. 'I love them and I'm very proud of them, but I can't ever remember really trying to please them.'

Even when her youngest daughter became nationally famous, Helen refused to discuss her. She would immediately start talking about her other children whenever a rare visitor to Birtle Edge House spotted Victoria on family photographs, and would later take to hiding them in a drawer. 'My mother won't discuss me with other people,' Victoria once said. 'If someone says "You sound awfully like Victoria Wood" she might admit through gritted teeth we're related.'

Stanley, however, basked in Victoria's glory and even introduced himself as her father to complete strangers at bus stops. 'He was a frustrated entertainer. He'd done shows in the Navy and things like that. He would have loved to have done what I do,' Victoria said. Stanley would share a double act of sorts with his daughter in the wryly ironic letters they exchanged in later life. Victoria believes he too would have achieved success as a comedian or musician if he had been of a different generation, but there was never any question of Stanley forcing Victoria to live his ambitions for him as he enjoyed his insurance work so much.

Stanley was the more obvious influence on Victoria's career, but Helen did contribute in part. Despite claiming to have no sense of humour, Helen was, according to Victoria, unwittingly funny and very observant, and was used as the basis for many of Victoria's older comic characters. Ultimately though, Victoria is reluctant to give her parents total credit for her talent. She concedes that she inherited her mother's industry and determination and her father's creativity, but she does not omit 'whatever's thrown in on top of that to make me an individual'.

Television comedy shows were a welcome relief to the lonely, young Victoria. She claims she 'wasted' her childhood slumped in front of the box, but the ideas and dreams it planted in her were a vital part of her adult success. It enabled her to see how comedy worked and, in the absence of close friends and family, it was the performers who set an example. 'When I started watching television a lot, I wanted to do that, to "do television" as a job,' explained Victoria, whose biggest pleasure was discovering comedy programmes.

Comedy was something of an antidote to the grim lifestyle of Birtle Edge House. 'I think it was more my own thing,' Victoria said. 'Obviously, I gradually realised how witty my father was, but humour wasn't a particularly frequent thing. We didn't all roll around on the floor together . . . So comedy didn't feel to me a family thing, but something I was into.'

Domestically, Victoria's years at Birtle Edge House were lacking, but culturally there was stimulation that formed a rare bond between the family. Bolton's Octagon Theatre was a popular destination, but seeing one of the actors greeting his wife at the station amazed Victoria – she did not think actors did such mundane things. Every Christmas there would be a family outing to the pantomime at Manchester's Palace Theatre where the Woods sat at the back of the gods. The theatre trips were not limited to the festive season and Victoria was lucky enough to see some of the great entertainers of the day in concert. It was on one such outing that the foundations of her own career were built.

> I saw Joyce Grenfell on stage in Buxton when I was about six. It was the first time I'd ever seen anyone stand on their own on stage. I didn't realise there were jobs like that before – that one could stand on stage and speak, with no props except a nice frock, and people could die laughing. I was very taken with the idea. The idea of working alone, doing something for yourself but also for all those in attendance. I can remember much of the dialogue even now. Grenfell was terribly

observant and her voice was superb. Using humour to communicate
rather than attack – which I think women generally can do better than
men. She made a great impression on me.

Victoria added: 'She did the whole two hours, or whatever, just her and
the man at the piano. I was made aware that that was a job, that you
could go on stage and stand on your own.'

Grenfell's performance that night left an indelible impression on
Victoria and the gauche comedienne became a role model. 'It had such
a huge effect on me that when I was deciding what I wanted to do for
a job, when I was about fifteen, I decided that's what I would do. I
wanted to stand on stage on my own doing something like Joyce
Grenfell.' The newly discovered career also matched Victoria's
psychological make-up. 'As a very sort of isolating person I find that
appealing: the idea of standing on stage and not being with other
people.'

British comedy owes a huge debt to Grenfell, not only for her own
talents, but for passing the baton on to Victoria, who admits: 'If I hadn't
seen her it might never have occurred to me.' The seed was planted.

After the performance, the family momentarily tore Victoria away
from her starry-eyed dreams by snapping her back to the reality of her
lowly status.

'At the end of the show my sisters went round backstage to say hello
to her, I don't know why. And it was decided that I couldn't go because
I was too young, so I had to wait outside and I felt a bit miffed. And I
was standing at the stage door and she came out because they told her
that they had another sister and so she came out to find me and say
hello. I remember her saying, "Is this Vicky?" '

Grenfell died in 1979, but had she lived it is highly likely that she
would have been recruited by Victoria. The two did 'appear' together in
1996 thanks to the South African caricaturist, Nicky Taylor. He was
commissioned to design a pack of cards honouring 54 exceptional
women to mark the 50th anniversary of Radio 4's *Woman's Hour*.
Victoria and Joyce were the jokers of the pack. Victoria paid her own
tribute to Grenfell by incorporating a 'Mrs Comstock' in a 1988 stage
routine about a holiday flight. It was the same name of the nice but

nervous woman played by Grenfell in her monologue, 'First Flight'.

Besides outings to the theatre there were weekly trips to Bury's cinemas, the Art being a Wood family favourite. Comedies such as Tony Hancock's *The Punch and Judy Man* were, not surprisingly, Victoria's favourite type of film. In fact, she would sometimes refuse to join the family if she didn't approve of the selected film. But there was laughter to be found in even the most serious films.

'They always seemed to be showing Biblical epics,' recalled Victoria. 'I saw a different Jesus being nailed to the cross every week.' The memory of the Bury audience calling out 'Don't drink it!' to Victor Mature during the drugging scene in *Samson and Delilah* still makes her chuckle, but not all her visits to the cinema are as fondly remembered. A man once stroked her leg throughout an entire film but she was too shy and embarrassed to complain. She was just thankful it was not a double feature.

An attempt to alleviate the isolation of her home life and overcome her shyness came when Victoria joined Birtle Parish Church Brownies. Unlike her brother, who had worked diligently towards a Duke of Edinburgh Award gold medal, Victoria was not suited to group activities. Despite her young age, Helen expected her to press her own uniform, and the crumpled result and subsequent embarrassment may have contributed to Victoria's short stay in the pack.

When the family moved to Birtle, Victoria transferred to the nearest school, Fairfield County Primary on Rochdale Old Road. Her world was upturned in more ways than one as, for some reason, the classes at Fairfield were numbered in reverse order.

'It was a fairly strict school, but enjoyable with a friendly atmosphere,' says Kevin German. It did not dawn on him until the 1980s that the Victoria Wood he saw on television was the same Vicky Wood who used to play chainy, tag and bob in the playground with him and Marilyn Wood.

Her classmates remember Victoria as a plump, scruffy, red-faced girl who was rarely seen without sweets or her thumb in her mouth. Accounts of her personality vary, but years later the impression Victoria made is still vivid in their minds. 'She was a bit of a loner,' recalls Dave Roscoe, while Graham Bentley remembers her as 'outgoing, lively and a bit of a chatterbox who had a lot to say for herself'. Graham Spencer says: 'She was funny, but not funny ha-ha. She was a bit of a queer girl. She was very pushy and forthcoming and clever, but she wasn't a show-off.'

One girl in Victoria's class lost a leg when she was knocked down outside the school. 'She's the one who later tried to commit suicide by driving into the East Lancs Railway Station,' Graham Bentley reveals. Another classmate became a transsexual. 'He caused quite a rumpus when he went into Huntley Mount Union Club dressed as a woman. He joined the RAF and later had a sex change. He calls himself Rita now, I believe,' says Billy Armstead.

Victoria herself felt similarly out of place and wanted to be a boy. She felt she had nothing in common with the other girls in her class whose play consisted of pretending to be passive housewives, which made Victoria feel like she was 'trapped with 47 middle-aged women'. Such frustrating sexual stereotyping was something that she would come up against again and again in her early days of stand-up. But her yearning to escape the limits of her own gender would later help her to develop and shape an act that she hoped would appeal to all sexes.

Victoria said that at Fairfield her thing was 'being clever' and her competitive streak was already evident in the way she vied with Ann Kilgowan and Graham Howarth to be first at everything. There were also early signs of her creative talent. Janet Robinson (née Ashton), her teacher in Class Two, says: 'Her handwriting was awful, her books were messy, but she wrote some wonderful stories. I remember an inspector, Mr Page, looking at her work and saying "Watch this girl. She'll go places."'

Victoria even made a positive impression on the strict Norman Rushton, who taught her in her final year at the school. 'We had a very good relationship. Her command of language was exceptional, she certainly stood out. Victoria worked hard and had a good imagination. She was ebullient and a real extrovert.'

Hard working, but by no means saintly, Victoria found herself attracted to the notorious twins, John and Robert Mahon, who were always getting into trouble. She demonstrated her affection during one outing to Bury Public Paths. John was the first boy she kissed on the lips. It was underwater and she was so excited she had to leave the pool immediately to have a sixpence cup of chicken soup.

Her early ambition to appear on stage did not have much of an outlet at Fairfield. 'I narrated the nativity play once, but I was never an angel or anything like that. I never even got a chance to dress up, which was a sad disappointment to me.' Instead, it was her piano playing that was to provide her with her first public audiences.

Stanley introduced her to the instrument and nurtured her interest in it. He wrote the names of the notes underneath 'Polly-Wolly-Doodle', a song Victoria knew, and from that she taught herself how to read music. Delighted with her enthusiasm, Stanley was determined to encourage her further and at the age of seven she began having piano tuition, as her siblings had before her. But Stanley's good intentions had not taken Victoria's shyness into account and the lessons only lasted for a matter of weeks.

'I couldn't cope with the embarrassment of being alone in a room with a man,' she explained. 'It used to make me sweat and I'd have to go and wash my hands. I stopped going in the end because I didn't have enough social skills to handle it.' She found the lessons extremely uncomfortable, but Victoria had become attached to the piano and had no intention of giving *that* up.

'I started playing on my own and I thought: "Well my parents will be cross if I play the piano because I'm not having lessons." So I used to play the piano in secret. And when they'd gone out I used to run to the piano – I used to dream about playing the piano – and then, when I heard their car come up the drive, I used to get up again and close the lid and the piano was still steaming, and I'd run into the other room and put the television on. For years I did that.'

There was no need for such secrecy at school, and from around Class Four onwards Victoria was called upon to perform recitals for her teachers and classmates. Sadly, she found herself trying to entertain an audience of one during one of the most traumatic occasions of her childhood.

'I was invited to her birthday party in juniors,' says Graham Howarth. 'She would have been about eight or nine and she invited a group of us. The plan was to be picked up at the bottom of Castle Hill Road one Saturday afternoon. Vicky came down in the car with her dad, but I was the only one that turned up. We even drove round to Dennis Ford's house but his mum said he was out playing.'

Although Victoria tried to put a brave face on it, she was secretly devastated. Poignantly, the party went ahead with just Victoria and Graham, who recalls: 'I stayed for a couple of hours and we went on the swing in the garden. We didn't play any party games, though: you can't really play pass the parcel with just two people.'

The birthday party was not the only humiliation Victoria had to endure. She was too shy to react when somebody stole her bobble hat from her head, but at other times her sense of self and strength of character overcame her timidity. At the age of fourteen she decided she wanted to be a boxer, but an aggressive side to her personality was already evident at primary school. Graham Howarth remembers a boy jumping onto her back as she entered a sweetshop and Victoria grabbing both his hands and flinging him over her head so he landed flat on his back. Teacher Janet Robinson also witnessed a display of fury when Victoria was accidentally humiliated in front of the entire class.

'I was giving a dance lesson and told the children to sit on the floor but Victoria, who wore kilts, wouldn't stop dancing. Ian Taylor reached up to pull her down, but her kilt came down too. She absolutely pummelled him. He was a little thin boy whereas Victoria was square. We had to pull her off him.'

In general though, Victoria had a comparatively happy time at Fairfield, where her intelligence was recognised and there was little competition. This security would be ripped away at Bury Grammar School for Girls.

CHAPTER 2

'WE suffered in silence. We thought everyone else was such a high flyer. I wouldn't say Bury Grammar schooldays were the happiest days of our lives, like schooldays are supposed to be,' says Gail Branch (née Melling). She was one of a group of women in their late thirties dining at The Crimble Restaurant near Rochdale after revisiting their past one Saturday in November 1989.

Hilary Wills (née Pollitt) was also one of those present. 'The funny thing about the day was that we all ended up realising we all felt exactly the same way about school. It was a pity it took so many years for us to acknowledge how miserable inside we all were. Everyone thought everyone else was fine at school.'

Earlier that day they had been among 55 former pupils who had returned to Bury Grammar School for Girls to mark the 25th anniversary of the start of the misery.

'It's a pity Victoria didn't come to the meal after the reunion. She would have found it very helpful,' says Gail. Instead it took her former classmate a course of counselling to deal with 'things that might have been bothering me about my past' before she could finally exorcise the pain of adolescence.

Sanctas clavis fores aperit is the motto of Bury Grammar School for Girls. The school song of the same title expresses the hope that besides finding the key that opens holy doors, the girls will also find a faith in the school that sends their spirits soaring. As Victoria and many of her classmates soon found out, real life rarely lives up to expectations.

The school was typical of most grammar schools of that era: disciplined but not excessively oppressive, and with an emphasis on academic achievement. Its failing was its inability to cater for its more psychologically fragile, insecure and timid pupils. If Victoria had expected a respite from her dismal home life, she was about to be very badly disappointed.

She began at the school in the September of 1964, the same time that her mother embarked on an O-level course of study in English Language, English Literature, History, Geography and Social Studies at Bolton Technical College. 'I wanted to catch up with what I had missed when I was younger,' Helen told the *Bury Times*. It meant the gulf between her and Victoria would grow wider, with Helen having very little time to think of Victoria or support her during her teenage years.

The foundations of Bury Grammar School for Girls had been laid in the early 1880s. Funding to buy and furnish a house in Bolton Street was provided by a company of local gentlemen and in 1884 Bury High School for Girls opened its doors, with Miss Jane Kitchener, a relative of the famous lord, as headmistress. The Bridge Road building which Victoria would attend was built in 1906. During her time there the school, which has had its own swimming pool since 1940, consisted largely of the daughters of the professional middle classes. They lived in fear of the teachers who patrolled the corridors in their gowns.

'Those great, black-robed figures were quite daunting to a ten-year-old,' says Hilary Wills. Gail Branch remembers feeling lost, scared and shell-shocked at being transplanted from a happy primary school to such a cold and formal institution. But the prospect of going to the school had not intimidated Victoria. Both Penny and Chris were past pupils of the Girls' and Boys' Grammar Schools and had enjoyed the experience. If they told horror stories about it, Victoria was not deterred and she had actually made an earlier attempt to join the school's junior department. Rosalind Wood, too, had applied to the school but did not make the grade and so went to Rochdale Convent instead.

Despite Victoria's optimism, she got a rude awakening at Bury Grammar. 'It was the first time I'd been with people as clever as me, and I didn't like it,' she said.

Gail Branch recalls: 'I think the nature of the place made everyone competitive. You either competed or you sank. You had to play the game.' Hilary Wills adds: 'It was very, very qualification-orientated. We were not exactly encouraged to all work together as a group.'

Instead of trying to compete, Victoria withdrew. If she could not be the best why subject herself to futile efforts to keep up with the academic high flyers? It is interesting to note that years later, when

Victoria began carving a niche as a stand-up comedian, it was a field free of female rivals.

Although intelligent, Victoria's self-acknowledged laziness at school meant she quickly sank to the bottom in some subjects. Gail Branch recalls: 'She was very bright, though not academic in the sense of slogging. She didn't need to work at the things she was good at because she was naturally good at them. And what she wasn't good at, she wasn't particularly interested in.'

Victoria may have derived some amusement from a couple of the teachers. The distinctly Grenfell-like Miss Orme taught Classics and wrote the school song ('I've always been a bit of a versifier, either in Latin or English'). An omnipresent photographer, she enjoyed 'marshalling people into groups and making them pose'. Mrs Starkey, the History teacher, had a habit of punctuating her speech with 'erm' (a trait Victoria later gave some of her comic creations). The girls whiled away her lessons by counting the number of times she would make the utterance.

Presiding over the school with the same authority she displayed when sitting on the bench at Bury Magistrates Court was the headmistress, Miss Lester. 'She was very much the iron fist in the velvet glove. She never raised her voice but her name was enough to strike the fear of God into one,' says Hilary Wills.

Victoria was unfortunate with her first form teacher, and found Miss Smith, the games teacher, 'very frightening'. Her form mates agree and remember her as stern, harsh and strict. Being unsuited to sport did not endear Victoria to Miss Smith. By comparison Penny Wood, who attended the school from 1956 to 1963 before going on to study Fine Art at Leeds University, was a star of the hockey team, and Chris excelled on the cross country track.

'I quite liked Gym because I was fairly bendy,' said Victoria. 'I wasn't very good at it, though – I could never get up a rope to save my life!' Organised games were not her forte either. 'I once got on the hockey team by mistake, because they needed somebody wide to go in the goal. Anyway, I let in thirteen goals, and nobody spoke to me on the bus back.'

In later years, Victoria became less disparaging about her athletic abilities, but this was after she had attended confidence-boosting therapy sessions. 'Because I was fat I didn't think I was good at anything. But I suppose I could have done lots of things if I'd tried, but I just thought that I couldn't.'

Her least favourite subjects were Geography, Biology and Physics ('I just used to waffle my way through them'). She liked Art and thought Domestic Science was 'a good laugh', although she admits she was no good at it. A disastrous attempt at making a gingham apron ('It was like an old dishcloth by the time I finished') showed she had not inherited her mother's needlework skills.

As with all other aspects of school life, uniform regulations were strictly enforced. Skirts had to be knee-length and the hated stiff, grey felt hats had to be worn at all times, even on bus journeys to and from school – prefects would report anyone they spotted hatless. The hallmark of teenage rebellion was to wear a school tie. Gail Branch recalls: 'When we first went, there was a school tie and then they changed the blouses to open neck. So what did we all do? We started wearing ties just to be awkward, to rebel.'

Other attempts at insubordination included defying the school's blue underwear policy by wearing psychedelic knickers. 'There was a fad for dyeing underwear,' said Victoria. 'It was when all psychedelic colours had come in so everything had to be lime green or purple or orange. We were supposed to wear navy blue knickers every day, but people only used to bother on gym days, which was Friday.'

For Victoria, who was never fashion-conscious, school uniform was an irrelevance. 'I never minded it as much as most people, because I only liked wearing trousers, and I knew that they would never be allowed. So I didn't really care – one skirt was much the same as another to me.'

The school song includes the line: 'Here may we know the comradeship of youth', but the ethos of Bury Grammar meant more importance was attached to developing academic excellence than social skills. 'It took a long time to establish friendships and get to know people,' remembers Gail Branch. 'I think a lot of us weren't so much shy as introverted because of the situation.'

Victoria was a loner to begin with, but she wanted friendship. 'I had *some* friends, but until later I was never in the groups I wanted to be in. I used to look at the girls who rode horses, or were good at games . . . and I'd think "Oh I wish I was one of you" . . . Now I think thank God I wasn't! But I did get in with some amusing girls.' One of these was the calm, intelligent and ambitious Lesley Fitton, whose friendship with Victoria has endured to this day. Although she and Victoria were in different forms, they grew closer as they progressed through the school.

Typically for the unfortunate Victoria, Lesley, who went on to work as a research assistant in the Department of Greek and Roman Antiquities in the British Museum, was one of the 'Rochdale crowd'. This made home visits difficult so Victoria was still pretty much isolated outside school hours. Within her form, Victoria chummed up with the mischievous Patricia Ogden, who shared a love of music and window-shopping. Dorothy Kershaw's boutique in Bury town centre was a favourite haunt. 'We used to look in the shop window wishing we had money,' remembered Victoria, who, with Patricia, would also mooch around the Co-Op and Bury Market eating sweets.

Individuality was frowned upon at the school and inevitably the girls would sometimes react to the starchy regime. Misdemeanours tended to be thin on the ground, however, such was the discipline. The fear of incurring Miss Lester's wrath was an effective deterrent in itself and the cane was not needed. Detentions and lines were meted out for such offences as not walking on the left-hand side of the corridor, chewing in public and not wearing school hats. Victoria was a frequent offender and joked that she was kept behind so often her parents thought she was on the night shift. 'I never went home, I was always in detention. I was always doing lines. I'd only been in the school for about three minutes when I was put in detention for not having a name tape on my pumps – my mum had used magic marker instead. And then I got in deep trouble for writing a message on a notice board in chalk.'

It was not the only time attention would be directed at her.

'I suppose I was a bit naughty,' admitted Victoria with classic understatement. Her natural Puckishness could not be suppressed: she pocketed the £13 sponsor money she made from a school walk across the moors, and she found an ingenious way of avoiding yet another detention for not doing her homework. Having secretly swiped half the essays from the teacher's desk and thrown them away, she added her own indignant voice to those of the more conscientious pupils and insisted to the puzzled teacher that she, too, had dutifully handed in her homework assignment.

Classrooms were turned back to front, there were stink bombs in the music room, knickers flying from the flagpole, organised desk lid banging and book dropping, but it took a truly elaborate prank to cause Miss Williams, the French teacher, to flee the classroom in tears.

'There were collapsible desks and string was tied all the way around. We each held a piece, but those sitting at the four corners had more. In the middle of the lesson they pulled them and the desks all went . . . I remember Victoria tying the desks together. I think she owned up for that actually,' recalls Hilary. 'And I'm sure she Sellotaped the piano keys before a concert. Everyone just erupted when the teacher sat down to play.'

But not all the pranks were without malice. 'There was one girl, called Gail, and we always used to shut her in the cupboard, because everyone hated her,' confessed Victoria once. Quite why Victoria singled her out is a mystery. While admitting they were never best friends, Gail Branch remembers sharing jokes and a seat with Victoria on the top deck of the number 9 bus on the way into school each morning. 'She used to joke about having spots and lank, greasy hair and I used to say about how I got called Twiggy because I was as skinny as a rake.'

Perhaps it was the survival-of-the-fittest ethos that influenced Victoria and encouraged her to view Gail as an easy target. Disabled by a hip complaint, she was a year younger than everyone else, came from a working-class family, lived in a terraced house and was interested in religion. An apology of sorts eventually came in 1996 when, after reducing Melvyn Bragg to sniggering incredulity by revealing her torture skills on *The South Bank Show*, Victoria turned to the camera and said sorry to her victim by name.

'I don't know why she said that, I wasn't the only one to get tied up,' is Gail's indignant response.

Victoria was not bullied herself and unlike many other entertainers she did not have to 'perform' in order to escape intimidation. She has never claimed to be 'The Class Joker', but has acknowledged that she used humour to give herself an identity and a pathway through school. Despite being on the receiving end of Victoria's cruel streak, Gail was not unappreciative of her 'tongue-in-cheek and down-to-earth' sense of humour. Hilary Wills was a fan of her dry sarcasm.

What Victoria's sense of humour made of a visit to dreary Birtle by the epitome of 1960s Hollywood is easy to imagine. The incongruity must have certainly appealed to her sense of the ridiculous.

Down the road from Birtle Edge House is the Church Inn where, rather bizarrely, the American actress Jayne Mansfield celebrated her 35th and final birthday in April 1967. The then landlord had met the pneumatic star at a horse race and invited her to pull a pint at his recently refurbished pub. She took him up on the offer to become a temporary barmaid and spent 45 minutes at the 'simply wonderful' pub en route to an engagement in Westhoughton.

The idea of such a glamorous Hollywood star visiting her distinctly unglamorous home patch must have tickled the young Victoria and it was around this time that she wrote a song about a flat-chested girl who took pills to grow breasts. Such pills would not be needed by Victoria once she entered puberty. Indeed, she soon realised her developing breasts could become a valuable asset. That is, until Twiggy struck.

The flat-chested look was suddenly in vogue thanks to the waif-like model and Victoria's breasts became as frowned upon as her greasy hair. In later life she said her bosom was the thing she most disliked about her appearance, but back then there were more serious underlying problems. It was only natural that her unhappiness and sense of inadequacy should manifest itself externally and with Victoria that meant her eating habits. 'You choose food to deal with other problems, the way other people choose cigarettes or drink or drugs,' she said.

Victoria felt that being fat was some sort of criminal offence. Her guilt complex was not helped by her mother Helen, who marched the self-conscious twelve-year-old to the doctor and had her put on diet pills. Helen, who was not interested in whether Victoria's clothes were ironed, whether her daughter had washed or whether she had a packed lunch for school, did find the time to encourage countless diets. They included slimmers' biscuits and drinks, hot water and lemon juice, and a belief that by eating grapefruit before a rasher of bacon, the grapefruit would 'eat' the bacon. Each time a fad failed Victoria consoled herself by eating more sweets. 'I hated being fat but I didn't do anything about it,' she said. 'I just felt wrong.'

In slimmed-down adulthood she was able to joke about the plump, spotty, spectacle-wearing mess she had been: 'I was the one with the insulating tape round the glasses and a face like Dick Whittington's hankie.' But as a schoolgirl she was painfully aware that she did not meet the ideal. 'When you're a teenager being fat is "not on". The only saving grace was that there was a girl who was fatter than me in my class and she took all the stick.'

Victoria did suffer at home, though, where her unhealthy habit of comparing herself to others continued to eat away at her self-confidence. When she held herself up to Penny and Rosalind, she was bound to feel gauche and unattractive.

> *I felt that my sisters were much cleverer and much better at everything than me. It never occurred to me that it was just because they were older; I thought they were naturally endowed with more brains and more looks . . . just better at everything. So I tended to disassociate myself from the things they did. I stayed at home, and often sneaked round their rooms – privately taking an interest in their doings.*

Penny was not interested in boys, but she was well-liked according to her school friend, Sheila James. 'She was good fun to be around. She was popular because she was good at Games and she was the complete opposite of Victoria: tall, dark and thin.' But it was Rosalind whom Victoria hero-worshipped.

> *She's a brilliant dancer, she used to go to all the clubs in Manchester and dance and meet boys. There wasn't that in me – I couldn't have done it, but I was very envious. I think I wanted her approval. She went to art school and used to make all her own clothes. And I felt very pathetic in comparison.*

Being overshadowed as the youngest child was what Victoria blamed for her early passivity. The effect of being put down, overlooked and patronised would linger even after her sisters had left Bury. 'It took me a long time to get the adrenaline and energy together to say, "I am going to go for it".' The treatment she received from her sisters not only taught Victoria the importance of developing a thick skin, it also formed her determined nature. 'It made me, has made me, very competitive – so I'm glad really. Because it made me want to get even with them!'

Victoria's sensitivity to her looks blighted her formative years and turned her into a virtual recluse. Bury 4645 was not telephoned often and few friends visited Birtle Edge House, which was a blessing as it meant the state of the house did not become public knowledge at school. Stanley and Helen shared the chores, but housework was evidently not a priority. Helen was a hoarder and thought nothing of collecting bits of timber from building sites, buying job lots of stage costumes and purchasing masses of books. She even accumulated 200 shoe lasts for the left foot. Stanley added to the clutter with his 1930s sheet music and collection of old dance band 78s, which he played on an old wind-up record player.

'The house was in a really bad state,' says Joan Lloyd. 'My son, Paul, was an apprentice plumber and he did some work there. He couldn't believe it, it was a shambles. Dirty and tatty.'

Gigg Lane Social Club on Friday nights and the Farmer's Arms were the in-places to go in 1960s Bury, but while her classmates looked forward to an illicit rum and coke, a dance and a furtive snog, Victoria stayed at home. 'I couldn't go to clubs with my mates because if someone had told me I was ugly I wouldn't have coped. I wasn't good-looking. And I knew the score. Lads don't say, "She looks a bit rough but God, she's funny."' Never learning to dance is one of Victoria's biggest regrets.

The closest she got to socialising with her classmates out of school was occasionally stopping off at Hilary Wills's house for a cup of tea if the snow was really bad, before taking a short-cut home across Walmersley golf course. Even within school Victoria felt isolated and was not a mixer. 'I don't like to exaggerate this too much. I wasn't completely unpopular or anything like that but I didn't feel I was in the mainstream with people who were really having a wonderful time.' She said she experienced a sense of 'dislocation' from those around her and was not so much unpopular as not needed by anybody.

The idea that the national press would one day lay siege to the school and even try to gain entry through a toilet window just to get a photograph of her would have seemed like an impossible fantasy to Victoria back then. But that is exactly what happened at the 1989 school reunion. The press had presumably been alerted by an interview Victoria had granted the *Sunday Times* a month earlier, in which she announced she would be attending. On the day of the reunion the school register was used to ensure old girls only were admitted into the school.

Back in the 1960s Victoria only existed on the sidelines. 'I'd look at the other girls and wish I could be like them, interested in boys, meeting in the Wimpy Bar on Saturday mornings and going to discos,' she said. Her poor self-image, combined with low self-esteem, meant she was even reluctant to acknowledge her burgeoning musical and comedic skills. 'She'd put her own talents down and be very modest. She didn't have a very high opinion of her capabilities at all,' says Gail Branch. Secretly, though, Victoria would treasure any compliments and carefully write them down in her diary.

There were opportunities to socialise outside school, but her motive was music, not friendship, and Victoria joined Bury Orchestra and Bury Military Band. Robert Jackson, who coincidentally later lived in the former Wood home on Tottington Road, still remembers Victoria's arrival at the military band. 'She must have been about twelve when she joined. There was an open day to attract new members one Sunday. I remember Vicky turning up with a trumpet. She was one of the youngest there.'

Armed with her trumpet, Victoria left Jericho every Wednesday and Sunday for practices at Elton Conservative Club. Band secretary Eric Bentley felt sorry for her and would sometimes drive her back to Birtle after rehearsals. 'She usually had to make her own way home. Her parents didn't seem to be bothered about her. They just weren't interested.'

Because it was a military band there were no contests, apart from an unsuccessful audition for the TV talent show *Opportunity Knocks!* Instead, the musicians performed at Bury's Clarence Park and took part in the Whit parade. On Christmas Day and New Year's Day there would be charity performances in the town's streets. Alan Haydock conducted the band when Victoria was a member. 'Sometimes, when I stood at the front, I thought I was talking a load of rubbish and Vicky had a way of looking at you that suggested *she* knew what *she* was doing – as if she could see through you,' he recalls.

Victoria also projected this sense of being a removed observer at school. 'She *watched*. She certainly didn't mix in a lot,' recalls Gail Branch. 'I sometimes think back and remember her being withdrawn on occasions, but you didn't ask what was up. You just didn't. And she could definitely sulk. She'd go very, very quiet and have certain expressions on her face. I can still remember them. She'd withdraw herself. It was very much "You are not going to get through" – as if she'd built an invisible wall around herself.'

Miss Lester, the headmistress, also remembered her watchfulness: 'Victoria's acute powers of observation were noticeable in all she said and did.'

Victoria did not realise it at the time, but the misery and loneliness would be of immense value in later life. 'I think it was all going on inside,' she said. 'I was biding my time. I don't think you can write unless you've been in a position where you're isolated. You can either take part in things or observe. I think if I'd been thin and gone out with boys I wouldn't have had anything to write about. If you're fulfilled you have nothing to say. And it's a joy to me now that all that happened, because it got me where I am. I wouldn't change any of it.'

In retrospect she believes being a 'fat, desperately shy teenager' was the making of her. 'If I'd have gone out a lot I'd never have learnt to play the piano. I wouldn't have developed my talent. But at the time that was no consolation. It really hurt.'

The pain was lessened somewhat by seeing the rise and fall of others during her schooldays. The realisation that 'fame' was fickle was a valuable lesson. To go the distance it needed to be cultivated, developed and respected. 'Some girls at fourteen were terrific and by the time they were eighteen they were finished. It must be sad to be eighteen and to know all your best years are behind you,' reflected Victoria.

Being an observer meant she was more receptive to the minutiae of life around her, which she would unconsciously store up for use in later years. 'I think *if anything*, most of my inspiration comes from . . . my childhood in Bury and schooldays. From stuff that's all tucked right at the back of the head.'

A good example of this is the school's debating society. During Victoria's time it was highly active with motions such as 'This house believes that blood sports should be abolished' being defeated and the Conservatives inevitably winning mock elections. It was not until twelve years after leaving the school that Victoria would speak in a school debate.

'This House Believes' was performed in her 1983 stage show, *Lucky Bag*, and saw Victoria, inspired by Bury Grammar, as a priggish schoolgirl speaking against the motion 'This house believes school uniform should be abolished'.

After pointing out that there is a lot of uniform in the Bayeux tapestry, Victoria's character cites the finest schools in the country – including the one her brother attends – as examples of the positive effects of school uniform. But, she says, she has not chosen these schools for snob value; ordinary children, such as the offspring of architects, go to them. She then imagines life without school uniform and envisages parents waiting in their Range Rovers while their children dither over their wardrobes and a fourth year not knowing she is the punishment monitor because she is not wearing her red punishment tie. Warming to her subject she answers those critics who claim uniform puts financial pressure on poorer parents by pointing out that they would not be poor if they had taken the trouble to pass exams in accountancy and business management. Summing up, she says uniform promotes a sense of identity and team spirit and prevents class discrimination, before revealing that her father is now the sole supplier of uniform for the school and anyone voting for her will get a discount.

More inspiration came one lunch break when Victoria was

sunbathing on the school fire escape with Ann Sweeney. Another girl, whom they had asked to get some raspberry yoghurt or a suitable alternative, returned from the shops. She explained that she could not get the yoghurt and so she got a meat and potato pie instead.

'Everybody used to eat yoghurt the whole time cos everybody was always on a diet the whole time, but they never could keep up with it,' explained Victoria many years later. 'They couldn't do it for more than about three hours so they used to start off with the yoghurt and then go and have a bag of chips or whatever.'

It might be thought that when Victoria was the only remaining child at the house, Helen and Stanley could at last pay her some attention. But they were too preoccupied with their own lives – Helen with her studies and sewing and Stanley with his job and writing. 'Doing something creative is the only reason for my existence,' he told the *Bury Times*. Victoria's process of withdrawal accelerated.

'Once my sisters left home I had three rooms, a television and a piano to myself, and I used to spend all my time there letting my brain go in all sorts of directions.' No one would see her for days on end, but whether her parents even noticed her absence is open to question. Stanley would sometimes attempt to inject a spark of fun into the bleakness, only to be slapped down by Helen's rebuke 'Oh Wood, don't be silly.' It was typical of how their relationship had deteriorated. In the early days they would do fun things such as make a record in a booth, but during Victoria's adolescence the rot set in and they either argued or isolated themselves. Victoria sadly joked it was only their consumption of sugar that stopped them killing each other. When the atmosphere grew tense Helen would pop a wine gum into her mouth and Stanley would chew on some Thornton's toffee.

Victoria said: 'I was left to my own devices. So I lived in a very odd world. I don't know whether I was obsessive because I had nothing else to do or whether I was just like that anyway . . . And even if I'd lived on a road and had tonnes of friends I think I would have been a bit like it. But . . . it was a way of filling up time as much as anything.'

One way of filling up the emptiness was to submerge herself in literature. Reading was an obsession she shared with her mother who would descend on second-hand bookshops armed with an empty pillow case and depart with a full load. The extra space at the roomy Birtle Edge House was quickly utilised by an ever-expanding library. 'You couldn't move for books,' Victoria once said. 'At one point you couldn't walk down the corridor except sideways because my mother is a mad second-hand book collector. She once did a thesis on minor Victorian novels, of which there are about 29 million, most of which we had in our house.'

Victoria would sometimes contribute to the bulging bookshelves courtesy of Bury Library. She was not a member but that did not stop her going in and stealing books that took her fancy. These thieving expeditions were nothing to do with childish thrill-seeking or bravado: they were caused by her insecurity and crippling shyness. 'I didn't know how you joined the library, and I didn't know what you were supposed to do and I was too shy to ask the woman at the desk if I could join. So I used to go in and I used to sit in the reference library and read and I used to take books away in my satchel.' In 1999 Bury Library received £100 in cash in the post along with a letter of apology.

Books were a salvation for Victoria during her lonely childhood and she cited one as a particular favourite. She was about seven when she first opened *The Swish of The Curtain*. The novel, written by Pamela Brown, had inspired a teenaged Maggie Smith to choose acting as a profession and it had a similar effect on Victoria. It tells the tale of a group of stage-struck children who live in Goldenwood Avenue, Fenchester. They find a disused chapel (in one of a number of irreverent streaks the former minister is in prison for forging bank notes) and the vicar allows them to make use of it providing they clean it up. With breathless enthusiasm the children decide to form a theatre company, writing and mounting their own productions, designing the sets and making the costumes themselves. Their goal is to become famous actors.

'It was my life, that's what I wanted to do,' said Victoria, who still cherishes her battered copy of the book. Like Joyce Grenfell, the children of Goldenwood Avenue set an important example. If they could write and perform their own shows then why couldn't she? 'I was stage-struck. Whether I was stage-struck anyway because of that book I don't know, but I have remained stage-struck. I have remained wanting to go into a church hall and paint the chairs blue and do shows.' The doors of Victoria's ambition were truly opened by the exploits of the children in the novel. 'I was lost in that world of possibility that you could take control of your own life aged eight . . . that was my driving force.'

The children could be regarded as Victoria's surrogate friends. There was even a chubby little one named Vicky, but Victoria preferred to identify with the embryo actress, Lynette Darwin. She shared the children's aspirations and delighted in their creation of the Blue Door Theatre Company. Blue was the colour of the chapel door in the novel; it was also the colour of the door to Victoria's bedroom. That was where she could let her mind take flight and dream of a theatrical career which would open a door into a life she could actually enjoy.

The Swish of The Curtain provided Victoria with some badly needed joy, but even in the midst of such pleasure she found something to be melancholic about. 'I felt terribly jealous of the author who, I think I'm right in saying, was thirteen when she started to write it and fourteen when she finished it. So when I hit fourteen and did not have a hardback best-selling children's novel to my credit I felt really inferior,' said Victoria. 'I thought "Oh, that's it now. My life is over. I'm not Pamela Brown." '

Throwing herself in front of a book not only helped Victoria deal with her lonely life, it also provided her with a useful tool. 'I've a good vocabulary because I read all the time and that's been very useful to me.' Had she not entered the world of entertainment, she believes she might have become a writer.

Reading gave Victoria more than just a good vocabulary. She thought one book, *Modern Masters of Wit and Laughter*, was 'absolutely hysterical'. Aspects of Victoria's own style can be traced back to this collection of short humorous pieces by comic writers such as A.A. Milne. She owed a particular debt to W.C. Sellars and R.J. Yeatman's *Practice and Fury of Knitting*.

For Victoria, reading was an inspiration, a refuge and a release. It was a cruel irony that one of the few things that gave her pleasure would ultimately betray her. Even while she was happily losing herself in the antics of the Blue Door Theatre Company and 'living in a world of books', she was unwittingly making herself vulnerable to future depressions. 'I learned everything I knew about life from books so life was a constant disappointment.'

'The 60s sexual revolution passed Bury Grammar by,' says Gail Branch. 'There was a lot of naiveté.' Sex education was limited to learning about the reproduction of frogs. In the light of such ignorance it was hardly surprising that Victoria was unable to tell the police the name of what she had been told to touch by a pervert who indecently assaulted her on the way home from school. She was terrified by the encounter – rightly so, as Ian Brady and Myra Hindley were preying on youngsters of a similar age not too far away – but her embarrassment at having to describe it was almost as painful for her as the assault itself. The psychological effects of the incident, along with the earlier assault in the cinema, may have left Victoria confused and even more unsure of herself. Despite reassuring words, she must have wondered what it was about her that attracted sexual deviants.

The school did not encourage the sexes to interact. Even during Victoria's early years there, when the building was occupied by both girls and boys, there was strict control. The classroom doors were colour coded: pink for girls and blue for boys. The only sparks came when the adolescent boys, in a confused attempt to impress, threw fireworks into Victoria's form room.

Fate decreed that just as Victoria entered puberty, the boys moved into a new building of their own, which stood tantalisingly on the other side of Bridge Road. 'We'd heard rumours that there was an offer to have the school co-ed, with the lower school in the old building and the upper school in the new building, but our headmistress said no, she didn't want that,' says Gail Branch. In view of Victoria's low opinion of herself and her looks, the segregation probably made her situation slightly more bearable. She found the academic competitiveness bad enough, so to be outshone in the fanciability stakes would have eaten further into what little self-confidence she had left. She already knew she looked unattractive and did not need the boys to remind her how she fared in comparison to her stunning classmates. It was far better to insulate herself from harsh reality by daydreaming about Paul McCartney.

The removal of the boys meant there was no one for the girls to develop crushes on during their day-to-day school life. Ironically for the disinterested Victoria, it was her passion for the trumpet that enabled her to cross the border into the boys' school.

'In those days you weren't allowed to congregate with the boys – barbed wire and Dobermans! – but music lessons and rehearsals were held in their school,' explains Hilary Wills. 'Pat Ogden, who played the drums, was allowed to go over there too, so they were quite envied.'

The lure of the piano proved even stronger than Victoria's shyness and lessons recommenced when she was thirteen, after her parents informed her that they knew all about her furtive sessions on the piano at home. She was back at the keyboard with a vengeance. 'I played anything, anything I could read. I was very good at sight-reading.' The Steinway piano presented to the school in 1964 by the Guild of Parents and Friends was at her command, and Victoria played for the annual Founders' Day service. Stanley presented her with a piano of her own on her fifteenth birthday, which she installed in the sanctuary of her bedroom.

Public performances at the piano, in the school choir and in the school orchestra allowed Victoria to shed some of her shyness by losing herself in something she enjoyed and at which she excelled. A yearning to write for an audience, to show that she was something more than a fat, spotty oddity, could not be quelled by her natural timidity, and Victoria became a form representative on the school magazine committee. Although she was a member from the outset, it took three years before she had her work published in *Cygnus*. Perhaps encouraged by an appeal for 'contributions of a lighter and more humorous strain' she put pen to paper. Her first published work, simply entitled 'An Ode', appeared in November 1966. The twelve-line poem addressed to a safety pin was hardly exceptional, but when compared to the preceding poem, 'Protest Prototype' – a rather worthy rant by Margaret Pannikar attacking 1960s radicalism – it was indicative of Victoria's talent.

By the time she had reached the Lower Vth she had gained enough confidence in her abilities to experiment. The previous summer had seen the height of psychedelia with The Beatles' 'I Am The Walrus' causing widespread bewilderment. Victoria's 'Pardon?' probably had much the same effect on the population of Bury Grammar. It was a fascinating stream of consciousness, deliberately devoid of punctuation, which made it clear that Victoria was not afraid to explore her creativity.

'I suppose they'll all be looking at me now,' said an excited Victoria a month before the 1989 school reunion. Over the years she had dropped hints in various interviews that she would like to see Bury Grammar again and now the opportunity had finally arisen. But when she made a late entrance with Lesley Fitton, Victoria had no idea that she would be cheated out of revenge by her own success. So keen to avoid accusations of sycophancy and hypocrisy were her former classmates that pacts had been made beforehand to prevent her being the centre of attention. It was agreed that she should not be approached and conversation would only take place if she initiated it. 'We all sort of said, "If you see her and she smiles and she says hello then say hello back",' says Gail Branch.

The idea of a reunion is to catch up on each other's lives, but what fresh information could Victoria supply? Her marriage, motherhood and career had been documented on television, in newspapers and on stage. Once again she was an outsider – this time it was her fame that excluded her. There was the discreet nod or quick glance, but the real interest lay in hearing about lives lived outside the public eye. For many of those present, it was the first time they had seen each other in eighteen years. The physical changes in Victoria could be studied in any magazine rack.

An encounter with Miss Lord, the Maths teacher, was a humbling experience. 'Victoria!' barked the elderly woman, 'Come and sit down over here and tell me how your sister's doing, because we know what you're doing.' It was little wonder that Victoria stuck with the security of Lesley Fitton and Patricia Ogden for the day.

Two years later, after the experience had passed through what Victoria calls her 'barmy filter', she used the reunion in her stage act, painting her classmates in the most unflattering of terms.

CHAPTER 3

VICTORIA regards the summer of 1968 as one of the happiest periods of her life. The sun finally came out for her, she said, and the world changed, when she joined Rochdale Youth Theatre Workshop. The adored Rosalind had been a member since its creation in 1966, starring in its very first production, *Our Town*. Bury had nothing vaguely similar on offer so, when she was old enough, Victoria tagged along.

Had she headed nine miles south instead of seven miles east, Victoria would have found herself learning under the direction of Mike Leigh. At that time Leigh, who grew up on the Prestwich/Salford border, had taken time out from London life to return to his roots. Between the autumn of 1968 and the summer of 1969 he devised and directed plays for the Manchester Youth Theatre, among which was *Glum Victoria and the Lad With Specs*, described as an exercise in alienation and not feeling wanted.

That could have accurately described Victoria's own feelings up until the moment she entered the top storey of Hey Brook County Primary School, which the Rochdale Youth Theatre Workshop had converted for its own use.

'She arrived with her talent, that was already there; I think the Workshop gave her the confidence,' says David Morton of Victoria. As Rochdale's drama adviser he led the group, but it was the town's chairman of education, Cyril Smith, who was directly responsible for its formation and who enjoyed some of Victoria's very first performances.

'I adored the youth theatre,' she said. 'It gave me the pointer to what I was good at. I had such a rush of adrenaline when I walked into that building. I was first in and last out every day.'

It was a place where she could live out the exploits of the Blue Door Theatre Company for herself. In light of her home life, it was hardly surprising that she virtually lived at the Rochdale school. She was not exaggerating when she described it as her 'salvation'.

'There was a marvellous atmosphere, it wasn't like we were children at all. You were treated as an adult . . . I just loved it all,' she said. 'I think I learned more there than anywhere.

'It didn't matter if you had spots or you were fat or you were 15 or you were 45.'

The summer months were the busiest, attracting around 100 youngsters. Membership was dependent on enthusiasm, not ability. The days were spent rehearsing for one of three productions, which were usually performed in September.

'There was a very high degree of professionalism. I've never seen anything of that standard since,' says former member Joe Dawson. 'It was unique and very special. We learned so much. We were allowed to explore and develop ideas. It was all so new to us.'

They were taught about design, lighting, sound and costumes and there were workshops in mime, clowning and movement. Talks and demonstrations were given by visiting professionals. Smaller productions would take place throughout the year with twice-weekly evening meetings. These were attended by a core of around fifteen, of which Bob Mason, Rosalind Wood, Joe Dawson and his future wife, Jeanette Hynes, were considered the leading lights.

'They were a very talented group and Victoria, largely because of her age, was on the fringe. I think she was in awe of them,' says David Morton. 'She always regarded herself as the one who didn't know anything.'

Comparisons between the two Wood sisters were inevitable. The dainty, dark and artistic Rosalind was regarded as the better actress, but for once Victoria did not simply give up and withdraw. Her first part was a comedy char (an early Mrs Overall?) in a semi-devised production of *The Rising Generation* by Ann Jellico who, for years afterwards, Victoria believed was called Angelico. The post-nuclear protest play about the peace and youth movements was set in a stadium during a rally and called for a large cast.

'The char was a smallish role, but a great character part,' recalls Joe Dawson. She worked at the stadium and her purpose was to represent a contrasting outlook to the youngsters. Although Victoria had few lines she certainly made an impression, thanks to her football boots, curlers, padded bosom and the bottles of booze secreted about her person which fell out at comically inopportune moments.

Another early production, *Dracula*, saw her as a wolf and a prompter. This caused some difficulties as it meant her offstage moments were spent squinting down a cornflake packet muzzle trying to read the script.

Irrespective of the size of the parts, the whole workshop experience led to her developing self-esteem. 'I just suddenly thought, "Oh yes, this is the thing I can do" . . . After being told at school that you can't do this, you're hopeless, you're bad at that, you're so naughty and dirty and messy. And this clicked, and I thought, "Well, this is the thing I can do."'

She was still not totally confident, however, and the security blankets of childhood remained. David Morton remembers her sitting in the corner a lot, nursing her trumpet and sucking her thumb. But he was aware of her originality. 'Her acting was imaginative and intuitive and interesting. She was not as disciplined as the others and she just about kept within the parameter of what we were doing, but she was inventive. Her comic invention stood out, as did her writing skills.'

Like others after him, Morton did not think Victoria had the necessary qualities to be a professional actress. 'Musicianship was her strength. I can't honestly say I saw a future for her as a performer. She didn't really have the ability for serious roles. She had a shy manner, except when she got behind the piano and she'd break into songs she'd written.'

In *The Swish of The Curtain* the Blue Door Theatre Company performed at Sunday School Christmas parties and a garden fête at the vicarage in aid of the South England Bible Campaign. But the sketch show Victoria wrote for the Workshop was for a very different kind of audience.

'We did it at Buckley Hall Youth Detention Centre. It was a one-off but they loved it,' says Diane Leach.

As Victoria entered her O-level year in September 1968, Rosalind set off to Loughborough Art College and Helen, who had gained A levels in History, English and Geography, was about to embark on a degree course at Manchester University. The news made the front page of the *Bury Times*, and she revealed she planned to teach teenagers after graduating. 'I get on very well with them,' said Helen with a straight face. She had already gained experience of teaching younger children by assisting at Victoria's old primary school.

The story appeared just days before Victoria began a new school term and would have been a topic of conversation for her fellow pupils. Although Victoria was undoubtedly proud of her mother's achievements, the publicity was unwelcome as it exposed her to ridicule and embarrassment. The photograph of Helen which appeared in the newspaper showed her engaged in her unusual hobby of making dolls of characters from English literature in period costume.

Someone else was getting publicity in the local papers during that new term and, along with Pamela Brown's example, it demonstrated to Victoria that youth was no obstacle to being a successful writer. The subject of the attention was Bob Mason, one of the Rochdale Youth Theatre Workshop crowd. He had won first prize in the *Daily Mirror's* young poets competition with 'Loughrigg Autumn', a poem about 'autumn with a dead sheep and life' as the sixteen-year-old Rochdale Technical College student explained to the *Rochdale Observer*.

In *The Swish of The Curtain* Lynette nearly falls downstairs with delight when the Bishop invites her and her chums to Stratford-upon-Avon for a Shakespearean festival. Victoria was equally excited when Bury Grammar organised a similar trip for the Upper Vth in July 1969. 'We stayed in hotels for about four days and that was really good fun,' recalled Victoria.

Fired with enthusiasm by the visit, Victoria was unable to prevent her own ambition to perform from spilling into her school life. One of her greatest successes came on 15 July 1969. As an end-of-term lark, each year of the school had to perform a one-act play. The Upper Vth as a whole were credited with devising and producing *Pearl* ('a melodrama sponsored by Cupid's Kiss Corn Plaster'). In reality it was a Victoria Wood production.

'It was based on the old silent movies. Victoria wrote the play, did the music and played the piano,' says Hilary Wills. 'Pat Ogden was the

Pearl White figure and Joy Mendelsohn was the villain with the big tall hat and the moustache and cape. Pat was tied to the railway track. They used dustbin lids for the wheels of the train.'

Performed on the new school stage, which had only just been completed (there were no curtains to swish), *Pearl* was the undoubted hit of the day and the school magazine singled out the 'hilarious' play for special praise.

The 'sponsors' interrupted the piece with adverts for their product and Victoria, who once considered copywriting as a career, still remembers one of the jingles:

> *With a Cupid's Kiss cornplaster*
> *You'll have feet like alabaster,*
> *Be a Mrs, not a Miss*
> *With a Cupid's Kiss.*

This marked the advent of a lifelong obsession with advertising and brand names for Victoria. It is hardly surprising that she should have been influenced by the art form as the first British television advert appeared in 1955 – commercials shared Victoria's infancy and developed alongside her.

The summer of 1969 was a major breakthrough for Victoria. She fell in love. Naturally, it was the Rochdale Youth Theatre Workshop that facilitated her happiness. Bob Mason, the seventeen-year-old son of a coachworker, with his studious manner and a Beatles haircut his grandmother disapproved of, became her first boyfriend.

The precociously talented poet and playwright must have cut quite a romantic and exciting figure to Victoria. He was a fan of Dylan Thomas and a painter of abstract art. Bob shared Victoria's ingrained melancholy, confessing to the *Rochdale Observer* that he was perturbed that most of his writing ended tragically. Significantly, he also had a lot in common with Stanley Wood, from the playwriting to a fondness for jazz. Bob had even played father to Rosalind in a production of *Hobson's Choice*.

His charisma, ambition and success proved an irresistible

combination for Victoria. Just as the Blue Door Theatre Company brought Lynette Darwin and Nigel Halford together, the Rochdale Youth Theatre Workshop acted as Cupid for Victoria and Bob.

'We were always writing songs,' recalls Mason. 'That's where the real deep connection was. Vicky had an old 78 recording by the jazz pianist Art Tatum and I remember us listening to that. We loved plonking about on the piano.

'She was a kindred spirit – somebody who was as creative as I was then. It was very exciting to be with someone who could also make up rhymes and be funny, and who was a similar wacky type to the type I was.'

He adds: 'It was all very rumbustious and kind of rolly-abouty. I didn't think we were terribly romantic about it. We were great mates. She probably had high hopes for us. There was a huge romantic attachment, a dream attachment – and a fantasy attachment as well.'

The *Daily Mirror* poetry competition had not been his first success. In 1967 he achieved the sort of acclaim Victoria dreamed of when he beat 3,000 other young writers to win the Rediffusion Write A Play competition for under sixteen-year-olds. *To An Audience of Cork-Lined Ears* was a ten-minute play about an institutionalised man articulating his reaction to his situation and the world around him. When it was screened Milton Shulman of the *Evening Standard* described it as 'very impressive', and Hilary Spurling of the *Spectator* said that, in parts, it was as good as professional television plays.

Where Victoria was inert, Bob was pro-active and he was actually on the verge of submitting his unsolicited play to television companies when he heard about the competition. The press made a fuss of him when he returned from London after the judging and he was photographed on a patch of land known as 'The Tip' gazing into the distance with his jacket over his shoulder. He handled his success with a mixture of diffidence, indifference and arrogance; Victoria would later ape such behaviour when she too was fêted. Bob told reporters: 'I really don't care what people think – I'm just the same person.' His prize was a weekend in Stratford-upon-Avon where he saw plays and met the leading actors. 'It's not a Mothers' Union coach trip,' he told the press.

'I'll be going behind the scenes there. You can't just pay to meet the actors. They just wouldn't listen to you.'

Victoria and Bob's first summer of love coincided with the first-ever Bury Lions Carnival. Although the theme of the day was 'Lancashire Through the Ages' the populace did not cotton on, hence a float of a large silver foil Apollo space rocket in the parade. The highlight of the day was a timed competition in which men in vests, armed with sledgehammers, had to smash 34 pianos, much to the delight of the cheering crowds. It was time for Victoria to think about escaping, and Bob Mason was signposting the way.

Pearl gave her the confidence to audition for the school play, a production of *The Winter's Tale*. Having discovered her dramatic feet at Rochdale Youth Theatre Workshop, Victoria's enthusiasm was ignited and she successfully auditioned, winning the part of Autolycus, a rogue.

The production was one of the most elaborate ever attempted by the school and there was more excitement than usual as it marked the debut of the new apron stage and lighting system. Besides acting, Victoria was one of several girls who composed the music.

A performance for the school was given on 15 December 1969, with public performances the following two evenings.

'It wasn't a main part but she made the role her own,' says Gail Branch. 'We all knew then that she'd got something.' Hilary Wills says Victoria's performance was 'brilliant', and the school magazine was similarly impressed, describing her as 'hilariously roguish'.

Despite the plaudits, Victoria did not regard it as a beneficial experience. 'You couldn't be in the school play unless you did your homework, so that left that out,' she said. 'I didn't get in the school play until about seventeen and a half, by which time it was too late to do me any good.' Her enduring memory is not of her performance, but of her unflattering costume: 'horrible brown tights that hadn't been washed for about a million years'.

The evidence that she could shine on stage, coupled with the creative outlet she found at Rochdale Youth Theatre Workshop, strengthened Victoria's conviction that becoming an actress was the career she should strive for. But Bury Grammar was not the sort of place which encouraged girls to risk a life in the theatre. 'I knew what I wanted to do, but I didn't really like to say to anybody "I want to go on stage and be famous" so I just used to say that I wanted to do English because that's what I was good at,' she said. 'The expectation was, of course, that you just went to university. I remember saying to somebody that I wanted to be an actress and the woman saying, "Just don't. That's not possible." ' Such a reaction deterred Victoria from admitting her real goal. 'I always wanted to be a comedienne, but I never told anyone because I thought it was such a stupid thing to want to be, and that no one would really understand.'

Instead, she sought advice from Peter Ustinov, writing and asking him what he did to achieve a foothold. 'He said: "What I did bears no relation to what you would do", which is the right answer,' she recalled. Willie Rushton did not reply to her letter.

Performing for those who already knew her gave Victoria some security, but auditioning for drama schools was another matter altogether. Strangers usually made her feel timid, but her determination to break into showbusiness drove her on. However, she still lacked the courage to try for RADA or the Central School of Speech and Drama, so instead chose some lesser-known institutions. Victoria was rejected time and time again; at one audition for a drama school in Swiss Cottage she was even told she had a deformed jaw and could not pronounce her 's's.

For her audition piece the bespectacled Victoria chose to do the death scene from *Romeo and Juliet*. At Manchester Polytechnic's School of Theatre she performed this in her green cardigan, a midi skirt and a green PVC maxi-coat. She was not accepted.

The day was significant, however, as it was the first time Victoria met Julie Walters, an event which made an impression on both of them. The twenty-year-old Walters was a first-year student. Her journey from her home town of Smethwick in the Black Country to Manchester had not been without incident. After a series of unsuccessful stints working in an insurance office, a shoe shop, a cigarette factory and the canteen of United Cattle Products, she trained to be a nurse. When she told her fiery Irish mother that she was giving up nursing for acting she had to get her two brothers and father to stand between them for protection.

On that fateful day at Manchester Polytechnic in 1970 Julie had been assigned the task of giving the young hopefuls a tour of the building. Dressed in a leotard and brimming with confidence, she entertained them with a stream of anecdotes.

'Somebody's mother must have said to her, "What did you do before coming here?",' recalled Victoria. 'She just launched into this huge impression of being a nurse and how she used to wheel commodes down the ward, with lots of acting out and showing off. I was quite mesmerised by her. She had these teeny-weeny eyes, tons of eye-shadow and tons of hair.'

Julie remembers Victoria as a 'little girl with glasses who was being quietly sick in the corner'.

But despite the series of rejections on the audition round, Victoria still had the stubbornness and presence of mind not to desperately accept the one drama school that did offer her a place. As someone who felt unhappy surrounded by the beautiful and bright of Bury Grammar, it was curious that she rejected the place because 'everyone there was like me – fat with glasses'.

Victoria knew she had been academically indolent during her first five years at grammar school. Being forced to go to a place she did not like did not sit well with her independent nature. But despite the pressure exerted on the girls to continue their education (and 22 of her 30-strong form group did), entering the Sixth Form was still a personal choice for Victoria. It helped that sixth formers, in Hilary Wills's words, 'were treated like we had brains, as if we could think for ourselves'.

Opting out of those competitive initial few years for fear of being outshone was all very well, but the consequences of dropping out of school at sixteen were unpalatable. The teachers painted a bleak and unfulfilling future of life without A levels. For Victoria, who dreamed of fame, the idea of ending up working in a Bury bank, shop or office was unthinkable.

'I was really lazy, and I never did any work for the first five years, so I was always in trouble,' she said. 'If there was a bottom stream for a subject, I was always in it. It was only after I'd failed my O levels 74 times that I perked up, and I was actually quite clever in the Sixth Form. But before that, everyone used to get annoyed with me because

I never did my homework. I didn't win any prizes at school – not a thing. I wasn't stupid, I was lazy.'

General Studies was a mandatory A-level subject, and Victoria's English skills and musical talent made them natural A-level options. Years later Victoria's own monologues would be linguistically analysed by students as part of their A-level examinations. Her third subject choice was Scripture and her decision may have been influenced by the dry, sarcastic humour of its teacher, Miss Carney. A real character, she had been a pupil at the school herself, which no doubt helped her empathise with Victoria and her classmates. She also impressed them by refusing to sing 'Jerusalem' at the end-of-term assemblies because she regarded it as theologically incorrect.

English teacher Mrs Jean Marshall was Victoria's favourite. Victoria was one of a small select group to be taught A+ English by her, alongside the standard A-level course. The group was a sort of academic hothouse for those who had shown a particular aptitude for the subject. Besides her unique and inspiring approach to teaching, it was Mrs Marshall's warm, maternal personality that most endeared her to the class. Being married, with children of her own, made her quite a rarity among the staff, and her trusting and sympathetic nature made her extremely popular with the girls. She was one of the few teachers to champion Victoria.

'Mrs Marshall obviously appreciated Vicky's writing and I think the two of them had a very good teacher/pupil relationship,' says Hilary Wills.

The relationship continued after Bury Grammar, with Victoria and Jean Marshall exchanging letters for a while. They met up again once, but a planned second meeting had to be cancelled because of Victoria's busy schedule. After Jean Marshall's death her daughter, Sheila, allowed Victoria to choose one of her mother's paintings.

'My mum was in favour of those who wanted to do something different. The ones who had more about them . . . she always stood up for them. She'd say, "Just because they're mischievous it doesn't mean their heads are empty." Victoria was a different sort of person to the others.'

Performing on stage, where Victoria could shed her own personality and hide behind a character was one thing, but, for someone so fundamentally shy, it was more of an achievement to perform as a version of herself. The recently built Sixth Form common room became her stage and Victoria entertained her peers by singing folk and show songs. She would also play the piano in assemblies if the music teacher had not arrived.

'As she got older you noticed her talent more and she was very confident where it was the things she was good at,' says Gail Branch. 'She was shy but the confidence would come through when she was playing the fool or the piano. She certainly wasn't a show-off though.'

The piano inspired a unique entry by Victoria for the school magazine. Even had it not been sandwiched between two unremarkable poems ('Autumn' and 'Bluebells and Buttercups') the quality, attention to detail and assured style of 'A Scaly Downfall' would have still made it stand out. In this highly descriptive work of prose, Victoria delighted in revealing the frustration of receiving a piano lesson from an elderly teacher.

Victoria would go on to gain Grade VII with Merit in Pianoforte before leaving the school, but not continuing with piano lessons beyond that is still a source of regret to her. The ability to be a brilliant jazz pianist is the one talent she would most like to have.

Another famous native of Bury who did continue with lessons, and went on to make a successful career at the keyboard, was Peter Skellern. His and Victoria's paths never crossed in their home town and it was not until years later that they met.

'A television producer – I think it was Greg Dyke – organised a lunch for us once. He had the idea for us to play two characters in a drama series, but nothing came of it,' recalls Skellern.

By the time they entered the Sixth Form Victoria and her classmates had discovered there was more to sex than frogs and tadpoles. In fact, the subject had become a major preoccupation. 'It was the main theme of conversation . . . only five pupils in the sixth form had "done it", and we kept an elaborate chart of how far everyone had gone . . . it was a scream,' said Victoria, who with the security of a boyfriend was able to confidently join in the discussions.

There were rumours that one girl had left the school because she was pregnant, and stories spread about the most respectable girl in the Scripture class. The teachers did not escape the sex gossip-mill either, and there was a rumour that an English teacher who suddenly disappeared had run off with a priest.

Victoria's final year at the school was one of her happiest. The countdown to A levels, and the fact that her best friend, Lesley, was made Head Girl, did not prevent them from having fun. It was virtually unheard of for eighteen-year-olds to be sent out of the dining hall, but Victoria and Lesley achieved it after being caught making a mould of the Head Girl's medallion in the mashed potatoes.

That year's school magazine saw Victoria writing with relish of the 'many and various' activities of the Literary and Dramatic Society, but it was her final contribution to the school magazine that is the most interesting. The untitled piece bears all the hallmarks of Victoria's idiosyncratic style, and displays her typical irony and dourness. She lovingly describes the moment a beautiful young actress, spotted playing a bit part in *No, No Nanette* in Wigan, is about to make her West End debut and bring the house down. Her transition to stardom is humorously easy and Victoria wryly ended the piece by promising readers how next week she would tell them how easy it is to become Queen of England.

Clearly, it was the future Victoria fantasised for herself, but in her wryness she showed she was not blind to the hardships that her chosen profession would present. Without doubt the article was inspired by a description of Lynette's moment of glory when she accepted the Seymore trophy on behalf of the Blue Door Theatre Company in the all-important competition in *The Swish of The Curtain*.

Victoria shared a similar sense of elation in her final performance for the Rochdale Youth Theatre Workshop, stunning those who thought her incapable of playing serious roles.

'I had the main part in *The Caucasian Chalk Circle* at the end, just before I left to go to university. Pity you have to move on, really, but I finished in a *blaze* of glory.' Joe Dawson agrees and remembers her giving a 'very moving' performance as Grusha Vashnadze.

By the summer of 1971 Victoria had accepted a place to study Drama and Theatre Arts at Birmingham University. She was free at last to 'join' her Fenchester friends from *The Swish of The Curtain* as they lay in the sunshine on a day 'between the past and the future', wondering what was to come. For the children of Goldenwood Avenue, 'the past was clear and colourful as a tapestry as they gazed out across the sea that was shrouded and misty as the future'.

Victoria's future, too, was unclear, but the greyness of her past made her determined the years ahead would be brighter.

CHAPTER 4

WHEN Victoria departed for Birmingham it was effectively a permanent exile. There was no regret at leaving a place that had been the scene of her unhappiness.

As she prepared to start university, her mother graduated from Manchester University with a General Arts Degree. Once again Helen made the front page of the *Bury Times* – this time she was photographed in a pinnie polishing a chair from the University union that she had purchased as a souvenir. She had enjoyed being a student and was active in the drama department, making costumes and even performing in Brecht's *Baal*. Helen toyed with the idea of studying for an MA or teaching Liberal Studies at a college. Instead, she became an English and Drama lecturer at Bolton Institute of Technology.

It can be assumed that Victoria looked forward to university with some optimism. Wood family life had already made her adept at independent living, and while Bury Grammar had been a largely unhappy experience, things had picked up towards the end. If she could consolidate on that, and the confidence she had gained from the Rochdale Youth Theatre Workshop, life might improve.

The Birmingham course covered everything from the Middle Ages to Noel Coward. 'It was very innovative,' says Gerry McCarthy, one of Victoria's tutors. 'It was a course which was designed to enquire into the ways in which performance worked. It was intellectually highly structured.'

It was an experience Victoria hated.

'I was intimidated when I got there. It was a poncey place. It was the first time I had come up against glossy looking girls from Hampstead who talked in posh voices,' was how Victoria dismissed her fellow students. In actual fact, the other undergraduates were people like George Irving from Newcastle, working-class Londoner Terry Johnson and Leeds girl Chrissie Poulter. There was the theatrically named middle-class Southerner Fidelis Morgan, but the only student who matched

Victoria's description was Jane Wymark, who actually became a good friend.

Victoria likes to suggest she was the neglected ugly duckling of the course: the humble Northerner without pretensions who did nothing but sweep the stage on which her graceful fellow students dazzled one and all with their dramatic talents. She said she was so self-conscious she wore her treasured leg warmers beneath her trousers.

'Everybody could act, and they could all do it better than me . . . or so I imagined,' she said. 'I've had this repeated pattern throughout my life of always thinking people are better than me.'

Gerry McCarthy was puzzled by Victoria's poor self-image. 'I wonder if she ever considered why she was admitted. There must have been several hundred people trying to get those ten or so places.'

The fundamental problem was caused by the collision of her egotism with her sense of inadequacy. She was not the best actress on the course and so, in her mind, she was a failure. By writing her rivals off as faceless, ethereal beauties she could console herself that theirs was only a superficial triumph. Setting herself apart from them could be interpreted as a manifestation of her low self-esteem. On the other hand it could also be seen as a demonstration of a belief in her own superiority.

The lecturers too came in for criticism. Victoria claimed that they were dismissive of her, telling her she lacked the ability to be an actress and advising her to aim for a career in stage management instead. They were justified to an extent. Part of the problem was Victoria's impatience to demonstrate her flair for writing. Instead of producing an essay on a playwright she would write a play in the style of the playwright – Joe Orton being a particular favourite. Needless to say, her puzzled lecturers were not impressed.

Gerry McCarthy had an inkling that Victoria was not going to be a typical student. 'Whenever her name was mentioned the other lecturers sort of scratched their heads and said "Oh. Victoria".' He adds: 'In a way she was just one delightful quirk. She was not a good actor, but she was a really terrific act.'

By the time he came into contact with her, Victoria's relationship with the rest of the group had deteriorated to such an extent that she exiled herself into a class of her own. 'The thing is Victoria was always an interestingly self-critical person and I think she managed to fall out with a number of people,' he recalls. 'She ended up the only person who wanted to do a particular thing and she didn't want to do it with anybody else because she'd fallen out with them.' In their private lessons Victoria expressed an interest in studying comedy, especially Victorian farce.

The academic emphasis of the degree course disappointed Victoria, who preferred the idea of *performing*. It found an outlet in her frustration. 'The performance was Victoria telling me what was happening in her life, which was good enough material,' says Gerry. 'I thought she was extremely funny and rather a bright person.' But he also detected a certain vulnerability and felt that she saw the world through the eyes of a two-year-old.

Victoria's claim that she was overlooked in the casting of plays does have substance. Lecturer Clive Barker recalled directing a production of a Greek tragedy and being ordered to give her the leading part. He protested, but was told by his departmental heads that she had to play the role as part of the course requirement: she had not been given any parts in productions throughout the year and this was the last one.

In the play, *The Phoenician Women* by Euripides, Victoria was given the role of Antigone. She used a Northern accent and performed most of the play with her back to the audience.

'Looking back on it, having seen other productions which cast very good-looking actresses as Antigone – good middle-class well-trained actresses – I had an advantage in having Victoria because Antigone is a dumpy, ill-considered girl trying to grow up . . . Victoria at that time was absolutely as Antigone is depicted in the play,' says Clive.

'I think basically what you would say about Victoria at that time was that she was trying to break out of a cocoon. Life had defined her from her shape and her looks, and I think, the family as well. I think Victoria was looking for a way out of that.

'She was, I think, slightly in the shadow of her father who wrote for *Coronation Street* and various things at that time and I think she was trying to escape from that.'

He remembers Victoria as an 'oddball' who 'lived in a different world to everybody else'. But he also detected an underlying strength. 'She was a very strong character . . . even when she was shy and uncertain she was still *strongly* shy and uncertain. You can't ignore Victoria and you never could. She was a presence.'

Her professed shyness and uncertainty did not prevent her from attending university parties, where she entertained those present with a selection of self-penned comic songs. Because of *The Phoenician Women*, she gravitated towards Clive. 'She was mad.' he laughs. 'She ruined my social life for three years. Every time we went to a party Victoria stood beside me and told me all about her sad love life. All the stuff that she would put into the songs later – all the material was there at the beginning. She was shy but there's some idiot feature in my make-up that leant itself to her standing next to me and telling me intimate details of her life.'

This included her fondness for the smaller of her boyfriend's testicles – which interested her enormously and for which she felt very maternal – and the goings on at the house she lived in on Priory Road.

Clive feels it was his unthreatening personality that drew Victoria to him. 'You're dealing with someone who's safe, who's not going to put you down, who's not going to hurt you or harm you or attack you, so you stand next to that person.' Because she trusted him, Victoria allowed Clive to read a play she had written, a touching cross-generational comedy about an old man and a young woman. 'It was a very good play,' he says. 'The two of us were going to perform it, but never got round to it. I think she wanted to re-write it.'

He feels Victoria's talent for writing only began to emerge towards the end of the course. On one occasion she wrote a final-year practical for another student to perform. It was about someone trying to commit suicide but getting it all wrong, which said a lot about Victoria's outlook during that period.

It was her frustration at being overlooked yet again – after unsuccessfully auditioning for the part of Fay in Orton's *Loot* – that provoked Victoria into making her mark. As compensation for losing out on the role, she was allowed to play the piano during the interval and at the end when everyone was filing out. The song, which she described as 'very evil', was her chance for revenge. It was all about how it should have been her on stage playing the part and it got a huge round of applause and lots of laughter every night. In terms of her career, it was a moment that was as pivotal as seeing Joyce Grenfell perform.

By 1973 Victoria's romance with Bob Mason was over. The fact that she was in Birmingham and he was in London put the relationship under a strain, but it was Bob's wandering eye that was the final blow. 'He was at the Central School of Drama then and she was an actress. As different from me as can be imagined. Smart, dark and posh,' said Victoria. She discovered the affair when she found a letter in Mason's bag, written in a very over-the-top way by the girl he was seeing. Victoria was deeply wounded and described the betrayal as the most painful thing that had ever happened to her, which was hardly surprising considering the callous manner in which she was dumped.

'The worst part of it was at the time we split up I was putting flares in the side of his jeans and when he left he said, "You can send them on when you've finished." And, what's more, I did. Then he sent me a postcard saying "jeans very poor". So you can see what sort of person we are dealing with here.'

Explaining his infidelity, Mason says he was confused and naive. 'I was a working-class lad from a mill town and I was suddenly transplanted into drama school and surrounded by heiresses from Belgravia and all kinds of exciting people.

'I wasn't in control of what was happening to me. When you are young, you think you can behave a bit recklessly and get away with it.'

The break-up meant much more than just a failed romance. Having a boyfriend gave Victoria security and spared her from having to enter the university dating game with its risks of rejection. She had also seen Mason as a key component in the development of her career. Whenever they met they used to sit together at the piano: he wrote the lyrics, she wrote the music and together they mapped out their future. But, with just one year left at university, Victoria was alone and no closer to realising her dreams. The plunge into misery and despair put things into perspective. The shyness that had plagued her had been eclipsed by black depression, making her timidity seem inconsequential. This liberated her and enabled her to adopt a desperate remedy that would have been unthinkable before the trauma. She entered a talent show.

Her motives for entering the Pub Entertainer of the Year contest were a mixture of revenge and attempted reconciliation. She had the forlorn hope that she would win and that Bob would come and witness her triumph and regret ditching her. To increase the chance of him seeing her, she entered one of the London heats at a pub near the Victoria Palace. The piano was bolted to the floor, which meant she performed her three lovelorn songs with her back to the audience. Her revenge fantasy failed and she was placed third out of five, defeated by three enormous girl singers in hot pants and a man dressed as a skeleton who climbed out of a cardboard coffin and sang 'Taint No Sin To Take Off Your Skin and Dance Around In Your Bones'.

It was a valuable experience nonetheless, as it proved to Victoria that she did have reserves of confidence and could perform for an indifferent audience. Freed by this knowledge she began to play her comic songs in Birmingham pubs and folk clubs. She also entered another talent contest, this time in a Birmingham nightclub, where she came third on the clapometer (which she later discovered was nothing but a vanity case covered in paper).

It was around this time that Victoria got the only 'normal' job she would ever have. It said something about her growing confidence that she could take on that most sociable of professions and become a barmaid. Still at university, she worked nights at The Sportsman, a pub which was near the Pebble Mill studios and her bed-sit. Because of its location it was frequented by a number of BBC producers, one of whom invited Victoria to a party. She accepted and during the course of the evening, began entertaining them with her songs.

In an interview given years later, she said the producers were so impressed that they invited her to audition at the television studios the following day. Putting it down to drunken enthusiasm, she thought nothing of it until they phoned her the next morning to tell her they were all waiting for her. She jumped on the bus, auditioned, and was given a job singing on a local arts slot at 10 p.m. on Friday nights at £33 a time. 'They weren't songs I particularly wanted to write,' she said, 'I just wanted to be on television.'

The show, broadcast in the Midlands only, was a four-part series called *St John On* . . . in which St John Howell took a lighthearted look at Midland lifestyles and curiosities. She was commissioned to write four songs for each of the half-hour programmes with the themes of Home, Money, Food and Fashion. The songs were written in the university music practice rooms, which she would sneak into with only a carton of milk for company. The first show was broadcast at 10.15 p.m. on Tuesday 14 May, and Victoria sang about a student returning home during the holidays and finding the parental background embarrassing.

Producer Edmund Marshall, who described Victoria as 'a great, undeveloped talent', said the songs were witty, cabaret-style numbers. They were also all two minutes, ten seconds in length because one of the BBC group told Victoria this was the perfect length. It was a rule she adhered to religiously for years.

She told the *Sunday Mercury*: 'My ambition is to develop my songwriting and performing talents as far as possible.' And, just five days off her twenty-first birthday, it looked like she was already beginning to get things together. Not only did she have a television contract, she had also recorded a five-track demo tape of songs which was in the hands of a record company.

The moderate success with her own material – she made a couple more television appearances on the local folk programme *Springs To Mind* – nudged Victoria yet further away from the idea of becoming an actress after graduating. 'I thought, "Hang on, I don't look or sound like Ophelia, and I don't want to lose two stone or my Northern accent."'

The television work also strengthened her conviction that her way was right. She said she was too conceited to copy anybody else's style because she didn't think any other performers were worth aspiring to be like.

Whether these early television appearances were enjoyed by Victoria is unknown. 'It's difficult to say,' says Gerry McCarthy. 'She was always so objective and amusing about what was going on in this wide-eyed way that she had.'

Although Victoria did not request help from him when preparing her television work, she did seek advice on a more personal matter, namely, should she yield to one of the Pebble Mill producer's sexual advances in order to help her career?

'She only asked me really should she sleep with her producer,' says Gerry. 'I think we were discussing the likely state of this person's underwear and I think we came to the conclusion if we could be sure that the underwear would not be so appalling, maybe one could go through with it. The trouble was you couldn't say "Show me your underwear first."'

There is no indication at all that Victoria did succumb to the casting couch. However, years later her take on sexual politics would certainly justify an action such as sleeping one's way into a job. 'I believe feminism is absolutely to revel in your own sex and take advantage of every opportunity it gives you.'

After years of judging herself, Victoria took the drastic step of letting the country give its verdict when she auditioned for the television talent show *New Faces*. The programme was first broadcast in September 1973 and was an immediate hit, attracting huge audiences. The ATV show had an irresistible appeal: contestants would be routinely humiliated by the panel of judges, and the viewing public could participate and sit in judgement. Originally the audience could phone in to vote but such was the enthusiasm that the GPO switchboard in Birmingham was burned out, and so there was a switch to postal voting, with a coupon in the *TV Times*.

A television talent show had been Les Dawson's passport to fame. He was a resident of Bury between 1967 and 1974 and having such an example on her doorstep may have partly inspired Victoria to follow suit. But whereas Dawson got his break on *Opportunity Knocks!*, which used amateurs, Victoria's six previous television appearances meant her only option was *New Faces* with its professionals-only policy.

The audition was held at the La Dolce Vita nightclub on Queensway, Birmingham, and had it not been for a friend who was a make-up artist on the show and who ensured Victoria's application was at the top of the pile, she would never have been seen that day. She found herself surrounded by teenage rock groups, a troupe of old ladies in bonnets and wheelchairs singing 'We'll Gather Lilacs' and a dwarf who kept singing 'Welcome To My World'. Under such circumstances it was no wonder Victoria accepted 'a tablet' off someone. Whatever it was it worked, and producer Les Cocks, who was the sole judge of which acts would appear on the show itself, was impressed with her and awarded Victoria a place.

A total of 16,000 acts had auditioned all over the country and Victoria was just one of 300 who was successful. The odds were even greater than they had been for a place on the university course, but still Victoria felt unworthy. 'The rest of the hopefuls were a bit snotty. And I was ridden with guilt,' she said. 'They thought they should have won and they were right. They were all better than I was.'

Between the audition and the competition itself, Victoria graduated from university with what Gerry McCarthy describes as a lousy degree. 'If she didn't want to do something she probably would simply not do it and I think her willingness to see life as a very unsatisfactory process extended to her university career,' he said. It was not until 1996 that Birmingham University decided to award its old girl with an honorary degree (she collected others from Lancaster University (1989), Sunderland University (1994), Bolton Institute (1995) and Manchester University (1998).

Victoria decided she was not good enough to be a serious actress and believed the only good parts for somebody shaped like her were in comedy. 'But you couldn't say that then,' she told the *Guardian* in 1994. 'You couldn't say "I'm in comedy" – there was no such thing. So I said "Well, I'm going to be an actress", and I sort of vaguely imagined I'd be like Hattie Jacques or something. I hadn't really thought it through. On some basic level I wanted to be a comedian but there weren't any women comedians.'

She put herself at the mercy of the British public on Saturday 12 October 1974 when she made her debut on *New Faces*. Dressed in a borrowed frock and seated behind a piano and a model of *The Magic Roundabout* Victoria performed a song of her own composition called 'Dorothy'. Among those cheering her on was Celia Imrie, a friend of a university friend of Victoria's.

On the show Victoria was up against Davy Wanda, a unicycling ventriloquist from Whitby; Liverpool songstress Carol Christmas; singer Eddie Buchanan from Manchester; the group Wytchwood from

Wetherby; and Chas and Anabel of Bournemouth, who sang an 'old-tyme medley'. In between acts 22-stone 'mirthquake' Eric Fields kept the audience entertained.

Victoria won. She scored highly in the categories of presentation, content and star quality, gaining 116 points out of a possible 120. After collecting her £75 appearance fee Victoria caught the bus home to Priory Road in time to see Joyce Grenfell on BBC2's *Face The Music*. That same day there was an interview with Hattie Jacques in the *Daily Mirror*. She revealed her main ambition was to do a two-woman television comedy series with her best friend Joan Sims.

Winning *New Faces* lifted Victoria to a much-needed high, and she excitedly told Birmingham's *Evening Mail*: 'I just cannot believe all this is happening to me. This is my major breakthrough.' Bursting with enthusiasm she revealed her ultimate ambition was to do a one-woman show on television or on the stage – she had already got a trunkful of songs 'for when the time comes'. But even on the bus ride home there were niggling doubts. 'I was clueless about getting work. And I'd already shown my act. That was all I had.'

The problem was she was performing sophisticated cabaret, something that had died out with Noel Coward. Les Cocks said: 'The show used to get lots of phone calls and there was very little comment about her although she'd won the show. And the other interesting thing was that we'd had no calls from any agents.'

The solution came when an agent, a retired band leader from Hove, phoned offering his services. Because he was a friend of Les Cocks, Victoria believed he was a safe bet and agreed to him becoming her agent. It would turn out to be one of the biggest mistakes of her career.

As someone who deplored bad manners in others, Victoria did not read the three-year exclusive management contract before she signed, feeling that it would be rude to do so and would look like she did not trust him. Any doubts she may have had did not have time to germinate because, on 9 November, she returned to the ATV studios for the first of the *New Faces* winners' shows which were held every eight weeks throughout the series. If she won that she would automatically gain a place in the grand final.

Her rivals this time were impressionists Les Dennis and Tony Maiden; Leicester pop group Mint; the group Jess and the Gingerbread; and eight-year-old singer Malandra Newman. The show's adults-only policy was relaxed for little Malandra, provoking an outcry by the public and no doubt leaving her fellow competitors feeling rather sour towards her. In later life Malandra Burrows, as she became known, achieved stardom in the soap opera *Emmerdale*. Les Dennis, too, would make a name for himself in the world of light entertainment.

For someone desperately trying to establish a public identity the omens were not good for Victoria. The *Evening Mail* mistakenly called her 'Christine' and she was introduced on the show as 'Joanna Wood'.

Her nervousness was evident in the introductory shot of the hopefuls: she is seen drawing on a cigarette and flicking the ash on the floor. The inexperience of the guest host, a former runner-up called Nicky Martyn, also added to the unease. He tried to whip up excitement by informing the aspiring stars that they might get a recording contract or a summer season at a holiday camp if they won. In his stumbling introduction of Victoria, in which he mentioned her university credentials, he said: 'You would expect her to go on possibly to the Old Vic or, y'know, somewhere like that, somewhere very Shakespearean. But no.'

For this appearance Victoria wore a bright yellow shirt and dungarees. She sat in the spotlight behind a black piano and sang a song in the character of 'Lorraine', an office worker not looking forward to her marriage to the greasy-haired Richard who washed his Cortina more than his neck. She anticipated the vicious whispers about her at the wedding reception and the false bonhomie of the men married to boring women. She despondently concluded that marriage was better than staying single or death. She didn't know what she could do instead.

The dourness and poignancy of the song must have confused an audience that was anticipating some saucy, upbeat number. Although she did not win, she did receive praise from the panel of judges. 'Hasn't this girl got a great deal of magic, a great deal of charm,' said Derek Hobson. 'She's so cute-looking on screen.' Victoria smiled at the compliment, but her face dropped a few seconds later when he compared her to a female Jake Thackery. 'I really think this is a lovely singer, a lovely, clever song,' Hobson continued. His only criticism was that her piano playing was a little lacking in depth. It needed more 'oomph' to help carry the song along, he said, 'particularly in all those packed clubs I'm sure she's going to be playing to.'

The song contained the line: 'I ought to get thin for the wedding, lose a couple of stone' and Victoria blew Hobson a kiss when he told her: 'Don't lose a couple of stone because you're lovely the way you are.'

Losing was a blow to Victoria's fragile self-confidence. It was the start of what she called 'a long, drawn out, not very memorable disaster'. She got some club bookings on the strength of *New Faces*, but her act was so bad she was rarely invited back. Her career did not so much take off, she says, as reverse into the departure lounge. Victoria then endured being 'biffed about' by people who thought she was too fat, not funny enough and lacking in showbiz glamour. Her idea of dressing for the part was another borrowed dress and a pair of cowboy boots. It was no wonder she spent most of that period claiming dole.

'People were very dismissive of how I looked – which is very difficult at that age – and how I sounded,' she said. 'They seemed to think that if you spoke with a Northern accent, there must be something a little bit wrong with you.' She pottered around miserably, growing more and more depressed. The few friends she had from university left Birmingham to take jobs elsewhere, and the isolated bed-sit existence did nothing to alleviate her despair. She would often spend fourteen hours a day in bed and rarely ventured outdoors. 'I just couldn't seem to get it together, and my belief in myself was starting to dribble away.'

Looking back, she said: 'In my twenties I was like an unexploded bomb. There was something I wanted to do and I could not see a way of doing it. I had a real burning urge to be a comedian, or something, and I knew I was good. But I was singing little songs on television and people just said things like "You're too fat, you shouldn't wear trousers." I just seemed to get slapped down a lot and I didn't have any confidence in myself.'

The sense of frustration was no doubt increased by another member of her family demonstrating what it was possible to achieve. 'If you've got a creative talent, then it's your duty to belt it out,' Stanley Wood told the *Bury Times* in April 1975. It was a view that Victoria shared, but for her it was becoming increasingly difficult to find opportunities for showcasing her talent.

Stanley was getting publicity in the North because his musical melodrama, *Clogs!*, was premiered at the Duke's Playhouse in Lancaster. Set in a Lancashire village in 1887, *Clogs!* was inspired by *The Clog Shop Chronicles* written by the Revd Fred Smith of Burnley in 1890. The plot revolved around master clogger, Jabez, who felt work was more important than the villagers' plans to celebrate Queen Victoria's Golden Jubilee. The two sides were united by an outbreak of smallpox.

'It's the culmination of various kinds of writing,' explained Stanley. 'It started with a story line then certain phrases suggested songs, and the songs were developed with the help of an excellent composer, and then the whole thing took off.' He wrote it in just three weeks during 1966, and then spent the following six years revising and rewriting it. The precision and attention to detail (though certainly not the leisurely approach) was something which Victoria inherited.

By the time *Clogs!* reached the stage, Stanley was writing for *Northern Drift*, *Talkabout*, *Coronation Street* and Saturday afternoon radio. Despite his insurance work he spent at least two hours every night writing and revising his stock of material. 'The art of play writing,' he said 'is intertwining the story lines so that something is always happening, either a crisis, a confrontation, or whatever, and everything must be logical. It is almost an engineering job.'

His son believes *Clogs!* would have been a great success in the West End. 'We discussed this many times, but it would have meant him giving up control,' says Chris Foote Wood. 'It was his baby, he wouldn't let go. I think Victoria's the same. She insists on complete artistic, financial and editorial control.'

Back in Birmingham, Victoria had no control over her career at all, thanks to her manager. His idea of building her career was to turn down all job offers except television work in the hope that a big break would come along. As far as Victoria was concerned she would have been happy doing a twenty-minute performance for the West Midlands

Women's Institute, so desperate was she for a chance to develop her stage technique.

'Whenever I did work live, which was very rarely, I was diabolical because I'd had no experience. My idea of an act was to put together every song I'd ever written . . . and just sit there and play them. I didn't know how to walk on, how to say hello – I couldn't play the piano and look at the audience at the same time.'

Sitting in her bed-sit eating tins of mince heated on a communal Baby Belling cooker, with only the occasional song to write for such programmes as the BBC's *Camera and the Song*, it slowly dawned on Victoria that her manager simply did not like work. 'It was easier for him to send a girl along to a TV studio than traipse around the country fixing up a support tour.' Because she was still lacking in confidence she tolerated the situation, and thought nothing of travelling from Birmingham to Hove at her own expense whenever her manager summoned her. 'Fatty's not doing anything,' he told would-be employers in Victoria's presence. She silently took the abuse because she blamed herself for being overweight.

In many respects Victoria was fortunate not to reach the *New Faces All Winners Gala Final* at the London Palladium. Broadcast live in July 1975 it was a disaster. Badly presented, under-rehearsed, and with the sound off-balance, the hapless hopefuls died a death. They included sixteen-year-old impressionist Lenny Henry, Sheffield comedienne Marti Caine (who won) and impressionist Tony Maiden, who had defeated Victoria in her second *New Faces* appearance.

She may have escaped the final, but the ATV producers deemed her talented enough to appear in *The Summer Show*, a prime-time series of five 45-minute shows which began being broadcast a week after the gala final. For the first time on television she would be acting in comedy sketches instead of simply performing behind a piano.

The Summer Show was supposed to be a British version of *Laugh-In*, and each week the themed shows took a lighthearted look at such topics as mystery and crime, health and doctors, showbusiness and sport.

Victoria was one of only seven of the 62 *New Faces*' winners chosen to appear in the show. He exceptionally high score in the competition was obviously a key factor in her selection, but the producers may have also decided her plain and plump appearance could be used as a contrast to the pencil-thin and glamorous ex-beauty queen Marti Caine, another of *The Summer Show*'s stars. This may have also accounted for the inclusion of Lenny Henry and the 4ft 7in Welsh girl singer Charlie James. Making up the numbers were *New Faces*' very first winner, the Cumbrian singer Trevor Chance, and comedians Aiden J. Harvey and Nicky Martyn.

It was filmed in Studio D at Elstree Studios and the cast stayed in the nearby Spider's Web Motel. A scriptwriting team was hired (much to Victoria's chagrin) and there was a week's rehearsal time between the shows for the songs. The performers, who were paid £175 a week, were encouraged to develop their versatility: instead of simply doing their party pieces they were thrown together in various combinations for songs, sketches and dances.

Keen to get it off to a good start, a feature was arranged with the *TV Times* and the cast was photographed for the cover. On the day it was published Victoria and others excitedly crowded around, only to discover Marti had been made the solo cover star. Over breakfast someone stubbed out a cigarette on it.

For the first show Leslie Crowther was enlisted as a guest host to inspire confidence. In one number he found himself duetting with Victoria, who was dressed in a huge bustle skirt. Victoria, who was billed as a singer-songwriter, hated the whole experience. 'It was one of those really bad variety shows where they got the scripts out of other people's dustbins,' she said. 'It was just dreadful.' But at the time she was in no position to be choosy about accepting work. Marti Caine took a drop in pay to appear, but to Victoria the money seemed marvellous.

Besides the dismal quality of the material, Victoria had to endure personal humiliation. She felt bad because she was too big for most of the costumes, and the wardrobe department were unsympathetic, rifling through the racks and sighing to her 'If only you'd lose two stone you could wear this of Anna Massey's.'

The Summer Show resulted in Marti Caine being given her own television series and Lenny Henry becoming one of television's Black and White Minstrels. Victoria returned to Priory Road and unemployment. She could not even console herself with the thought that she had scored a triumph over her old boyfriend. Earlier that year Bob Mason had starred in a Mike Leigh television play, *The Permissive Society*, and before the year was over one of his own plays was broadcast on BBC2.

The Summer Show lacked the kudos Victoria would have liked, but for her professional stage debut the quality did move up a notch. *Wordplay* was written by and starred Roger McGough, who described it as

> *A play on words . . . a play about words . . . how people use words and are used by them . . . a Celebration of Words – the music, the pattern, the sense and the non-sense . . . how words fail us . . . how we fail each other in our own mis-use of them . . . despite desperate attempts to communicate with those nearest and dearest to us – we remain bound and gagged.*

The overall theme was non-communication, something that Victoria, who had an almost non-existent relationship with her family and found herself unable to confront her manager, was well-versed in.

The 75-minute revue used sketches, songs, running gags and comic turns. Besides McGough the poet and Victoria, the cast featured recording artist Andy Roberts, John Gorman who, like McGough, was a member of The Scaffold, and Lindsay Ingram, who had worked extensively in fringe theatre. As well as being older than Victoria, the other members of the cast already knew each other through previous projects. Fortunately, they were sensitive enough to realise Victoria might have felt it all rather daunting and were very protective of her.

Rehearsals were held in the Stanmore home of Andy Roberts and his wife in Middlesex, and Victoria lodged in their spare room for the fortnight-long rehearsal period.

'She was very withdrawn,' recalls Roberts. 'I remember thinking it was slightly odd really because we were all gregarious and the house always had a lot of people in but Vicky didn't seem to want to be around them. When we weren't rehearsing she would sit in the bedroom eating biscuits on her own.'

Roberts also formed a very accurate impression of Victoria's absent manager. 'This bloke was always phoning her up. It was like a throwback situation, like a sleazy agent somewhere who was completely invisible. You never saw him, he never turned up to see the show or anything like that.'

The bittersweet songs that Victoria wrote for *Wordplay* – including one entitled 'We're Throwing a Party for the End of the World' – impressed Roberts. 'They were absolutely beautifully crafted and she was singing them really well. I thought the music was the most interesting thing about what she was doing. I told her that if she cut out the comedy she could be the English Randy Newman.' It seems incredible to think now but, for a while, Victoria took Roberts's advice, and later wrote to tell him that she had written some new songs that he might like better than her others as they had nicer music and no funny words.

As well as the songs, Victoria also took part in some of the sketches. In 'Germs', she and Lindsay played two old women sitting on a park bench discussing germs. 'She was more nervous about the acting than being at the piano,' says Ingram, who found Victoria extremely witty.

Wordplay was deemed successful enough to transfer from the Edinburgh festival to the Hampstead Theatre where it ran from 11 December to 10 January 1976, again under the direction of Jim Goddard.

The Times's Irving Wardle described it as an 'interesting experience' and singled out 'the deadpan pianist Victoria Wood' as being one of the 'drollest personalities'. In the *Guardian* Michael Billington said she contributed 'genial songs', and in the *Daily Telegraph* John Barber conceded that she sang acceptably. Victoria's best review came from the *Financial Times*'s B.A. Young, who praised her for being 'particularly adept at socially-pointed songs'.

Although Victoria still considered herself naive, it eventually dawned on her that her manager was not acting in her best interests. She had not rocketed to stardom and she was still in her Birmingham bed-sit living on social security. The final straw came when she discovered he had turned down an offer from *That's Life*. Victoria was mortified and phoned the BBC herself to inform them there had been a dreadful mistake. She managed to salvage the situation, and extricated herself from her management contract. Seeking new representation she wrote to Tony Hancock's brother, Roger, who had managed the comedian and ran his own agency. Hancock turned her down and suggested she approach Richard Stone instead. Stone, who represented the likes of Benny Hill, Dave Allen, David Jason and Barbara Windsor, was impressed by the tapes Victoria sent and took her on.

During the 1976 season of *That's Life* when Victoria was its resident pianist, it was not a live programme but was recorded about an hour before it was broadcast on Sunday evenings. It was the most popular programme on British television with audiences of around 15 million and offered valuable exposure. Victoria reacted to the pressure by procrastinating.

Esther Rantzen would ring her on a Friday with an idea for a topical song (Victoria never read newspapers so was unable to come up with suggestions of her own), but Victoria did not begin writing until midnight on Saturdays, aiming to finish before her 2 a.m. clock alarm sounded. Even when she arrived at the studios with some jokey disposable song about the Sex Discrimination Act the problems were not over. More often than not she would discover her spot directly followed some grim item on plane crashes or mugged pensioners. But despite the conditions Victoria felt she was in her natural environment. 'I felt I was in the right place,' she said. 'The rest of the time I felt I was rather floundering.'

The £30 she received for her fortnightly appearances was saved and used by Victoria to buy a mini-van. The money was certainly welcome, but the *That's Life* experience was not entirely satisfactory. She had an uneasy relationship with the dominant Rantzen, who regarded the consumer magazine show as very much her baby; the public mistook Victoria for Pam Ayres (who had a similar hairstyle and surfaced on *Opportunity Knocks!* at about the same time Victoria appeared on *New Faces*); television executives were not interested in offering her anything else; and her television appearances led to problems at Birmingham Labour Exchange.

One man grew suspicious after seeing her on television on Sunday and then standing at his dole counter for her £11 allowance the next morning. He subjected her to countless interrogations in a back room, an experience which took some of the shine off her television appearances.

When her contract with *That's Life* was not renewed, she was signed up as a support act on Jasper Carrott's sell-out tour. Once again it was good exposure and allowed her to practise her stage technique, but Victoria was well aware that the public were not turning out to see her. 'It was supposed to be my big break, but it was terrible. I died on my arse wherever we went and people just sat tapping their watches and thinking "uuuhhh . . . when's Jasper coming on?".'

In the summer of 1976 Victoria's career path took a bizarre turn when she visited a friend in Leicester who was a member of the city's Phoenix Theatre Company. Her arrival coincided with a dramatic crisis: the musical director of the company's forthcoming production had dropped out at the last minute. Never one to turn down good money, Victoria readily agreed to stand in as a relief pianist.

The show was *Gunslinger*, a musical by Richard Crane and Joss Buckley billed as 'an action-packed celebration of the legendary Wild West'. Wild Willy Fifty Fingers underwent a sex change to become Wild Wilhelmina Fifty Fingers when Victoria was hired. Victoria was not mentioned in any of the reviews. Neither was Alan (Chief Blackmoon) Rickman, nor a 27-year-old overweight former librarian called Geoffrey Durham who played Buffalo Bill.

It had been three years since Victoria's last serious relationship and she found herself attracted to another member of the cast. She was therefore most disturbed when Geoffrey informed her that the object of her affection was gay. It was a lie, designed to advance his own romantic aims. The ploy worked. Victoria and Geoffrey had first met in the theatre's crowded bar where she was intrigued by his appearance: he was wearing tights and sandals. 'When I discovered that Geoffrey was doing a street show during the day and this was his costume, I didn't hold it against him. I thought, you'll do,' she said. They ended up spending a day together, chainsmoking and talking, and found they had much in common. 'Bumping into Victoria was the best thing that happened to me in my life,' said Geoffrey, who was amazed at how shy she was. She in turn said that she could not have met a better person at that time in her life.

Geoffrey was born in East Molesey, Surrey, on 22 July 1949, the son of a company director for a firm of dry cleaners. He had worked at Kingston public library – something that no doubt endeared him to the book-loving Victoria – but went on to read Spanish at Leeds University. After graduating he taught English in Spain before returning to Leeds where he worked as a stagehand in the local variety theatre. A year of acting in Glasgow followed before he embarked on his true ambition and became a director at Liverpool's Everyman Theatre. His rented room was beneath another member of the company, Julie Walters, who often used to pop in for a chat.

'After being fired, I became a busker, did a mind-reading act and stunts,' he says. 'I taught myself to eat fire, quivering in front of a mirror and reading instructions from a book.' His act also included lying on a bed of nails and a trick involving two members of the audience trying to strangle him with a rope. By his own admission they were not world-beating acts, but they provided quite a good living and experience in grabbing an audience's attention. Geoffrey's major creation was The Great Soprendo, an exuberant Torremolinos conjuror who was born at the Everyman in 1973.

Emotionally and professionally, Geoffrey gave Victoria the encouragement and support she needed. His influence on her career was enormous. He accompanied her on jobs and even ironed her costumes; he got her organised; he told her exactly what part of her fledgling act worked and what did not.

'It was my husband who first said, and made me think about – "Well, what the fuck are you going to do? How are you going to walk on stage? What are you going to wear and say?",' said Victoria. 'Those questions had honestly never occurred to me.' She adopted his motto: 'I will sit down and make some money every day' and, under his influence, she performed a children's show with magic, Abracawhat?, at the Young Vic. Most importantly, he encouraged Victoria to develop her act by punctuating her songs with comic patter. Thanks largely to

Geoffrey she crafted six minutes of workable stand-up material by 1977.

'I was a frustrated extrovert. Stand-up comedy was the perfect situation,' she said. 'You're doing all the talking and everyone else has to shut up and listen.' The woman who had been overlooked as a child understood that going on stage and making jokes was a way of satiating a craving for approval. By diversifying her act to take in more than just music and song she was taking a leaf out of her father's book: Stanley Wood always stressed the importance of having more than one string to your bow.

In an age where there are almost as many female stand-up comedians as there are male it is difficult to appreciate just what a revolutionary step Victoria had taken. Back in the 1970s she was very much out there on her own, the concept of the female stand-up was something that she had to invent herself. London's Comedy Store, which was the springboard for alternative comedy, did not open until May 1979. If such an establishment had existed earlier, it would have helped Victoria's career enormously. But there were advantages.

'I think it was fortunate that I managed to sneak in just before the alternative comedy explosion,' she said. 'It meant that I was that little bit ahead of the game.' If she had emerged as part of that bandwagon it would have been a more comfortable ride, but she would have been a participant rather than a pioneer and would not have been as memorable.

The entertainment milieu which Victoria was up against with her stand-up routine could not have been more unsuitable. The traditional working men's club circuit, with its crude and sexist male comics, dominated and there was no platform for her brand of cabaret. The clubs were totally alien to what Victoria was trying to do and, to her credit, she refused to compromise her act, her looks or her outfits. 'I wanted to wear a man's suit and talk about spare tyres and spots. But they wanted me to put on a skimpy evening frock and stand there,' she complained. 'No one understood what I was about. It was difficult for me to establish myself.'

Initially and ironically, Victoria sat down for her stand-up: she needed the security of the piano stool. Her lack of confidence was also reflected in the material, and she would make jokes about her weight to get easy laughs. There were not many 'fat' jokes, but in the absence of a catchphrase it was something that the audience could latch on to and Victoria became the 'funny fat bird'.

'I really don't think I was very good at first,' she said. 'But if it's comedy you're interested in you just have to wait, because you're not going to be good as a child. You can't be. It's a process you have to go through.'

A series of nightmare engagements followed where Victoria found herself performing to drunken squaddies in Catterick, trying to earn laughs from an Irish rifle shooting team and attempting to entertain at student balls where she went down so badly she felt embarrassed about collecting her fee. Applause was rarely heard; there was either silence, people carrying on their own conversations, or censorious statements like 'Well, I don't admire her dress sense.'

She admits she died in those early performances. Audiences expected blue material, not witty ditties and a bit of patter. It was only ego and stubbornness that kept her going.

'I didn't think about the obstacles,' she said. 'You don't when you're driven. You just go for it blindly.'

CHAPTER 5

VICTORIA returned to her native North in 1977. Geoffrey's first major job after quitting acting in favour of performing as The Great Soprendo was in the *Silver Jubilee Victorian Music Hall* staged at Morecambe's Central Pier by the Lancaster-based Duke's Theatre. Victoria joined him in the Lancashire seaside resort where Alan Bennett was conceived and which was the birthplace of Thora Hird and Eric Morecambe.

The thrice-weekly variety show commenced on 20 June and *The Visitor* described The Great Soprendo, with his high-pitched giggle and 'Olé Torremolinos' catchphrase as one of the highlights of the show. Lill Roughley as a bawdy Britannia also attracted praise and caught Victoria's eye: years later she would become a member of the Victoria Wood 'repertory company'.

When the show ended on 3 September Victoria and Geoffrey decided to remain in Morecambe. The decision was largely Victoria's – she had enjoyed an Alan Bennett television play (*Sunset Across the Bay*) set in the town and thought it would be fun to live there. A move to London, which offered better work opportunities, would have been the logical thing to do but Victoria preferred to recreate the isolation that she had known all her life.

They rented a first-floor flat at 12 Oxford Street for £13 a week and set about stamping their identities on their first real home together. The coconut welcome mat and the bean bags added a touch of domesticity, but it was the five wall-to-wall shelves crammed with Victoria's paperback collection which dominated. Equally as important to her was her upright piano (beneath a photograph of Bob Hope) and the blue painted table which served as her work desk.

The flat itself formed part of a terrace that overlooked the bus station and was only a few minutes away from the seafront. The cobbled back alley was the closest Victoria ever came to stereotypical Northern living.

They quickly established a work pattern which, although productive, was not conducive to a healthy relationship and caused many arguments. While Geoffrey crashed and *Olé'd* his way through daytime rehearsals of his act, Victoria worked through the night. Their next-door neighbours, who ran a boarding house, were far from happy with the arrangements. 'There were piano going at all hours,' says Harry Lambert.

Blue is supposedly a calming influence, but the colour scheme of Victoria and Geoffrey's flat did not have the desired effect and once again the Lamberts suffered. 'They certainly had their set-to's and fallings out,' recalls Harry. Volcanic shouting matches could be triggered by something as simple as Geoffrey spilling shoe dye on the carpet. The rows were glossed over in later life by Victoria who spoke lovingly of how she and Geoffrey struggled together, taking each other's bookings and buying each other's stamps. 'There were times when I couldn't tell you where I stopped and he started,' she said.

Their frequent separations made life more peaceful for the Lamberts. Geoffrey was getting more and more bookings at hotels, conferences and parties, and demand for Victoria was slowly growing. She did a short three-night stint at the Institute of Contemporary Arts in London with the Birmingham comedian John Dowie and, perhaps, picked up a few ideas from him for her own act. Dowie, after all, was credited with establishing the observational humour which became such an important part of alternative comedy. The *Sunday Times* preview of the show described Victoria as 'a rose with several thorns'.

Her forays to the capital continued when she did a musical comedy slot on Radio 4's *Start The Week*, an experience she loathed. Producer Dan Gardhouse remembers her as being so shy that she would arrive at the studio early, record her song and leave before the other guests arrived. But the reason for Victoria's hit-and-run approach was more complicated than mere timidity.

'I just felt completely out of place,' she explained. 'I found the atmosphere unwelcoming. I was new to it all, so it was difficult to relax and fit in. I thought, everybody knows more than me, and most of them are middle-aged men; I don't know how to communicate with them . . . I was only asked once to sit around the table with other guests. And they took my microphone away because I couldn't think of anything to say. Richard Baker asked something like, "have you ever felt alienated?", and it got to me. I said, "Well, I feel alienated now", and he moved on. He didn't want to talk about that.'

In At The Death was a revue that saw the birth of the career Victoria had yearned for. The production ran at London's Bush Theatre from 13 July to 6 August 1978 and was the most significant turning point in her professional life.

Director Dusty Hughes had been impressed by Victoria's songwriting skills when he saw one of her ICA shows, and he invited her to write and perform songs for the Alternative Theatre Company's sketch show about mortality. Victoria was initially reluctant. She had grown accustomed to the autonomy of her solo shows. To her, three weeks at the Bush was like committing to do a decade of *The Mousetrap*, and being just one of the six-strong writing team did not suit her individualistic approach to work. She only decided to sign-up after attending a cast meeting at writer Snoo Wilson's house. Alison Fiske, Godfrey Jackman, Philip Jackson and Clive Merrison all made a positive impression, but it was the 'jolly' girl who attracted Victoria's attention.

Ever since the unsuccessful audition at Manchester Polytechnic, Victoria had often wondered what had become of the amusing girl with the tiny eyes who had shown her around. She discovered the answer one lunchtime when Julie Walters, the sixth cast member, began talking about how she had studied at the polytechnic. 'Suddenly the face from the past, and the face in front of me, blended into one,' said Victoria.

The two girls hit it off immediately and spent their lunchtimes giggling and gossiping over liver and peas in a Shepherd's Bush cafe. Besides a shared sense of humour they were also connected by their uncomfortable upbringings. Like Victoria, Julie, who by that time had had a West End hit with *Funny Peculiar*, was the baby of the family and overshadowed by her older siblings. Her mother, too, was a difficult woman of Irish descent and Julie's education was every bit as unhappy as Victoria's. 'I've always been a nervous girl,' says Julie. 'It goes back to the sense of inadequacy I felt at school. I grew up thinking I wasn't good enough.'

The topicality of *In At The Death* made the revue a perfect vehicle for *That's Life* veteran Victoria. She was the major contributor, her enthusiasm fed by having an outlet for untapped creative energy on the professional stage. Work began on 4 June when the writers were asked to write their impressions of the week as seen through the newspapers. While Ken Campbell sought inspiration in the obscurity of the *Malaysian New Straits Times*, and Nigel Baldwin scoured the pages of the *Holyhead and Anglesey Chronicle*, Victoria remained strictly national and predominantly tabloid. Accessibility was all.

Of the six items in the first half of the revue, four were written by Victoria. There was a touching requiem for Guy the Gorilla, followed by 'Battered Wives' a song inspired by a story in the *Sun* about domestic violence. A third song, 'Road Blocks', based on the death of a teenage motorcyclist killed in a police chase through Surrey, was sung by Julie. 'Love Song', performed by Godfrey Jackman, is of particular interest since it is a rare example of Victoria opting for sentimentality over grim reality. Its origins lay in a Southwark man's attempt to allow his dying, hospitalised wife to spend her final days at home. The couple were portrayed as sweethearts, with the husband reminiscing happily about their early life together. There was the embarrassment on the honeymoon night, a war-time trip to the seaside, and his habit of making her breakfast. He takes a box of chocolates to her in hospital and discovers she has died. He collects her wedding ring and false teeth.

For the second half of the revue Victoria supplied 'Dear Mum', in which Alison Fiske played a middle-class woman who could not be bothered visiting her elderly mother in a nursing home. There was also 'Abortion', a haunting song about a girl lying in a mental hospital thinking about her aborted baby.

The critics were impressed with Victoria. The *Daily Telegraph* said her songs 'successfully blend a gallows humour with an unexpected touch of humanity' and the *West London Observer* said they made the poetry of Pam Ayres seem like the mutterings of a village idiot by comparison. *Time Out's* Ros Franey wrote: 'Victoria Wood's musical epigrams brilliantly embroider the action.'

By luck, Victoria was cast in Ron Hutchinson's 'Compensation' and

Dusty Hughes's 'Ghouls', two of the more understandable sketches of the revue. In the former she was cast as the gleefully malignant schoolboy, Munty. Since the piece was about a Belfast family's compensation scam, accents were called for. Victoria could not manage one so Munty was made a deaf mute. Like 'Compensation', 'Ghouls' involved the entire cast and Victoria played Michelle, one of a group of sightseers who treated disasters as a chance for a trip out. It was Hughes's response to the thousands who turned out for the Staines air crash.

Victoria almost discovered her true talent by accident. The revue was too short, and because she could not find any more deaths to write songs about, she tentatively asked Hughes if she could pen a comedy sketch instead. He agreed and during one lunchtime Victoria wrote 'Sex'. During the writing process she discovered her true voice. 'It was the first thing I'd written with proper jokes and I thought, "aha",' she said. 'I'd suddenly found something I could do. It was a blinding flash, like learning a new language.' She had locked into her unique brand of comedy and it felt wonderful. From that moment on she knew she had connected with something that was going to make it all work.

'Sex' was inspired by a *Daily Express* report about an Anne-Marie Sykes of Cheshire, who was determined to have a test-tube baby despite medical experts warning of the dangers of malformed embryos – not the most promising material from which to wring comedy. Victoria set it in a Manchester library with Julie as the panicky teenage girl who thinks she might be pregnant. She seeks family planning advice from Victoria's prudish librarian and then a concerned middle-class lady (Alison Fiske), searching the shelves for a copy of *Vegetarianism And The One Parent Family*, joins in the discussion. She asks the bewildered Julie what stage she is at in the menstrual cycle. 'Taurus,' she replies. It transpired that the girl had never actually had sex.

For the critics and audience who had sat with sympathetic embarrassment through such spectacles as Clive Merrison cavorting and mouthing jungle noises; an almost unbearable hot gospel duet about a Californian evangelist's claim that witches were out to conquer the world, and a sketch that utilised Gothic sounds and an overhead projector to tell the tale of a woman journeying underground in pursuit of her dead husband, 'Sex' was a welcome relief.

Irving Wardle in *The Times* rated Victoria as a 'great discovery' who got more poetry out of Manchester speech than he had heard for years. 'Had she coincided with the satire boom,' he wrote, 'Miss Wood would have walked away with *The Frost Programme*.' The *West London Observer* described 'Sex' as '15 minutes of sheer delight' and recognised the importance of culture clash in the humour, something that would become a central strand of Victoria's later work.

The critics were unanimous that all the most poignant and amusing moments of the revue were supplied by Victoria, be she acting, singing, playing the guitar or sitting at the piano. The *Financial Times* said she was a 'delightful discovery' and Francis King in the *Sunday Telegraph* predicted much more would be heard of her.

Encouraging though the reviews were, even some of the more perceptive critics felt compelled to allude to Victoria's size. The *New Statesman*'s Benedict Nightingale felt that with time she might have a future as a comic dramatist, but then he went on to describe how she 'plumply accompanies' and 'trundles out from behind her piano'. And *Plays and Players*' Steve Grant, after describing her as a superb performer who dominated the production, tainted the praise with the warning: 'Watch the coyness, Victoria. Everyone loves a fat girl but inside you there's good deal more.' He summed her up as a 'coy, tubby, mischievous mixture of Blossom Dearie, Randy Newman and Pam Ayres'.

But the combination of her songs, 'Sex' and her fortunate placing in other people's sketches ensured Victoria emerged as the one true talent of an otherwise mediocre revue. The critics were not the only ones impressed by her abilities. David Leland, then a director at Sheffield's Crucible Theatre, was so taken with the sketch and her songs that he invited Victoria and Ron Hutchinson to collaborate on a play for the Crucible's 1978 New Play Season.

Leland suggested they base their play on the strippers who worked in the pub beneath the Bush Theatre. Victoria had never thought of writing a play before so the seedy setting was almost immaterial to her: the important thing was she had been commissioned to write a full-length work for the theatre. So she and Hutchinson dutifully spent an evening watching the strip show as part of their research. The act consisted of a large girl walking out of the ladies' lavatory and removing her clothes before walking back into the lavatory. Typically it was not the display of flesh that caught Victoria's eye, but the poignancy in the detail. She noticed that the girl kept her boots on throughout because the floor was filthy.

When Hutchinson decided he was too busy to work on the play Leland took a gamble and asked Victoria to write it herself. She was not keen on visiting more strip clubs and instead came up with her own idea for a play. Following the age-old maxim, she wrote about what she knew and spent all night condensing her own experiences and ideas into a half-page outline, which she posted through Leland's letter box at six o'clock the next morning. The urgency was warranted because the Crucible had to have its publicity posters that week. Leland liked what he read and the play was one of six that would be premiered that season.

Rather audaciously, Victoria decided to name her play *Talent*. Its subject matter – the backstage goings-on at a talent show – made it an obvious title, but there was also a risk: if it failed then its name would haunt her and the critics would have a field day.

She returned to Morecambe to write *Talent* with a deadline of six weeks. Inspired, she completed it in just three. 'I found when I started writing that I had been fed in all sorts of ways I was not even aware,' she said. 'People were coming out of my pen that I had not ever been aware of hearing but all those voices and all those people, they had soaked into me somehow.'

Geoffrey typed the script out for her, an example of their improved relationship. Professionally, too, they were growing stronger, partly through their decision to take bookings together – Geoffrey with his magic and Victoria with her songs and stand-up. In fact one of the advantages of Victoria accepting the Crucible job was that she and Geoffrey could perform their own acts after the play.

Talent was set backstage at a nightclub where Julie nervously prepares for a talent show assisted by her dour, literal-minded fat friend, Maureen. Hope turns to disillusionment as Julie realises the contest is rigged, and to spare herself from humiliation she leaves the club rather than take her turn in the spotlight.

Along the way we are introduced to the World of Victoria Wood for the first time. It is a place where people refrain from carrying alarm clocks for fear of being mistaken for bomb scares; where a gynaecological operation prohibits the wearing of stretch-pants and the moving of spin driers; where a face pack could double as a tasty meal; where having 280 Kit-Kats is a status symbol; where a mother lives on Consulate and Smoky Bacon crisps; where nervous break-downs are only discussed on Boxing Day; and where too much tomato soup comes before a loss of faith as a reason for a disen-chanted nun to leave a convent.

Talent's inhabitants speak with a quasi-Ortonese precision (Maureen says a furniture store is having 'startling reductions on Formica kitchen units'). Added to this are Alan Bennett-style overtones and amusingly incongruous images (Sacha Distel playing Bingo in Morecambe; Pam Ayres stripping off her corset and reciting a poem about hedgehogs), which delight and surprise.

It is tempting to see *Talent* as an exploration of the relationship between attractive gutsy girls and fat plain ones. Victoria herself was fascinated by the dynamic and keen to elaborate on how pretty girls use their mousy friends. She once stated that *Talent* was simply. 'The Story of the Fat One and the Thin One' and it is true that there are a few disparaging references to Maureen's weight in the play – the arena in which judgement takes place is, after all, a nightclub called Bunter's. But *Talent* can better be seen as a metaphor for being trapped in an unsatisfactory situation – something Victoria (who was too independent to be anyone's fat adjunct) knew all about.

Julie is trapped by her circumstances. She is engaged to the unreliable Dave and stuck in a dreary job. She desperately clings to her showbusiness illusions as a means of escape, but the odds of winning the talent contest or a passport to the life she desires are against her.

Victoria cleverly invested the character with self-awareness, most notably demonstrated in the songs 'Fourteen Again' and 'Bored With This'. In the former, Julie looks back longingly to her schooldays when she was funny, famous and the centre of attention. She admits she had no idea then that she would one day wake up feeling bored. In 'Bored With This' she anticipates the future and, in a frenzy of frustration, describes with venom the likely fate that awaits: the marriage; the honeymoon; the keep-fit classes; the baby; the having the boss to dinner; the flirting with the milkman; the gin in the afternoon; the valium. 'Bored With This' was thematically similar to Victoria's *New Faces*' song, 'Lorraine', and even shares the detail of the stainless steel wedding present. It was also an early example of her tendency to recycle her own material (a few years later 'Fourteen Again' would, like 'Love Song' from *In At The Death*, be incorporated into her stage act).

Maureen, too, is trapped, but in her case she is held prisoner by her weight and her parents. Her fatness and her denial of it makes her defensive and sour. In depicting Maureen's relationship with her parents Victoria swings to the other extreme of her own family experience. Maureen's suffocating relationship with her appalling mother and father – she quotes them like others would quote their boyfriends and spends her evenings playing board games with them – was every bit as damaging as Helen and Stanley Wood's disinterest in the young Victoria.

The theme of being trapped is underlined by *Talent*'s claustrophobic setting. Apart from a brief exchange in a corridor, the entire play takes place in a small and cramped backstage room. Metaphorically speaking it is also dramatic shorthand for Maureen and Julie's inability to take centre stage in Life. To a certain extent the two girls represented different aspects of Victoria's own personality: the ambitious and dedicated Julie and the sullen and ill-fitting Maureen. Victoria returned to this technique and refined her approach sixteen years later with her screenplay *Pat and Margaret*.

Talent was crammed with a staggering amount of personal detail and autobiographical experience. Maureen, the part Victoria played, is 25, the same age that Victoria was when she wrote the play; the girls work at Benson's, the name of the sweet factory Victoria passed every morning on the way to school; Maureen has Irish blood on her mother's side; the compère tells Julie she has no act, no experience and a terrible Lancashire accent; Julie has to urinate in a container and leave it on the window-sill due to the poor sanitary conditions in Bunter's just as

Victoria and Julie had done at the Bush Theatre; Julie thinks her unfaithful boyfriend (whose surname is Walters) will be impressed with her for being in a talent show.

At university Victoria and Gerry McCarthy jokingly discussed that it might be OK for her to sleep with a television producer to get a job, so long as he did not have dirty underpants. Similarly, in *Talent*, Julie and Maureen discuss the idea of sleeping with a man in order to get a job on television. Julie says she would as long as he did not have bad breath. Julie believes an appearance on *New Faces* will lead to a life of wealth and fame, just as Victoria had. Among the talent show acts mentioned in the play are dwarfs and wheelchair-bound singers – Victoria encountered both of these at her *New Faces* audition. Cathy Christmas is the name of a singer described as a 'Muppet' in *Talent*; Carol Christmas competed against Victoria in her second *New Faces* appearance.

Acute audience awareness is one of Victoria's many strengths and it plays a large part in her phenomenal success. She knows and understands the frames of reference of the average person, and even in 1978 she was tapping into it. The play is littered with an accessible roll call of Cilla Black, the Black and White Minstrels, Leslie Crowther, Paul Daniels, Les Dawson, Freddie Garrity, Hughie Green, Russell Harty, Morecambe and Wise, Des O'Connor, Brian Poole and The Tremeloes, Harry Secombe and Lena Zavaroni. Likewise, the only phrases quoted or alluded to are advertising jingles for KP Discos, Palmolive and Tunes. Where other playwrights might have quoted great philosophers, Victoria quoted Larry Grayson and Paul Daniels.

Other aspects of the play that would become Wood hallmarks included a preoccupation with gynaecological matters (one hysterectomy and a prolapse); the use of the adjective 'barmy'; nuns as objects of amusement; and a fondness for brand names and rarefication (chocolates are 'After Eights', 'Black Magic' and 'Weekend', a car becomes a 'Cortina' and a bra is a 'Dorothy Perkins half-cup wired'). Victoria loves the straight-faced way jargon and product names are used in conversation. She finds the words funny in themselves, and is amused by their incongruity in everyday speech, but they also served the serious dramatic purpose of giving realism to her creations. 'What is important to me is that, beyond all the product name-calling, there is a *real* inner life within the characters I create that audiences can almost believe or identify with,' she said.

Some critics felt the play's originality lay in its aggressively female standpoint, but this also limited it, though not in Victoria's opinion.

'All my comedy is done from a woman's point of view, which doesn't mean that it's not accessible to men, just that it will always have a particular relevance for women.'

Since so much focus was put on Maureen and Julie, the male characters tended to be nothing more than walking jokes, prompting one critic to describe them as spectres at a hen party. Both Mel (Eric Richard) and the Compère (Peter Ellis) are insensitive and arrogant: echoes perhaps of Victoria's view of Bob Mason.

The Compère is a clumsy, chauvinistic, unfaithful lech whose seduction technique consists of putting first Julie's and then Maureen's hands on his crotch. A sexual braggart, he has no scruples about committing adultery while his wife is away brass rubbing, and he asks Maureen to bring a tissue to his suggested rendezvous in the back of his car. Just as one-dimensional and offensive is Mel, Julie's first boyfriend who turns up as the club's organist. We learn that he left Julie as soon as he found out she was pregnant. He assumed she opted for an abortion, and is unfazed when Julie reveals she gave birth to a son whom she gave away for adoption.

Talent's other male characters are retired factory worker George Findley (Roger Sloman) and his 59-year-old friend Arthur Hall (Bill Stewart). They were based on two elderly gentlemen Victoria met in Morecambe but their precise purpose in the play is questionable. They are at the club to perform a magic act that Victoria, no doubt influenced by Geoffrey – the play's 'Magic Consultant' – described in excessive detail.

After years of unemployment, frustration and fear of anonymity, one cannot help being dubious about Victoria's claim that she never intended to act in the play. Her ambition, competitive nature and the fact that she had poured so much of herself into the script makes it difficult to accept that she could happily step aside and be content to watch others performing her work. After all, writing and starring in a play was a way of making the girl who was 'not needed' at school indispensable. According to Victoria she only took the role of Maureen because she was playing the piano in the show and it made the play easier to stage.

'I've always wanted to do acting, but I'm not what you'd call an actress, I just pull faces. I can do comedy but I wouldn't do the serious stuff,' she humbly told Sheffield's *Star* newspaper. It seemed as if she could not believe her luck; possibly it was a get-out clause in case she fell flat on her face.

Talent premiered at the Crucible Studio on 9 November 1978. The first night audience lapped it up, but the Sheffield critics were less effusive. Tim Brown in the *Morning Telegraph* described it as 'a Thirty Minute Theatre of a plot, stretched to one-and-a-half hours' and he could not resist mentioning Victoria's 'ample form'. While Carole Freeman in the *Star* found the play 'very funny', it was its structure she most admired ('tremendously concise and well shaped').

A more generally appreciative view was found in the *Guardian*, where Paul Allen wrote: 'In its short and pithy span it incorporates a wealth of human disillusion and more comic one-liners than is altogether fair in a sad, sad story.' His criticism that the play was sometimes too 'knicker-wettingly funny' is unlikely to have traumatised Victoria.

The mixture of relief and pride she felt no doubt buoyed her along during November and December when she performed her 10 p.m. post-play stand-up act. Because she was energised by the positive audience response to *Talent*, what could have been a drain served instead as a further showcase for her talents. The shows were split into two individual segments with Geoffrey as *The Great Soprendo* ('That Slick Spick with the Spanish Vanish') taking first billing. Victoria called her 45-minute portion *Tickling My Ivories*, and described it as 'an evening of singing, talking, standing up, sitting down again and (possibly) one card trick'.

Her plans to write a situation comedy as well as material for Marti Caine's first BBC sketch and stand-up show were suddenly abandoned when Peter Eckersley made contact. A former *Coronation Street*

gift of a daughter (Lyn : Ann). Grateful thanks to Sister and Staff of Ward 4, also Ante-Natal clinic.

TORRANCE. — On May 18th, 1953, at the Rossendale General Hospital, to Gladys, (nee Riley), wife of James Torrance, a son, (David Andrew).

WOOD. — On May 19th, 1953, at Holyrood Maternity Home, Prestwich, to Mr. and Mrs. Stanley Wood, a daughter, (Victoria).

COMING OF AGE

ney wish
f age of
garet, of
ttom, on

you."
Marina.

greetings

Above: A star is born. The first time Victoria's name appeared in print was in this *Bury Times* birth announcement when she was four days old. (*Bury Times*)

Left: The Tottington Road house in Bury where Victoria lived from 1953 to 1958. It was in this garden that the infant Victoria decided she wanted to become famous.

Stanley Wood pictured with the script of *Clogs!* in 1975. His play was a musical melodrama about the outbreak of smallpox and was staged at the Duke's Playhouse in Lancaster. (*Bury Times*)

Above: Birtle Edge House, the bleak and isolated former children's home on the hills above Bury where Victoria spent her formative years.

Right: Mrs Overall – Victoria's mother, Helen, pictured in 1971 with the chair she bought from Manchester University. It was a souvenir of the time she spent there as a mature student. (*Bury Times*)

Above: Victoria looking ruddy-faced and anxious at Fairfield County Primary School, Bury, circa 1959.

Below: The 13-year-old Victoria in a Bury Grammar School (Girls) line-up from 1967.

Above: Victoria stole the show as the rogue Autolycus in a Bury Grammar (Girls) School production of *The Winter's Tale* in December 1969. (Arthur Hamer)

Below: Her most vivid memory of the play is of having to wear unwashed and unflattering 'horrible' brown tights. (Arthur Hamer)

Left: Bob Mason the Rochdale schoolboy, artist and award-winning poet was Victoria's first boyfriend. He made the local headlines in 1967 when he beat 3,000 other entrants to win the Rediffusion Write a Play competition for under-16-year-olds. (*Rochdale Observer*)

Below: The look of love – the 16-year-old Victoria gazes adoringly at Bob, who was also a leading light of Rochdale Youth Theatre Workshop.

July 15th 1969. Victoria pictured with the cast of *Pearl*, the comedy melodrama she wrote for the UVth as an end-of-term lark. Sponsored by 'Cupid's Kiss Cornplaster' it was the hit of the day.

Above: Victoria at the piano in the Oxford Street flat in Morecambe where she wrote *Talent*. (John Atkinson/Lancashire Evening Post)

Below: The 26-year-old award-winning playwright relaxes on a bean bag in the £13 a week flat. (John Atkinson/*Lancashire Evening Post*)

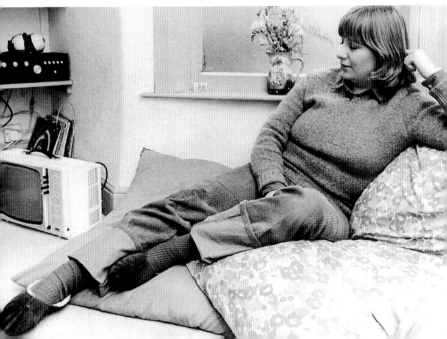

producer, he was then Granada's head of drama and, like David Leland before him, recognised Victoria's unique abilities. 'He went to Sheffield and I remember him coming home and saying that he saw this most wonderful girl and play – it was Victoria,' says his widow, Anne Reid.

When Eckersley bought *Talent* for Granada it marked the beginning of a short but prolific relationship with Victoria, who admired Eckersley tremendously.

'He was the thing that started me off . . . he was just one of the funniest people and one of the cleverest and just the perfect person for me to meet at that stage because you could bring a script to him that you thought was pretty good and he'd sit there and he'd tear half the pages out and hand it back and you'd think "Oh yeah, that's much better." He didn't do it in a nasty way. He was fantastic.'

Although undoubtedly excited by the deal, Victoria had to try and push all thoughts of the television version to the back of her mind and focus on the London transfer of the play. There were plans to put *Talent* on in the West End, but its running time of 80 minutes was deemed too uncommercial and instead it went to the ICA. The original cast remained intact, save for Bill Stewart and Peter Ellis who were replaced by David Ellison and Jim Broadbent, and Leland once again directed.

Talent opened for an eighteen-night run on 31 January 1979. The first national newspaper to publish a review was the *Daily Telegraph*, and its viciousness must have taken Victoria by surprise. The onslaught was relentless: 'She will have to do better than this crude and chattermagging little impression of an untalented Northern girl's attempt to win a singing competition at a club . . . No amount of fluency from the two fatuous females and comic wisecracks about local life can make up for absence of style and genuine zing and significance in the characters . . . One or two astringent songs with smart references to the zaggy let-downs of life have just a fifty-fiftyish chance of making it with a sympathetic audience.' Even the television and showbusiness allusions were condemned for being stale and weighing down the play.

Fortunately, the *Telegraph*'s verdict was the exception and the general consensus was that *Talent* was a hit. 'I cannot remember many debut occasions when I've relished the sheer pleasure of small details of small lives so precisely described and yielding such humour,' wrote

Nicholas de Jongh in the *Guardian*. He described it as a production of complete conviction that marked the arrival of a natural writer. Victoria Radin in the *Observer* felt Victoria had the potential to be the country's greatest female playwright. She admired the vitality of the dialogue, but thought there were too many personal memories pushed into it. As always, Victoria's weight did not escape comment in the reviews and this time the *Sunday Telegraph* obliged with the comment that her talent was 'as ample as her frame'.

That a play so anchored to the North, should be so well-received in the capital genuinely surprised Victoria. It need not have. The standard of writing and depth of perception was great enough to transcend regional and international boundaries – *Talent* even won some fringe awards when it was shown in Los Angeles. For Victoria, though, the important thing was to advance her career. She was mindful of how deceptive sudden success could be, thanks to her initial winning appearance on *New Faces*, and was impatient to consolidate the triumph of *Talent*. 'I just want to get home and get on with writing songs as well as plays,' she told the *Evening Standard*.

The theatrical acclaim she received swelled Victoria's belief in herself; she was being recognised for her own abilities. Consequently, when the BBC producer John Lloyd offered her a starring role in a new comedy series entitled *Not The Nine O'Clock News*, he was given very short shrift. Victoria was not remotely interested in diluting her new-found appeal by becoming identified as part of a group, and the place eventually went to Pamela Stephenson. On top of which she already had a commission for another play, from the leading impresario and producer, Michael Codron. He identified something special in Victoria and approached her after seeing *Talent*. He had a wealth of experience, having staged productions since 1957, and his client list read like a directory of British theatre, from Alan Bennett to Tom Stoppard via David Hare and Harold Pinter. Being commissioned by the man who introduced Joe Orton to the West End must have been particularly pleasing for Victoria.

She set about writing the play with a vengeance, determined to make up for those four wasted years of unemployment and idleness. Driven, she also managed to keep her hand in with the stand-up and fitted in an early evening performance of *Tickling My Ivories* at the National's Lyttelton Theatre on 9 March, as well as a couple of performances at Leicester's Phoenix and Haymarket theatres. In later life she gave a revealing insight into these early shows. 'I used to feel that the real me was on the stage and the rest of me was fumbling to catch up,' she explained. 'That when I was on stage it was talking honestly and communicating with people, that I had difficulty doing the rest of the time.'

By the spring of 1979 Victoria had completed her second play, *Pals*, but this tale of bed-sit life failed to impress Codron and the Crucible Theatre in Sheffield where it was to be staged. Victoria had confidently mailed it off, but grew increasingly concerned by their failure to respond. She was tempted to phone to check if they had received it, but gradually realised the silence indicated disapproval, so in the bin it went.

Meanwhile, preparations began for Granada's version of *Talent*. It was not Victoria's first encounter with the company. She had the odd slots in *Pandora's Box* and *This England* and a few years previously had applied for a job on one of its local programmes. On that occasion, by coincidence, Julie Walters had unknowingly crossed her path for the first time since 1971. Victoria was one of only two finalists shortlisted for the job and when she turned on the television to see who had beaten her, Julie appeared on the screen.

Other commitments had prevented Julie from appearing in the role created especially for her in the stage version of *Talent*, which was why the part went to Hazel Clyne. But now she was free, the two women would appear on television together for the first time.

CHAPTER 6

EVEN before *Talent* was broadcast, Granada commissioned another play from Victoria involving the central characters of Julie and Maureen. This added to her already busy schedule and meant that as well as juggling the demands of rehearsals at Granada with writing a stage play that Michael Codron found acceptable, she now had to think up a televisual sequel for *Talent*. An additional pressure came in the days leading up to *Talent* being broadcast when Victoria became the focus of mass media attention. The press screening had left her a bundle of nerves and in the round of newspaper interviews which followed, it became clear that journalists had already decided how to present her. Here was the perfect Cinderella story: a fat, plain-looking and seemingly working-class Lancashire lass emerging as an unlikely star. The fact that she was also a female stand-up comedian living with an even fatter magician in a Morecambe side street, and was one of the few *New Faces* success stories, provided additional grist for reporters.

Flimsy comparisons were drawn between *Talent* and *The Liver Birds* and the newspapers even elicited Victoria's weight, prompting Patrick O'Neill to remark in the *Daily Mail* that she was 'more than plump at 13st and too clever by half'. She and Julie were also portrayed as a double act following in the fat and thin tradition of Laurel and Hardy, Abbott and Costello and, most damningly, Little and Large. The fact that they were female gave them additional novelty value.

Victoria had assumed it was her work that would be judged and was taken aback by some of the attention. 'I was always very upset if they ever said I was fat. Even though I was. I felt they shouldn't mention it, I felt it wasn't relevant, but of course it's a British obsession,' she reflected. 'I was patronised either for being fat, for being a woman or for being Northern . . . I just felt I was living in a world of mad Southern people.'

Being presented as a fat, overnight success and having to share billing, even with a good friend, must not have been easy for Victoria who hated losing control. To speak out was to risk being branded a prima donna so instead of defending herself, she defended *Talent*, declaring loftily in the *Daily Mail*: 'This isn't sit com. This is the real thing.'

Talent was broadcast at 9.30 p.m. on Sunday, 5 August 1979, with Peter Eckersley producing and Baz Taylor directing. It was the second play in Granada's *Screenplay* series and besides Victoria, only Peter Ellis remained from the original Sheffield production. Bill Waddington, who later played Percy Sugden in *Coronation Street*, took the role of George and Sue Glover played Cathy Christmas, a character only ever referred to in the stage version. Forty minutes had to be cut for television and Victoria was only allowed to have her bust squeezed once by the Compère. Audiences that have only recently come to Victoria may be surprised by the raw vocabulary of *Talent* but mention of a 'twat' and two 'cock' references survived the television censors. However, a 'fuck' was removed, diluting Julie's celebrated line to 'I thought Coq au Vin was *love* in a lorry'.

Victoria wisely extracted some of the overly long magic scenes for the television version and certain lines were rearranged or sharpened, but fundamentally the play remained the same.

The television critics were unanimous in their praise. *Talent* was a rarity in being a television play with songs that actually worked. Only Dennis Potter had employed song so effectively before. The stage and television writer Alan Plater wrote Victoria a letter expressing his delight at seeing a new Northern writer, and John Le Mesurier wrote a letter full of praise, but the play was not to everyone's taste. Radio Blackburn's phone-in audience had a field day complaining about the bad language. One indignant woman even wrote to Victoria personally, informing her that Lancashire people never spoke as fast as June (sic) Walters and that the play's producer should be shot. Mischievously, Victoria responded with a letter informing the woman that June Walters was in fact from Manchester.

The wave of media attention that began with *Talent*'s press launch continued after the broadcast, engulfing Victoria and leaving her momentarily off guard. Her workload too may have meant she was not as in control as she would have liked. She viewed the press interest as a 'by-product', but seemed to realise the futility of fighting the media image that was being created of her, and gave in to it. Years later she complained that she was regarded as Northern Funny Girl by the media, but back in 1979 if getting her photograph in the *Daily Mail* or *TV Times* meant squatting on Morecambe Beach, gazing from the pier, posing in an amusement arcade or having her palm read in Gypsy Smith's booth, then so be it.

She obliged those journalists who tracked her down to the Oxford Street flat by swigging milk from the bottle and eating biscuits. She volunteered information about how she and Geoffrey only had a black-and-white portable television to watch the play on, and she revealed that she was down to her last 40 pence so could not afford to buy all the newspapers to read the reviews. The Granada money, she said, would come in handy as she had been hard up since university. She had already bought a Fiat with it – a colour television would follow – and was waiting for more money to last her the rest of the week.

But in the midst of all the acclaim Victoria presented a diffidence and modesty at odds with her internal drive and ambition. She dismissed *Talent* as 'just a little story, quite funny and also a bit sad'. Even the actual effort involved in writing it was shrouded in modesty: 'They paid me a hell of a lot of money for the TV rights. It was easy money really because all I had to do was take bits out of the stage play. I'm glad that people liked it, but to me it wasn't a fantastic play. I just wanted to get a few laughs,' she told the *Daily Mail*.

At times she seemed to want to collude with the press in projecting an image of down-to-earth Northern practicality; *her* head was not going to be turned by all this fame nonsense. 'Nobody in Morecambe knows who I am, thank goodness,' she told reporters, completely ignoring the fact that she had craved fame since childhood The double-talk also extended to Morecambe itself, which was painted as an idyllic place to live and where Victoria, with all her steely ambition, was apparently pleased to judge an old folks' talent show. 'We like Morecambe,' she said. 'It's nice. It's quiet and full of old people.'

Years later, when she was ensconced in her Highgate mansion, Victoria described her decision to live in Morecambe as mad, stupid and a strange, mental aberration, but the town, or rather its inhabitants, did once merit some genuine appreciation by Victoria who found inspiration in their dourness. She was particularly tickled by an exchange she overheard in the fish and chip shop. 'T'pier's burnt down' said one woman, to which her friend replied "bout time".'

Victoria's tolerance of the media in those early days did not extend to her own family and a rift developed between her and her brother because of comments he made to the press. It made an already remote relationship almost nonexistent. By that time Chris had left engineering, established a news and sports agency in Bishop Auckland and had married his second wife, Frances, a schoolteacher whose surname he incorporated into his own in the interests of sexual equality.

'An award-winning journalist phoned me up and asked what Victoria was like, if she was blonde, what her vital statistics were and things like that. I stupidly gave him her phone number and he rang her up and told her what I'd said. It was very hurtful,' Chris says of the falling out. It was not the only time Victoria's fame created problems for him. He successfully won a claim against a BBC North East journalist who implied that he was Victoria's half-brother. 'I won the case but it did me no favours and I've not been on television since,' laments Chris who, as a journalist and would-be Liberal MP, would have undoubtedly welcomed television exposure.

Once the fuss about *Talent* had died down, Victoria applied herself to writing the Codron play. She completed it in October and called it *Good Fun*. With it out of the way she could reciprocate Geoffrey's support and spent that Christmas Day at a York hotel where he had got a booking. The decade which had begun with such misery and frustration for Victoria could not have ended more differently. The end of the 1970s marked the end of the false starts for Victoria. She was about to enter third gear.

The first month of the new decade saw her gaining the professional approval and public recognition so necessary to her ego. The ICA production of *Talent* in London won her the *Plays and Players'* Most Promising New Playwright award, judged by eighteen London theatre critics. There were fourteen nominations and it was thanks to votes by Robert Cushman of the *Observer*, Kenneth Hurren of *What's On In*

London, David Nathan of the *Jewish Chronicle* and Irving Wardle of *The Times* that Victoria won.

That same month saw her sharing the Most Promising Playwright title with Richard Harris for his suburban cricket club comedy, *Outside Edge*, at the *Evening Standard* Drama Awards. The prestige of the occasion persuaded Victoria to renege on her usual dress code and she donned a frock bought from an oversize clothing company. It was too big for her. At the party afterwards she was rudely brought down to earth when an arm stretched across and flicked some cigarette ash into the bowl-like award she was clutching. Princess Margaret had assumed Victoria was an ashtray wallah. Typically dismissive, and eager to portray herself as domestically eccentric, Victoria later revealed one of the awards ended up in a plastic bag of Christmas decorations, and the other behind a rubber plant adorned with a string of plastic sausages.

Sometimes she seemed to be equally dismissive of her audiences, describing them as 'mainly young people or older people who think they're 21 but aren't'. Clearly, she wished to avoid ghettoising herself: her aim was to be enjoyed by a universal audience. If she could not achieve this, she stated, she might as well shoot herself.

Rehearsals for *Nearly A Happy Ending*, the television sequel to *Talent*, were completed in February 1980; a five-day shoot was scheduled for the same month; Granada had asked for another play for 1981; and in the middle of this rehearsals for *Good Fun* were due to begin. Somewhat perversely, Victoria decided it was a good time to fit in marriage.

Geoffrey had been badgering her to marry him almost from the start of their relationship, but, perhaps mindful of her own parents' marriage and the failure of her brother's first marriage, Victoria had been reluctant. 'I didn't get married for years because I thought the whole idea too naff for words,' she said. 'I didn't want to get married. *He* did. Every day he'd ask me to marry him.' In the end it was the number of rows about why they were not married that made her finally relent.

Today the celebrity wedding makes front-page news, and magazine deals make them a lucrative proposition, but back in 1980 Victoria and Geoffrey took the low-key wedding to new heights. Her heavy workload helped make the marriage merely incidental, which is what she wanted. There were no rings and, less surprisingly in view of Victoria's relationship with her family, no relatives present. They had plotted to marry on 29 February so anniversaries would only occur on Leap Years, but this plan was abandoned, along with Morecambe Register Office as the venue. Farcically, it was impossible to be married in the town because the register office was only licensed for deaths. Instead Victoria and Geoffrey drove over to Lancaster with their friend Alyson Lloyd, her husband and their baby, and were married at the Queen Street Register Office at 9.50 a.m. on Saturday, 1 March. The 'reception' was held at the cafe across the road and the honeymoon was a night in Buxton with Victoria returning to Sheffield the next day for a read through of *Good Fun*.

Not wearing a wedding ring and declining to take Geoffrey's surname were Victoria's ways of making a statement about her independence. 'I was a bit embarrassed by it all and didn't want people to know just by looking at me,' she explained. 'I felt marriage was an odd thing to do. Most of my friends just lived together. It took me a long time to get used to the fact I was married.' But once the act was done she had no regrets. 'We've got such an emotional bond together. That's why I married him. You only marry someone if you think them the best person possible and that's what Geoff is. I have a better time with him than anyone else.'

The idea of being a 'wife' had never appealed to her, which suited Geoffrey. 'I couldn't have married someone who wasn't an entertainer,' he said. 'Victoria understands the pressures. Other people might want a wife who does the dishes and stays home looking after the children, but that's not for me.'

Most brides-to-be diet furiously for their big day, but for Victoria weight loss was an occupational necessity. In *Nearly A Happy Ending*, Maureen is proud of reaching her target weight at a slimming club, which meant Victoria had to shed the pounds. She achieved this by swapping chocolate for salad and fruits and taking up swimming. Every morning Victoria, Julie and director Baz Taylor would go swimming at Salford Baths. In time she worked up from one length to twenty-six and slimmed down from thirteen stones to ten-and-a-half stones in the process, but there was to be no lasting record of the streamlined bride because the wedding photographs were mislaid on a bus.

Talent may have been aptly named, but *Good Fun* could not have been more inappropriately titled. It premiered on Good Friday 1980 and was an unhappy experience for those involved.

The central character of the play is Liz. She is ruthlessly exploited and manipulated by Geography teacher and avant-garde Punch and Judy man Mike (Gregory Floy), who, it emerges, is suffering from mental illness. Hovering around her is Frank (Charles McKeown), an immature and wimpish librarian who wants to bed her. Elsie is an old friend of Liz who provides a cynical commentary on events. Gail (Noreen Kershaw, who had also appeared in Stanley Wood's *Clogs!*) is the despised schoolmate lured to the arts centre under false pretences.

Liz, a community arts administrator, is thrown into a panic when she discovers the first big event she has been given responsibility for, a reception for 300 cystitis sufferers, is scheduled for the next day, earlier than she had expected. She ropes everyone in to help, including Lynne (Sue Wallace), a surly, pregnant nineteen-year-old who works in the salad bar, and her unemployed boyfriend, Kevin (Joe Figg). Adding to the numbers is Betty, a disco dancing cosmetics saleswoman and her husband, Maurice (Christopher Hancock), head of the Co-Op carpet department and a novelty hedgetrimmer.

Mike makes a move on Lynne, to Liz's chagrin. Her double bluffs fail and she strikes a deal with Lynne to take the baby off her hands. By lunchtime the next day the place is almost ready. A romance develops between Frank and Gail. Elsie takes a phone call from the cystitis woman who informs her that 300 of them will be marching down in about 20 minutes. Mike, who turns out to be the son of Betty and Maurice, reveals himself to be a pathological liar, but Liz continues to blind herself to his faults. All the signs point to disaster, but Liz gets a telegram informing her that the reception has been cancelled due to unforeseen circumstances. They tuck into the food and drink. Liz casually informs Lynne that the baby deal is off and, if it is not too late for an abortion, she could help with the bureaucracy. Gail proudly reveals she's played her first practical joke; she sent the telegram and the cystitis reception is still on. She and Frank leave. Lynne, who has taken an overdose, is taken to hospital by Betty and Maurice. Liz dismisses Lynne as a silly cow and Elsie is shocked by such callousness. She thought Liz's big thing was being a nice person. Liz is left alone on the stage.

In the play Elsie mockingly describes an incident where a theatre group performed a play about housewives outside Tesco's in an Arndale Centre. They made 'jokes' about Margaret Thatcher and expected a show of support from shoppers, who were not impressed and just wanted to get into the supermarket. Similarly, it could be said that *Good Fun* did not live up to *Talent* because Victoria did not heed her own satire. *Talent*'s broad scope was accessible to all, but the trials of a community arts administrator working in an arts centre had limited appeal to those unfamiliar with that world. Perhaps aware of this problem, Victoria compensated and tried to accommodate a wider audience by cramming less esoteric gags into *Good Fun*. The result was a work that fell between two extremes: a dark play of minority appeal shot through with unsubtle humour. Even the Islington crowd, who one might assume would have been the most knowing audience, were not impressed. When Victoria went to see the King's Head production during its six-week run in October of that year she heard a punter remark 'It's a bit witty witty, isn't it?' It was only eight years later, when the two plays were published by Methuen, that Victoria publicly acknowledged the play's failings, admitting she never got it right and did not really know what she was doing with it.

With the casting, Victoria once again presented herself as a reluctant performer, claiming that she only wrote herself into it under duress after the producers refused to stage it without her. She created Elsie, a cynical and candid 24-year-old bistro barmaid, whom she described as a version of herself 'with all the horrible bits knocked out'. Later she would dismiss the role as 'some jokes and an anorak'.

The lead role of the unsympathetic Liz, the 24-year-old community arts administrator, was taken by Annabel Leventon after Julie Walters turned it down in favour of playing Betty. Julie's choice was not surprising as Betty was a comedic tour-de-force and an irresistible part, even though it did involve ageing up by 22 years. The role was the first of Victoria's comic grotesques (at first Betty is mistaken for a drag artist) that Julie would play.

Annabel was the only established actress in the cast, having starred in the original production of *Hair* and a number of West End comedies. By coincidence she had directed the play *Morecambe* to great success at the Hampstead Theatre at the same time Victoria was performing *Wordplay* there. On first seeing the script of *Good Fun* she thought it was the funniest thing she had ever read and cried with laughter, but the laughter did not last long.

'It wasn't one of those relationships that gelled,' she says of the experience of working with Victoria. 'I wasn't comfortable. I felt out of it.' She attributes the problem to Victoria's insecurity and David Leland's weak direction, lack of sympathy and inability to create good relations between the cast. Matters were made worse when hopes of a West End transfer were dashed. After seeing an early performance Codron took Victoria and Leland out for a meal and all thoughts of a transfer were dropped. 'It was such a disappointment. They were all so sure it was going into town. It kind of fell apart,' says Annabel. 'There was an awful air of disappointment that hung over it. There was a big push towards the West End and everybody had high hopes because of *Talent* and then when it dropped I think everybody's confidence dropped.'

The rejection dented Victoria's pride and confidence. During her schooldays, when events did not go the way she wanted, she withdrew. This defensive mechanism was reactivated and Victoria concentrated on her individual performance, which, at times, meant others were upstaged.

'I think it was out of her control in a sense because we didn't have a strong director who allowed her to feel confident in what was happening. It's the director who builds the team and if you haven't got a good team builder people tend to get anxious and go out and protect themselves. She was on the line with that show and I think she went out and protected herself and unfortunately the effect of that is not necessarily very good on the other people on stage. It's not a pretty atmosphere and I don't think she created that but I do think she was a victim of it.

'I think she must have been very selective about the people she trusted and I suppose I'm not used to not being trusted and competed with on stage. It was a bit of a shock to find someone who'd written it not supporting you on stage when you're out there doing your best. She was *very* competitive on stage.'

Annabel adds: 'She acted like a solo performer rather than a member of a team so instead of you working together for a laugh you'd set up one thing and you'd find the laugh would be killed by a laugh that came from down over there which you knew nothing about, which is very isolating.'

She believes Victoria's behaviour came from an instinct of self-preservation, but it made for an extremely unhappy state of affairs. 'If you get on really well with a person you can say "What the hell were you doing?" but if you don't, you can't. I'm used to people who have a good time with each other on stage and who help each other . . . I didn't find that the case. It made it *very* hard work because you're working on your own, and to me theatre's teamwork and she's a solo performer.'

The crisis was exacerbated when Victoria realised Julie was not prepared to be in the planned revised version of the play. She had been offered the lead role in Willy Russell's *Educating Rita* and Annabel remembers Julie fretting that her defection might be seen as disloyal by Victoria. Wisely, Julie did go on to do the play at the RSC Warehouse and, later, at the Piccadilly Theatre in the West End. The role of the Liverpudlian hairdresser earned her the Drama Critic's Most Promising Newcomer Award, the Variety Club's Best Newcomer award and, ultimately, stardom.

The hallmarks of Victoria Wood first introduced in *Talent*, continued into her second play. The famous names dropped became even more frequent and eclectic (from Louis Armstrong to Raquel Welch). Textiles would weave their way throughout Victoria's career and in *Good Fun* she mentioned Lurex, cheesecloth, nylon and acrylic. Garments, too, pop up frequently, with Victoria preferring the unglamorous or impractical (such as surgical stockings, stretch pants and support hose).

During rehearsals for *Good Fun* Victoria was interviewed by the radio programme *Arena* and commented on why there were so few female comics: 'I suppose women think they shouldn't [go into comedy] because it's not quite nice – because all comedy's aggression and women have been brought up not to be aggressive.' She certainly illustrated her defiance of convention in *Good Fun* with unabashed mention of all things sexual and gynaecological. In the same *Arena* interview Victoria made plain her antipathy to the whole pseudo-political agit-prop community arts movement. 'I find it deeply depressing,' she said. 'There's no laughs in it usually. Well their idea of a laugh is to sort of dress up as William Pitt the Younger which I don't think is highly amusing.' She parodied this in the play, which includes an avant-garde Punch and Judy show where the crocodile is the DHSS, and Judy is pregnant because of faulty counselling by the Family Planning. An 'all-night Madrigal event' is given short shrift, and Elsie casts a satirical eye over Launderdrama, a theatrical group who perform shows in launderettes.

Afflictions, illness and bizarre injuries are things that Victoria likes to milk for humour. In *Good Fun* mention is made of everything from diabetes to impetigo, and even Punch has a colostomy bag! But it is the embarrassing and therefore comical cystitis that was used as an actual plot point. This led to letters of complaint from sufferers which Victoria dealt with in the same flippant way she had responded to those who criticised *Talent*. When one woman wrote to tell her 'I've got cystitis and it isn't funny', Victoria fired off the reply 'Send it back and ask for one that is.'

Nuns were once again used for comic effect, and 'Tupperware', 'raffia' 'tumble dryer' and 'barmy', which would, like coconut matting, become almost talismanic to Victoria, all got a mention. But the accusation most levelled at Victoria is that she is overly reliant on High Street/brand names, and these were already heavily evident in *Good Fun*.

The play is rooted in some of Victoria's own experiences, albeit to a lesser extent than *Talent*. The locale, the annexe of an arts centre in North West England, is described as being on the top floor of an old neglected building such as a church hall, school, or Conservative Club – environments that Victoria experienced through *The Swish of The Curtain*, the Rochdale Youth Theatre Workshop and Bury Military Band.

Passing mention is made to Radcliffe (part of Bury), *That's Life* and 'Christine Palmer' a name reminiscent of Chrissie Poulter who was on Victoria's university course and went into community theatre. In fact, Victoria's university tutor, Gerry McCarthy, believes Chrissie was the inspiration for the play.

Victoria freely admitted to being obsessed about her school days and this seems to have seeped into *Good Fun*. Gail Melling was her victim at Bury Grammar and a schoolmate character called Gail is victimised in the play. Gail Melling was extremely thin at school and the last Victoria knew of her was that she was going on to teacher training college. In *Good Fun* Victoria specifies Gail (who name drops nicknames and surnames of Victoria's Bury Grammar contemporaries) is 8st 10, a teacher and has a dreary Lancashire accent. For good measure she makes Gail dull, disapproving and humourless.

In spite of the internal difficulties, the critics gave *Good Fun* a generally favourable reaction, though not as effusive as that for *Talent*. More than one observed how plot seemed to have been sacrificed for a string of unsubtle jokes. The unrelenting unflattering portraits of men and the play's overlong, sometimes rambling, nature was also commented upon, and although Annabel Leventon, Noreen Kershaw, Julie Walters and Charles McKeown all drew praise, Tim Brown of the *Morning Telegraph* remarked: 'Miss Wood is clearly stretched keeping up with the rest of the cast.'

Before the modified version of *Good Fun* was staged, two events occurred that helped restore Victoria's confidence. Granada commissioned a pilot sketch show from her ('just sketches and songs – no big deal really,' she remarked with her customary self-deprecation), and she won the Pye Colour Television Award for Most Promising Writer. The award, which she received on her 27th birthday, was made in association with the Writers' Guild of Great Britain which gave Victoria a certain kudos. The £300 prize money was also welcome, but the fact that she was being rewarded for *Talent*, a play written two years previously, when her latest offering had failed to make it into London, gave a degree of negativity to her success. Mindful of this she remarked: 'Winning awards can be a bit of a handicap. It flashes your name around but people expect you to do something fantastic next time.' However, the praise (*Talent* also won an award at the Film and Television Festival of New York) reactivated her ambition and she began talking about making a film if the funding could be found.

Nearly A Happy Ending, the sequel to *Talent*, was broadcast on 1 June 1980. 'My real point is to show that people don't really know what they want,' said Victoria of her second Granada television play. It begins with a depressed Julie, whose boyfriend has been killed in a car crash and whose mother is back in a psychiatric hospital, suffering from depression. She has been spending her days watching *Playschool* and drinking coffee out of a vase. In comparison Maureen's life is on an upswing; she has passed her driving test and lost weight. The girls plan a night out but first Julie accompanies Maureen to the slimming club. In the car Maureen reveals to Julie how she had always planned to lose her virginity once she reached target weight. Her only criteria is the man who obliges her does not have tattoos. The car breaks down but randy businessmen Tim (Freddie Fletcher) and Ken (Mike Kelly) come to the rescue and invite them to their annual conference/convention at a nearby hotel.

At the bar the girls hit it off with the barman (Christopher Godwin). Tellingly, the first sympathetic male character to be created by Victoria was emasculated by his homosexuality. Later Julie fixes Maureen up with a character called Tony (Paul Seed). This prompts a genuinely moving and rhapsodic hymn from Maureen, revealing a lifetime of yearning and a long-awaited release from it. In his room Tony is taken aback by Maureen's stark and clinical request for sex. Meanwhile, Julie has formed a rapport with comedian Les Dickey (Peter Martin) and is seriously considering forming a double act with him.

Maureen returns, her virginity still intact. Julie tells her sex is over-rated, but goes ahead and plans a rendezvous with Tony for herself anyway. Julie arranges for Tony to drive her home in Maureen's car and fixes a taxi for Maureen. When Maureen is understandably upset at Julie's about-face concerning men, Julie justifies herself in song. At 26 she is already resigned to physical decline and as all men are the same anyway, she might as well take what's on offer. Such a defeatist attitude is a sad contrast to her final song in *Talent*, where she fought against her likely fate and the audience was left with the feeling that her self-awareness would take her further in life. Now she is going to settle for cigarettes and alcohol. The song becomes a duet and cleverly develops into an anthem of happy failure with both girls admitting they have not got a clue. To them, life is the soggy bottom sheet, a canteen dinner, a shopping list of things they can't afford. The girls are united in a belief that even if they do not go far or find their star they are nearly happy where they are.

The play allowed Victoria to target one of her pet hates: the slimming industry. The ritual of the weigh-in is shown in all its ridiculous tragedy with polite applause for those who are on target and rebukes for those who have failed. One character, Evelyn (Pat Roe), desperately assures guru Madge (Rosemary Williams) that 'the cellophane [wrapped round the stomach to achieve weight loss through sweating] didn't come off until Wednesday afternoon'. But it is not just weight that is disapproved of; on seeing Julie's rounded shoulders, Madge expresses a desire to get her on the floor with a broom handle one Tuesday evening.

Victoria highlighted the underlying deceit of the slimming industry – its success is based on peoples' failure – with the song 'Don't Get Cocky Baby'. With a chorus that is a musical pastiche of 'Keep Young And Beautiful', the song gives cautionary tales of 'successful' dieters, with the gloating refrain 'Don't get cocky baby you're going to be back next month'. Victoria had addressed the dangers of slimming in her *New Faces'* song, when Lorraine says: 'I might fade away and be just a veil and a pile of bones.' In 'Don't Get Cocky Baby' she again alluded to anorexia with the mention of Fiona who 'slimmed herself to bones and specs'.

So strong is Victoria's hatred of the industry that she has likened it to drug dealing, making money by creating neurosis and feeding off people's emotional reasons for overeating. She emphasised how dieting is not the solution to life's problems in Maureen's song 'I Might As Well Be Fat'. In fact, the most significant moment of the play comes when the spurned Maureen realises the phrases she has adopted from her parents and Madge, and on which she anchors her life, are actually empty and meaningless. When the barman asks her what she means by

'A stick of celery a day keeps the elasticated trousers away' she pauses, considers it and eventually replies 'I don't know'. In doing so she signifies her development and independence.

Victoria also used the play to pour scorn on the sexist attitudes she herself experienced in her career. Tony tells Julie: 'Comediennes are always a bit ugly and that's why they're comediennes. I've met a few, they're very hard ladies.' Maureen tells Julie that she can't stand up and tell jokes for the simple fact that 'Girls don't.'

Victoria's sharpened command of language yielded some unique and acute descriptions (Julie's long-suffering Auntie Kathleen is said to have a bum resembling frozen pastry that's been walked on by someone wearing stilettos, and Maureen says she was so fat she looked like she'd been badly sprayed with insulating plastic foam).

Victoria also developed the use of extraneous fine detail for humorous effect: Julie says the digital clock she threw at her mother didn't break but stayed on 15.42. Likewise, the double entendre of a Marks & Spencer's spotted dick is eclipsed by the comical specification that it was an individual spotted dick.

This type of detail was also applied to dates, a technique first used in *Good Fun* where Betty says her next-door neighbour has disliked them since 5 November 1967 when the Catherine Wheel flew off the horse chestnut. It is also a significant date for *Nearly A Happy Ending* as Les reveals his wife has had a continuous headache since Bonfire Night 1947.

Victoria's habit of relating the unrelated was heard in *Good Fun* when Lynne asks: 'How can I have a baby? I've never even had a goldfish'. Here it is used again when, on being asked if she's ever had a push start before, Julie replies that she's never even had Irish Coffee.

Namedropping, textiles/garments, sexual/gynaecological references, afflictions and High Street/brand names all got their customary mention. Nuns got yet another outing, with Julie saying that they have fun by playing billiards. Suburban lust is also revisited, with *Good Fun's* 'nude monopoly' here becoming 'strip tiddlywinks'. The tumble dryer once again merits a mention and the play is also littered with Margarets, Pams, Renees and Pats – names that would appear regularly in Victoria's 'register'.

The practice of using an older character for an added perspective that was first used in *Talent* and followed in *Good Fun*, is continued here with the brief appearance of the toilet attendant played by Jill Summers who, like Bill Waddington before her, would go on to become a *Coronation Street* regular.

As always there were autobiographical elements present, nowhere more so than in Maureen's address – Castle Hill Road – the Wood family home. The singers at the conference are named Silver Sensation; the group Sweet Sensation appeared on *New Faces* in the same year as Victoria. And Victoria would have known all about the plight of comedian Les, booked to perform for a businessmen's convention.

The play ends with Julie being bored to death by Tony and Maureen tucking into a box of Black Magic. It was the last time the public would see Maureen and Julie. Granada had tried to persuade Victoria to write another play about them, or possibly a series, but she knew she had exhausted the characters and sensibly decided to close the book on them.

Victoria's songs are always a bone of contention for critics. Personally, she is not a great listener of songs nor a fan of lyrics. For *Nearly A Happy Ending*, *The Times*' Michael Ratcliffe admired her 'exceptionally fluent and communicative' lyrics, but complained of the 'tuneless and self-effacing jingles' which accompanied them. The *Daily Mail*'s Herbert Kretzmer, on the other hand, thought the lyrics 'sometimes crashingly clumsy'. Ratcliffe likened Victoria to a sea lion on Blackpool prom, Kretzmer said she was stuck in a 'self-admiring rut' and even Clive James, who would later become a champion of Victoria as a performer and a person, said she looked like Orson Welles and her jokes fell into shape as naturally as her figure didn't. The *coup de grâce* came from the *Sunday Times*' Russell Davies, who was of the opinion that without Julie Walters, Victoria 'might not get away with it'.

There was little time to dwell on such reactions because later that same month the new, improved version of *Good Fun*, this time directed by Peter James, was staged, again at Sheffield. Sharper and pacier, James cut out Leland's gimmicky staging – the set no longer glowed and the band were in the orchestra pit as opposed to zooming in and out from the back wall – and encouraged a more naturalistic approach to the roles by the three replacement actors.

Annabel Leventon was not asked to reprise the role of Liz, which went to ex *Liver Bird* Polly James. Replacing Julie Walters was Meg Johnson, who made the mistake of attempting to play the cartoonish Betty as a realistic person. Sam Kelly took over as Frank.

Victoria's contribution was to prune the play of some of its wordiness, graft on some Plot and add two new songs. As with *Talent*, the play's songs enabled Victoria to give a greater insight into the characters than dialogue ever could. This is particularly so with three numbers given to Liz. 'Liz's Song' opens the play. Through it she seeks to establish the fact that she is 'nice', but there is a seam of discontent running through it, realised by some imaginative similes. 'I'll Do Anything' shows her willingness to sacrifice her ego in order to have Mike. She is comically prepared to learn enamelling, buy lavatory paper in bulk, diet, live in Tring and wear Littlewood's blouses. Victoria's obvious antipathy to such a lifestyle would soften in future years, the scorn turning into a more light-hearted mockery.

Liz's final song, and the song that ends the play, is the extremely caustic 'Good Fun'. We learn her niceness stemmed not from compassion, but from poor self-image. She surrounded herself with the sick and socially deprived to make herself look and feel better. She has always envied Elsie for breaking her rules about things an ugly girl should do. Selfishness is her new resolve – she does not care who has lost as long as she can win.

Other songs of note were 'Handicrafts', an affectionate swipe at arts, crafts and evening classes, 'Bloody Clowns', a song about disillusionment, and 'I've Had It Up To Here'. This is a litany of complaints about men who see women as bits of gynaecology and leave them cold and wet. It also heralded a preoccupation which would surface throughout Victoria's career: disillusionment and dissatisfaction with sex. As she later explained: 'I do think there are a lot of people out there who don't like sex very much so that's why it makes a good comic target.'

Despite the changes *Good Fun* remained unsatisfactory and, as the *Doncaster Evening Post*'s Stephen McClarence pointed out, attempting to turn it into a Well-Made Play was comparable to trying to turn *Coronation Street* into *King Lear*.

CHAPTER 7

GOOD *Fun* was not good enough to earn Victoria a place on the London stage; for that she turned to stand-up. When it opened at the King's Head in September, the punningly titled *Funny Turns* was presented as a new revue by Victoria and Geoffrey. In reality it was largely a re-hash of the revue they had been touring on and off since 1977, with material from *Tickling My Ivories* and songs from Victoria's back catalogue thrown in for good measure.

Geoffrey went onstage first and the reaction he got from the critics as The Great Soprendo debunks the popular assumption that he rode on the back of Victoria's success. It took a particular skill to bedazzle jaded Metropolitans with traditional tricks and revive the art of magic into dynamic entertainment. The character of Soprendo ('I am very big in The Canaries'), with his waxed moustache and Liberace shirts, gave Geoffrey's technical conjuring talent an extra edge. He peppered the act with such gems as 'You have been a wonderful audience, everything I have done, you have given me the clap', which were eagerly lapped up.

Included in Victoria's routine was 'Fourteen Again' from *Talent* and 'Love Song' from *In At The Death*. Another old song, 'Music and Movement', which is a nostalgic look at a 1950s childhood through the eyes of a disgruntled and indignant schoolboy, was already two years old, having first been aired on a radio show in Manchester. Her decision to use *Good Fun*'s 'I've Had It up To Here' led some of the uninitiated to assume it was a feminist anthem written from the heart, rather than for a character. It was modified slightly for *Funny Turns*. The original had the lyrics:

> *I've had it up to here with blokes*
> *And all their stupid dirty jokes*
> *About poofs and wogs and nigs and*
> *Buying pokes in pigs and*
> *Here's a funny one about John Noakes.*

But for the *Funny Turns* version the last three lines borrowed from the song 'Make A Joke':

> *It's not a lot of fun*
> *To hear the one about the nun,*
> *the marrow, the banana and John Noakes*

which, besides removing the racist and homophobic elements, made sense of the 'dirty jokes' aspect of the lyric.

Taking the supermarket counter, suburbia and the surgical ward as the landscapes for her routine, Victoria expounded a dissatisfaction and disinterest in sex and a scathing opinion of Morecambe. New was the character monologue, a device inherited from Joyce Grenfell that has remained a staple of Victoria's stage work. Her first creation was a condescending Women's Institute president outlining events for the coming season, such as Mr Ripley's talk 'Life has a lot to offer even if you've got no bowels'.

For once, the press laid off Victoria's appearance, apart from Eric Shorter in the *Daily Telegraph* who described her as 'a plucky, buxom singing blonde from Lancashire'. Far more perceptive was *The Times*' Irving Wardle, who was spot on in his analysis of her delivery ('as if serving a pound of crumbly Lancashire cheese across the counter of a corner shop'). He described her as 'a voice from the social junk heap: inspired by supermarket queues, slimming aids, Women's Institute meetings, handicraft hobbies and the inexhaustible heap of modern trash with which we while away the time.'

Funny Turns may have originally been regarded as an hors d'oeuvre to the King's Head production of *Good Fun* (featuring a cast independent of Victoria), but it turned out to be the main course. The critics were even less impressed with the play than they had been by the Sheffield productions, and the *Guardian*'s Nicholas de Jongh branded it a 'tiny disaster in which Miss Wood's marks of individuality have coarsened into repetitive sequences of sniggering knockabout'. The troubles the play had caused her did not prevent Victoria from naming the production company she set up in 1982, with herself as director and Geoffrey as co-director and secretary, after it and in doing so she erased its negative associations.

After *Funny Turns* was over Geoffrey momentarily had the spotlight solely on him when he appeared as Abanazar in the Crucible's pantomime of *Aladdin*. He spoke to Victoria on the phone every day and she sent him a synopsis of each *Coronation Street* episode he had missed. They did not meet up until the afternoon of Christmas Eve when Victoria went to see the matinée. Afterwards she drove them to a York hotel where Geoffrey was booked for a Christmas Day cabaret; money, as always, came before pleasure. The festivities were short-lived and on Boxing Day Victoria dropped him back at Sheffield while she returned to Morecambe to continue work on the Granada play. Her pilot sketch show was in the can and Granada presumably liked what they saw because the next day they commissioned an entire series.

The weight Victoria lost for *Nearly A Happy Ending* did not stop her worrying about her shape. She hated people mentioning her weight but masochistically drew attention to it herself by naming the New Year's Day 1981 pilot sketch show *Wood & Walters: Two Creatures Great and Small*.

Although Victoria wrote the entire show and shared the acting and singing duties, Julie merited equal billing as her presence was vital in shoring up Victoria's confidence. Even when Peter Eckersley had offered her a series, Victoria's fundamental insecurity meant she only agreed on the understanding that Julie was in it too.

Considering she had only written one sketch three years previously, the faith Granada placed in Victoria by giving her a show was remarkable. The pressure of expectation was felt by Victoria and she reacted by resorting to her stage show defence tactics. She still felt at her strongest with a song and a piano, which accounts for the unusually high ration of four songs in the 30-minute sketch show.

The sketches themselves concerned computer dating, keep fit class gossip, the joys of DIY and the Marriage Guidance Council, but their scarcity was a portent of the problems that would occur when *Wood & Walters* became a series.

Victoria later described the pilot show as dire, but to her great surprise it was nominated for a BAFTA award, along with *The Stanley*

Baxter Series (which won), *The Kenny Everett Video Show* and *The Two Ronnies*.

Although Victoria did not appear in her next project for Granada, *Happy Since I Met You*, she hung around for the filming. Whilst in Manchester she performed a one-off show at the Royal Exchange Theatre and in May, keen to build on her stand-up routine, she undertook a five-date tour of the North West. It is not widely known that during this period she was also the musical support for Radio 2's *The Little and Large Party*. Earlier she had written material for Su Pollard to perform on Granada's *The Comedians*. Perhaps understandably neither of these jobs appear on her CV.

While Geoffrey was away in Margate for the summer season, Victoria busied herself writing the *Wood & Walters* television series, which distracted her from nervously anticipating the reaction to *Happy Since I Met You*. 'I thought it was about time I wrote something I wasn't in,' she said of the play. The decision was probably prompted by self-defence rather than modesty. Sensitive to criticism, any hint that she was somehow lacking, made her recoil. The critics had made it plain in previous reviews that Julie was the better actress and, as at school, if Victoria could not compete she withdrew. Her increasingly heavy workload may have also been a factor. Besides, she realised that stand-up was becoming her real strength and an area in which she dominated.

Happy Since I Met You had the same team as Victoria's previous television plays, with Peter Eckersley producing and Baz Taylor directing. It was shown on 9 August 1981 and once again it got a Sunday evening slot. The gritty realism Victoria used to chart a relationship was a perfect antidote to the fairy tale marriage fever that had swept across the nation with the marriage of Charles and Diana.

The role of Frances Gordon, a 28-year-old drama teacher, was obviously Julie's. Her boyfriend was Jim Smith, a placid, struggling actor who holds the distinction of being the first major male character that Victoria wrote realistically and sympathetically.

The role was awarded to Duncan Preston, best known to the public as PC Fred Pooley in the 1973 television series *Hunter's Walk*. The RADA-trained actor had grown up in Bradford and started out as a lorry driver until he was spotted in amateur theatre. Victoria and Julie, in high spirits after a long lunch, sat in on his audition. 'It was absolutely terrifying, but I read a couple of scenes and then Julie Walters said "Ooh, I want him to do it because he's so big" and she jumped up and gave me a playful punch,' recalled Duncan. 'Later I rang my agent to tell him it had been a horrific interview, but he said I'd been offered the part.' The bond between Victoria and Julie was intimidating to the newcomer who likened joining the cast to entering a secret club.

It is apt that the play begins at Christmas since its framework resembles *A Christmas Carol*. Outwardly chirpy, Fran is fundamentally unhappy. She is presented with various case studies of relationships to mull over. Her neighbour (Eileen Mayers) is not in one and faces a lonely Christmas; a sister, Olwen (Sue Wallace), is embittered and in the throes of a divorce; another sister, Karen (Tracey Ullman) is devoted to and dependent on her boyfriend; a friend, Mary (Carol Leader), talks about the emotional benefits and conveniences of being in a relationship – it's less boring than being alone and better than going through the rigmarole of having to get used to being with someone new; a colleague, Judith (Kathryn Apanowicz) illustrates the material benefits of marriage.

Fran then has to analyse her own past relationships and make a decision whether or not to enter into a new one with Jim – whom she meets at a dire dinner party – in order to ensure a happy future. Along the way she faces pressure from her family, Jim himself, and even her pupils who buy her make-up for Christmas to help her get a bloke.

Fran and Jim's first date is in a wholefood vegetarian restaurant (the healthfood movement would become a popular target for Victoria). Fran launches into a speech about her new resolve regarding relationships. She does not want a one-night stand or a big heavy relationship. She won't let him into her flat in case it puts him off her. She tells Jim that she is determined not to repeat past mistakes by changing to suit the man she is with. She decides sex would be too much of a risk; afterwards he would go off her and she would be miserable again. The way she reels off her intentions is every bit as clinical as Maureen's approach to sex in *Nearly A Happy Ending*.

Attempting to control Love is of course futile. It is a gamble but Fran adopts Victoria's musical advice, holds her breath, takes a jump and ends up in bed with Jim.

She is in love with him and they move in together, but she has anxieties about being regarded as his appendage. Romance is replaced by banality and the little things begin to irritate her. In a playful mood Jim attempts to seduce her. Fran's response is to ask him to get some bin-liners.

Fran grows increasingly unsympathetic and crabby. Jim has a cold and even his sniffing irritates her. A walk in the park develops into a row and poor Jim eventually snaps. She tells him she is fed up of never being alone and having to explain every little thing. To her, a trouble shared is a trouble dragged out until bedtime. They give each other a slap.

Back at the flat there is another row, this time triggered by Christmas cards, and a rather unnerving fight breaks out – such was the force of one of Julie's slaps that Duncan got a swollen cheek. Fran leaves for a friend's cottage but, in an update of *Brief Encounter*, Jim catches up with her at the train station cafe. Fran tells him she loves him but knows she makes him miserable. He tells her he loves her and she reveals she had already decided to give the relationship another try. She affectionately points out that his shirt is untucked, signifying that her irritation has transformed into tenderness.

The shifting nature of their relationship was brilliantly charted by Victoria in the episodic song 'Living Together'. In the early days of Fran and Jim's romance she sings of the fun that living together brings. Living together then becomes work. In time it becomes mad, like sharing a prison cell.

The use of High Street/brand names was, partly, Victoria's way of rooting her plays in reality, but it is ironic that this, the most naturalistic of her three television plays, should feature so few. She downplayed the namechecks too, and on the gynaecological front, only sanitary towels were inserted in the script.

All the other hallmarks were present: Raffia; rarefication (an engagement ring is a 'diamond half hoop'); advertising jargon (a home is a 'three-bedroomed executive bungalow with Georgian portico');

unfashionable garments of particular fabric (nylon quilty housecoat, an angora jumper and a lime green canvas coat dress with mandarin collar); quirky figurative terms (Fran says she has got hands like the Magna Carta and breath like a car crash) and afflictions (hospitalisation with a neck injury caused by unscrewing a jar of beetroot).

Nuns are not only referred to, but embodied by Fidelis Morgan, a fellow student of Victoria's at Birmingham. Similarly, we get to see an auntie in the flesh. In her previous plays characters had quoted and alluded to various aunts – an irony since Victoria never knew any of her own – but in *Happy Since I Met You* Majorie Sudell is a comic highlight as Auntie Edith. She inflicts herself on the Gordon family Christmas and gives such miserly presents as a knitted waistcoat to be shared and a toilet roll holder.

Specific detail from Victoria's own past crept in via the mention of the Farmer's Arms pub. This was the Bury hostelry where her classmates socialised while Victoria stayed at home. Also worth a mention is the headwear of Fran's neighbour (Eileen Mayers). The beret would feature often in the years to come.

The play showed Victoria still had some shortcomings as a playwright. Songs were once again favoured over speech to convey deeper emotions, and there were rather too many scenes of Fran soliloquising in the mirror. But the *Daily Mail's* Mary Kenny rated it the best thing she had seen in a long time, remarking that Victoria's dialogue had the idiomatic drollness of Les Dawson with the refinement of Jean Anouilh. On the other hand, the *Guardian's* Stanley Reynolds complained: 'It was padded out with vulgar speeches . . . lines delivered as if they were heroic truths, as if they were not only great gems of wit but also terribly socially significant.'

Victoria achieved her aim of making a film in the September of 1981, but it was far from the grandiose project she had envisaged for herself. However, there was a sign of her growing reputation in that she was invited to perform in *The Secret Policeman's Other Ball* alongside some of the leading lights of British comedy. The show, an Amnesty International Gala, was filmed and recorded over three nights at the Theatre Royal, Drury Lane and later released as a video and LP. Victoria shared the bill with such luminaries as Rowan Atkinson, Alan Bennett, John Bird, Jasper Carrott, Graham Chapman, Billy Connolly, Dame Edna Everage, John Fortune, Griff Rhys Jones, Alexei Sayle and John Wells. The only other female performer on the bill was Pamela Stephenson, but since she was so closely associated with the *Not The Nine O'Clock News* team, a role Victoria had turned down, it meant Victoria had a unique place in the line up. Recalling the shows she said: 'On the first night I died the death, and on the second night I had to go on and swear, because that was the only way I could compete. I was following such filth, I sounded like Mary Poppins.'

The remainder of her year was spent rehearsing and recording the *Wood & Walters* series while Geoffrey was in pantomime at Newcastle. It was not a happy experience as shortly before work on the series began, Victoria's mentor Peter Eckersley died of cancer. It was a tremendous blow to her as he had been one of the few people she could trust. He was important to her not only as a friend, but as an experienced and critical eye. As a result of his loss the series was without an anchor.

'He had lots of ideas for the series . . . but he never told me what they were. His value to me was inestimable,' said Victoria. 'He had a marvellous eye for what was unnecessary and great attention to detail. He had liked the first material for the series but never saw any of the other stuff.'

Brian Armstrong took over as producer and Victoria was not impressed, complaining that he did not know what it was all about. Although Duncan Preston appeared in a couple of the sketches, Victoria was also of the opinion that several unsuitable actors had been hired.

In times of stress her critical faculties sometimes failed her, as witnessed during *Good Fun*. Not being used to writing a series, she had not anticipated the sheer volume of material that was required for *Wood & Walters* and only wrote enough for six half hours. Quality control was an unavailable luxury and when she did cut out poor material it left the series a whole show short. That was why episode six became a 'best of' compilation, a measure unthinkable in television today. Additional pressure came from seeing her comedy partner's stock begin to soar – 1982 was the year in which Julie would appear in both Alan Bleasdale's *Boys From The Blackstuff* and Alan Bennett's television play *Intensive Care*. Work would also begin on her first film, playing opposite Michael Caine in *Educating Rita*. Meanwhile Victoria's *One Cal* television advert (in which she put profit before principle to sing the praises of a diet drink), and her appearances on Radio 4's *Just A Minute* kept her financially afloat.

A more appropriate studio audience might have helped Victoria's self-confidence, but the pensioners Granada imported for *Wood & Walters* did not share her sense of humour. Before one sketch the warm-up man had to explain the concept of a boutique and on another occasion he was so desperate to get a reaction from the stony faces that he actually mooned them. During one recording a disgusted audience member was overheard saying to her friend: 'You realise that we're missing *Brideshead* for *this*.'

Up until this period the one unchanging source of confidence for Victoria had been that she had no rivals. As a female comedian she was unique and possessed a distinctive style. But now even this insurance policy was beginning to crumble. A young and largely unknown Rik Mayall had been given his own spot on *Wood & Walters* as Mitch, a chauvinistic feminist, and he enlightened Victoria that there were other female comics out there who were not of the working men's club ilk. He told her about Dawn French and Jennifer Saunders and Victoria later admitted that she grudgingly thought they sounded funny and was consequently concerned that they might invade her territory. As a result she steered clear of them for years. The Lancashire alternative comedian Jenny Eclair, who had filmed slots for *Wood & Walters*, found herself edited out when the series was aired.

The 'Two Creatures Great And Small' adjunct was dropped for the series, but the critics had got to Victoria, or 'the fat one who delights in playing puddings' as the *Daily Mirror* described her. Even though she had started buying her clothes from Fiorucci and having her hair cut at Vidal Sassoon, her self-image was still extremely fragile and some of the sketches in *Wood & Walters* had a savagely masochistic streak.

'I would set myself up as a victim and Julie would be the cruel one . . . I think that was my own chip on my shoulder and my own insecurity about being fat or Northern or whatever I felt insecure about I worked through in those sketches,' she explained. In the sketch 'Skin Care', for instance, Julie plays a sales assistant on the cosmetics counter who destroys Victoria's self-confidence, but much more savage is 'The Boutique'. When Victoria requests a size 14, Julie, again playing the assistant, informs her that it is a boutique, not the Elephant House. The insults come thick and fast, with Julie complaining that it is depressing dealing with the overweight all day long and expressing her reluctance to let obese people in the cubicles in case they sweat on the wallpaper. She calls her 'Porky' in much the same way that Victoria's first manager had called her 'Fatty' and likens an eight-stoner to a waterbed with legs. This sketch also saw Victoria borrowing from *Nearly A Happy Ending*, but where Julie said she wore her clothes so tight that she needed anaesthetic, the assistant requires surgery to remove things from her pockets.

The series included a version of 'Leader Of The Pack' sung by Julie, 'Northerners', discussed earlier, and 'What We Find'. Although only 29 Victoria tackled the ageing process in this bouncy song, which she premiered at the Bolton Festival. She highlights the Canute-like futility of fighting cellulite, falling bosoms, grey hair and dentures and she ridicules the preventative measures ('You rub your neck before you sleep with cream that's made from bits of sheep'). Here the textile of choice is 'crimplene'.

Of all the songs that featured in the series, 'Don't Do It' a duet sung by Victoria and Julie, was the most startling. Stripped of brand names and bare of humour, this was a plea for life to be lived without compromise that seemed to come from Victoria's own experiences. In it she depicts the bleakness of a dead marriage to warn of the dangers of simply accepting an unhappy situation. Perhaps reflecting how her own drive had helped her through the 1970s, she formalises her own philosophy. What could be worse than the pain and stupidity of a lifetime of nothing? she asks. It's one life and one chance that is easily ruined, why miss out on laughter, joy and elation? It's soft to give in or give up or go under. The message 'Don't Do It' is repeated throughout. 'Still you keep on smiling so the pain cannot be seen', sang Liz in *Good Fun*. But in 'Don't Do It' Victoria asks 'Why bother smiling in public and privately scheming?' and advocates shouting, kicking and screaming.

The first episode of *Wood & Walters*, which was broadcast on Sunday, 17 January 1982, included the sketch 'The Woman With 740 Children' in which Victoria played the unfortunate mother who had overdosed on a fertility drug. Much to Victoria's surprise and bemusement Granada used 70 real babies, including one from Rochdale who shared her name. Victoria's attitude had not softened to those who dared to write in and complain about her work. One foolhardy correspondent took exception to the use of the babies, wondering whether Victoria would be using cripples and blind people next, to which Victoria replied 'What a good idea.'

Elsewhere in the series we were introduced to Dotty who like Betty in *Good Fun* was another middle-aged Northern grotesque which Julie delighted in playing. Dressed in shocking pink, she dispensed advice and had no embarrassment at mentioning her groin strain caused after she got carried away behind the cistern with a crevice tool. In many ways Dotty was an early incarnation of Kitty, who Patricia Routledge would bring vividly to life in a later series, *Victoria Wood As Seen On TV*.

That series would also feature weekly 'documentaries' a device which was first used in *Wood & Walters'* *Girls Talking*. Parodying the stark documentary style and grim subjects of the early 1980s, this has Victoria and Julie playing the bored schoolgirls Marie and Jeanette. No strangers to shoplifting (the crime which Victoria always uses for amusement), both come from broken homes and live in Liverpool. They don't like school because they don't learn important things like how to inject themselves. Bored by child prostitution, they spend their time sniffing burning lino. They would like to get married because it is supposedly easier to get Valium.

At this stage in her career Victoria was getting used to being accosted by the public who tended to bluntly criticise her and her work, or mistook her for anyone from Pam Ayres to Virginia Wade. This may have inspired the sketch 'Groupies' in which Victoria and Julie played Bella and Enid who stage door a star (Alan Lake). They tell him they liked his show, but qualify this by saying they are easily pleased. The two typists do not want a signed photograph of him and they don't know anyone who would; most people in the office think he's really dated.

The piano had inspired one of Victoria's contributions to the school magazine and it also inspired the sketch 'The Practice Room'. Julie played the crass, chain-smoking cleaner with fond memories of *Dream of Olwen* which was on in Women's Surgical the night she had her cervix cauterised. Victoria played the stuffy piano student irritated by the cleaner's interruptions. The sketch sailed extremely close to snobbery about the working classes but Victoria prevented this at the last minute by showing how the cleaner, a supposed Philistine, actually had an in-depth knowledge of piano technique.

'Some bits of it were good; some were deadly,' was Victoria's bald verdict of the series. In spite of the mixed reception Granada, keen to keep the double act together, offered Victoria a second series. In Victoria's mind that would have only prolonged the failure; anything that was not totally successful was abhorrent to her and she declined. Eager to elevate herself from the series she began talking about her 'dark side' and the importance of developing her craftsmanship. Even Julie was distancing herself from the show, telling the *Daily Mail*: 'I want now to do something more serious than *Wood & Walters*. Comedy can get you down awfully after a while, and I have done so much that it becomes depressing.'

The most sensible thing for Victoria to have done at this time would have been to move to London. She was already making thrice-monthly visits but a permanent base there would have made it easier for her to raise her profile and take advantage of the comedy venues that were springing up all over the capital. Her middle sister, Rosalind, had already relocated and lived near Islington with her son, Mazda, named after the Greek god of light. She had her own market stall selling 1950s clothes. Penny, meanwhile was based in Oxford and sang with rock bands.

'All four of us have made our own way in life,' says Chris Foote Wood. 'No one's followed in any of the others' footsteps. Penny and Rosalind are more at the cutting edge. They're very individualistic at what they do. They are not concerned about populism. If people like it, fine. If not, hard luck. Penny is the artist. She's painted, sculpted, all sorts of things . . . She's very avant-garde.'

Victoria and Geoffrey, however, retreated further and bought their first home together in the village of Silverdale, 25 minutes from Morecambe. Number 22 Stankelt Road was a semi-detached stone cottage with a sea view from the toilet window. Silverdale was a rural idyll of dry stone walls, hedgerows, winding tree-lined country roads and meadows. Explaining the move, Victoria later admitted: 'I suppose I wanted to be odd in a way. I wanted to cut myself off. I wanted to be separate. I didn't have the nerve to go to London. I didn't want to compete.'

This distancing also applied to the villagers of Silverdale. 'She was a stuck-up bitch. She was her person and we were just riff-raff,' says Chris Taylor. He was one of the first villagers to encounter the local celebrities as Number 22 was his grandmother's former home and he had to turn on the power for Victoria and Geoffrey. 'It was basically "Thank you. Goodbye". There was no concern, no "how do you do". You didn't see much of her at all. She'd walk around occasionally, if it was a sunny evening, but she wouldn't speak to you. She never involved herself. She wasn't interested.'

Wood & Walters had failed to meet Victoria's own high standards, and with the disaster of *Good Fun* still galling her, she decided to concentrate on what she did best and take her stand-up act on the road again. However, she was aware that Geoffrey's career was struggling so they decided to reactivate *Funny Turns* in the hope that it would enable them to achieve something like steady earnings. It was the perfect solution to the enforced separations of work that were beginning to get the couple down. It was also to be their most ambitious outing yet.

A short eight-date tour was arranged prior to a four-week trial run at the King's Head, beginning in March 1982. The theatre pub's Dan Crawford had heard good reports about their act and asked them to fill in when another performer had let him down. Then, through Michael Codron, they would take the act, which Victoria described as 'Him – Interval – Me', into the West End for the first time. On the surface Victoria was confident and optimistic, still planning to write a film as well as a new play for Julie. She was not averse to elevating herself above any possible rivals either, telling the *TV Times*: 'A lot of women [comedians] aren't very good – that's the trouble.' But deep down her insecurities remained. By the time she was preparing for the nerve-wracking prospect of entering the arena of the West End, she had given up reading all reviews of her work because they caused depression. One, in which she was described as dominating the stage like a witty tank, particularly affected her.

'I don't read the reviews because I get so depressed. If they're very good, I don't believe them and if they're very bad, I do! Geoffrey sifts through them and says, "You've got quite a good one here . . . not such a good one in this paper." If they say "Victoria Wood is weak in this area", I get paranoid,' she said. An additional worry was how audiences would respond to Geoffrey as he tended to attract hecklers.

Exiling herself from Morecambe left Victoria with no qualms about savaging the town she had once praised. It was, she said in *Funny Turns*, so boring there that the tide only bothered to come in once a week. Evening classes were the only release but the choice was confined to Handling Your Pension, Coping With Cystitis, Good Grooming For the Over 90s and Keep Fit Beginners.

Victoria's act covered the traditional music hall subject matters of class, regional snobbery and sex, but her experience as a playwright gave her the edge. Very few comedians in those days had such a literary advantage. She was less reliant than others on punchlines and the humour tended to stem from exquisitely observed descriptions: the Hush Puppy slit for the bunion; the keep fit slippers that curl up as if they are about to devour your foot when you take them off; Victoria in a red leotard and tights looking like an eager salami.

Her musical instincts allowed her to employ phonetic comedy, savouring such words as 'Culottes' and 'trews'. And once again she juxtaposed garments with textiles – a tweed bodystocking – for comic effect.

'Maaarjorie', one of Morecambe's more sophisticated hostesses, wears such a low-cut dress it looks like she is standing in a carrier bag and her black hair is so heavily lacquered it looks like a 78 with a parting. Like the hostess in *Happy Since I Met You*, whose jarring attempt at sophistication is demonstrated by her serving up a plate of liver at a dinner party, Maaarjorie also gets it wrong by serving sprouts on cocktail sticks.

It was noticeable that Victoria's earlier awkward innocence had been replaced by a slick, calculated, sly professionalism. She was out of kilter with the trendy, right-on inhabitants of Islington, but instead of being intimidated as she may have been in the past, she went on the attack using a stage persona of down-to-earth Northern common sense as her weapon. 'Don't worry about being mugged when leaving the theatre,' she told the audiences, 'you're more likely to be subsidised'. The posey cosy world of stripped pine and wholemeal bread was also swiftly demolished in her stand-up act, and the political climate of the day was also mocked by Victoria chirpily threatening to sing a 'jolly chorus song' entitled I'm Not Worried About Unemployment Because There's Going To Be A Nuclear War'.

Geoffrey would not have informed Victoria of Milton Shulman's review in the *Evening Standard* ('Miss Wood is a big girl with few pretensions to glamour'). But the *Sunday Telegraph*'s review by Rosemary Say may have reached her ears ('She is sharp, observant and outrageous, but with it all she invites us to join without malice in the sheer hilarity of other people's behaviour').

A friend had once remarked to Victoria and Geoffrey that their act was so good because he was not totally masculine and she was not totally feminine; the *Guardian*'s Tom Sutcliffe put it more plainly when he wrote that Geoffrey had a higher voice and was less butch. This androgynous quality had been identified by Victoria in Max Miller, one of her favourite comedians, and she happily embraced it. This extended to her stage costumes and the jacket/blazer, trousers and tie became something of a trademark look for her. Just as wearing a tie had been an act of rebellion at Bury Grammar, so it was for Victoria as an adult female performer. So closely did she become associated with a tie that in October 1982 she became the first woman to be nominated for Tie Man of the Year (she lost to Trevor McDonald). Offstage too, she never wore a skirt and did not possess a handbag. Combined with the camp aspects of her act, the Northern caricatures, the exquisite detail and the mockery of the heterosexual male, it was hardly surprising that Victoria attracted a large gay following. Indeed, in later years she became a patron of the London Lighthouse Aids charity and was a public supporter of the campaign to lower the age of sexual consent for gay men.

'I used to get a lot of lesbians dressing like me actually,' she said. 'I had very short hair and a tie and I suppose it was a very masculine look . . . and I did used to get these enormous women coming back with cropped heads and ties. It was a bit scary . . . I think I was probably giving off androgynous signals because it wasn't a sexy look, it wasn't saying "I am a sexy woman", or "I am a butch woman". I think what it was saying was that whatever I am just take it and don't analyse it and just listen to the comedy.' The non-sexy look did have advantages. 'If you're not being glamorous or particularly feminine, people aren't feeling uncomfortable because you're twice as good looking as they are.'

Her stage presence too was getting more masculine. In the early days of stand-up she remained seated behind the piano. In *Wood & Walters* she had graduated to standing in the crook of the piano. But now she strode purposefully on stage and only had a stand mike between her and the audience.

After a short break for re-writes and adaptations *Funny Turns* opened at the Duchess Theatre on 12 May with Russell Harty giving an onstage introduction. The show still featured the old songs 'Fourteen Again', 'Music and Movement', 'I've Had It Up To Here', 'Don't Do It' and 'Northerners', but for the Duchess shows Victoria composed two new numbers. In 'Dear God' she succinctly summed up the utter misery of her impressions of student life.

'Thinking Of You', one of Victoria's 'anti-man' songs, was also new for the West End show. In it Victoria addresses an ex-lover and lists examples of how he reminds her of all her idiosyncratic pet hates (dripping wet towels, Dick Van Dyke's attempt at a Cockney accent) and veiled references to his impotence (a jellied eel, a pink blancmange that won't set).

The *Financial Times*'s Michael Coveney said her 'fast, brilliantly worked out and devastatingly funny' lyrics were the best available on the London stage with the exception of *Guys and Dolls* and created real poetry of the streets. Robert Cushman in the *Observer* went even further and said she was the best British lyricist since Noel Coward.

For the show, Geoffrey gave The Great Soprendo an additional catchphrase ('Olé Placido Domingo') and continued to delight critics with his malapropisms and mispronunciations ('I want you all to be as quiet as pins. I want to hear a mouse dropping', 'You are sitting there with one card; I am standing here with piles'). He was still prone to hecklers, which enraged Victoria. Sharing the bill with him meant the weight-watching critics moved their focus from Victoria's figure. So while Geoffrey was described as 'elephantine', Victoria was now being called 'attractive' and 'sexy'.

Funny Turns had a successful run until the end of June, repeats of *Wood & Walters* on Channel 4 no doubt helping raise Victoria's profile, and while not quite conquering Theatreland, Victoria had proved to herself that she need not fear a London audience. By delicious irony Bob Mason, the old boyfriend who so callously dumped her and who had gone on to gain a degree of fame as Terry Bradshaw in *Coronation Street*, had begun work on a biographical play about George Formby, arguably one of the most famous Northern comedians. It dealt with a pivotal moment in Formby's career, when he attempted to find success in London. Unlike Victoria, he failed.

CHAPTER 8

A PANIC attack seized Victoria the night before her 30th birthday. In a Maida Vale hotel room she came to the conclusion that the best of her life was over. Her childhood dream of being famous had been realised, she was an award-winning playwright, television star, stage actress, stand-up comedian, singer-songwriter and was living in an idyllic place with the husband she loved, but still the inner demons lingered. She discovered what many celebrities find out; fame does not eradicate fundamental psychological problems. There was still the sense of unworthiness, the impatience, the low self-esteem and the feeling that time was running out. Victoria needed to make a decision about where her career – which in those days was essentially her life – was heading.

It was not surprising that she chose the path that led to instant gratification and decided to concentrate on her stand-up work. 'When I go out there and make them laugh I'm saying "this is my personality and I hope you like it",' she said, demonstrating the almost masochistic extent she was prepared to go to gain assurance. But in order to truly test herself it had to be a solo venture, praise or criticism would be diluted if she continued performing with Geoffrey and so the end of *Funny Turns* marked the end of their professional stage partnership. Publicly, she blamed unsympathetic audiences for the break-up and claimed she was worn down by her worries that they would not like him: 'I overheard someone in the audience say "I don't like magic, but I suppose we'll have to sit through it until she comes on." It didn't bother him, but it was too much for me.' The claustrophobia of their relationship did not help either. 'I think our problem was that we worked together, lived together and did everything together. We never did anything separately.'

Performing alone was nothing new to Victoria, but previous outings had tended to be one-offs at universities, festivals and clubs in Northern England. For her new show, *Lucky Bag*, she was booked into the King's Head, Islington in October for a five-week run. It would be the last time she performed at that theatre, but she did not sever her involvement. She has performed charity galas for the theatre since and in the 1990s was made its life president.

Lucky Bag was a 90-minute show based around Victoria's CV, school, life in Morecambe and a trip to London. These were filled in with the sort of finely observed comic detail that was as much her hallmark as brand names.

'You have to distance yourself, be detached,' was Victoria's answer when asked what made a successful stand-up comedian. She had distanced herself from her family, from Geoffrey, from Julie, and from the town and the city. This isolationism became apparent in her material for *Lucky Bag*. But the more she distanced herself, the more her audiences grew.

As with *Funny Turns* the trendies and middle classes were targeted. She mocked the friend who lives in a converted mill chimney ('the rooms are very small but they have nice high ceilings'); time-share apartments in disused collieries; health food restaurants ('where you queue for 50 minutes for something that would do you a lot of good if you could get it out of your back fillings'); the Arts Council ('like the town council except the decisions they make don't affect anybody'); the alternative cabaret featuring a juggler who juggles three copies of the *Guardian* and a wok. A play is described as so boring it should win a Fringe award.

Victoria swept-up and dispensed with such a world using down-to-earth common sense. Yet that is not to say she was identifying herself with a no-nonsense, working-class, unsophisticated and welcoming North. 'See Naples and die – see Morecambe and feel as if you already have,' she said. Her savaging of the town was now total with description of the waxworks ('four shop dummies in de-mob suits labelled Bucks Fizz'), the pier ('a council house on a stick'), and the fair which consisted of a Big Wheel with antimacassars on the back of each seat and a liniment stall. The place is the domain of the pensioner. Old ladies wearing 'Kiss Me Quick, But Wait While I Get My Teeth In' hats grab men, take them into a dark corner, and show them photos of their son-in-law in Australia. In the 'Gifte Shoppe' hangs the sign: 'You don't have to be mad to work here, just old, deaf and incredibly irritating'.

Victoria's look and choice of career prevented her from being compartmentalised as feminine stereotype, but that did not mean she was about to embrace militantism. An unresponsive audience was assumed to be a deputation of Feminists Against Laughing and Victoria jokily introduced one song as: 'Don't Bother Buying Us A Port And Lemon As Freda And I Are Lesbians'.

Schooldays were increasingly influencing her work – she admitted to being obsessed about them – but she even managed to distance herself retrospectively. In one routine she describes half of her schoolmates as being common and the other half as being posh and in the process removes herself from the equation.

New for *Lucky Bag* was a surrealistic strain (knitting an orgasm and escaping from a mental hospital by knotting sheets together to make a moped). For the character monologue, a mainstay of the music hall tradition, Victoria created Paula Duval, a Northern club comedienne and 'vocaliste' who wows a hen party before playing the ukulele and singing the philosophical song 'Nasty Things'. 'She's a blue comedienne . . . She's the type of comedienne I can't bear,' said Victoria, even though she was happy to get laughs from Paula's material.

'I can't bear the fact that they're reversing the role of the male comic. I don't think it rings true. There are a few women blue comics on the club circuit. But I don't particularly go along with what they do – it seems pointless to alienate the whole of the other sex just because a few women complain that male comics tell mother-in-law and headache jokes.'

Lucky Bag also saw Victoria creating non-professional characters who found themselves having to 'perform'. This was a device which would serve her well in her career, both for other characters and as 'Victoria Wood'. The comedy was mined from the idiosyncrasies the character would inadvertently betray when called upon to speak in a formal situation. *Lucky Bag*'s schoolgirl debater has been discussed previously, but the show also featured the Haworth Parsonage Guide and the auditioning actress. The former is no respecter of twee, National Trust preciousness; she leaves her poncho on the Reverend Bronte's chair, parks her moped in the parsonage and makes inappropriate jokes. It was a brilliantly written and performed monologue but it did reveal Victoria's snobbishness. The crass commercialism of the souvenirs (Bronte pedestal mats and novelty tea-strainers) was a fair target, but the tourists – the Yorkshire Heritage coach party – are painted as gawping philistines who sandwich the Brontes between three dark Satanic mills, *Emmerdale Farm* and Nora Batty's front room.

The third character monologue was the actress whose career résumé includes children's theatre – playing *Winifred Wibbly-Wobbly* and a less creatively satisfying raspberry – followed by a spell with a troupe called Lorryload. This was an in-joke as Julie Walters had toured the working men's clubs of Liverpool in the early 1970s with her then boyfriend, Peter Postlethwaite, in a theatre company called Vanload. 'You don't know how near the knuckle I can go' Victoria warned in the song 'Put It Out Of Your Mind' and she certainly demonstrated this in *Lucky Bag* with jokes about cancer, Auschwitz and how anorexia is a middle-class accessory.

Sex continued to be shown as a largely unsatisfactory process (Victoria's Dutch cap was too small and made her ears itch; her dyslexic boyfriend bought a sex manual and spent half the night looking for her vinegar). A joke about the bed bolster with broken glass in it was recycled from *Nearly A Happy Ending* and she also adapted *Happy Since I Met You*'s sexual climax-puncturing request for bin-liners for the show.

But despite such boldness there were still hints of insecurity. The fact that she felt obliged to signpost the phonetic humour ('I was thinking what a funny word Twyfords is') suggested a lack of confidence. In this respect she had not advanced from *Talent* where Julie, after mentioning a Mivvi ice lolly, adds: 'Funny word isn't it'. Later in her career Victoria would trust an audience to respond to an amusing-sounding word without her prompting.

The self-deprecation remained present in *Lucky Bag*. She voiced the audience's disappointments ('It's the other one I like, the thin one'). 'I hope you like it' she says of a song, 'nobody else does'. Depressed, she phones the Samaritans and is cheered up, only to realise she has phoned C&A Outsize Department by mistake. She runs into The Body Shop and asks for 'this' in a size 8. 'I'm trained,' she says, in between playing an impressive piece of piano during 'Put it Out Of Your Mind', 'I'm trained to handle alsatians.' But Victoria was also beginning to turn her barbs outwards, devoting one song to 'fat people who go into a boutique and find the only thing that fits them is the cubicle curtain' (an adaptation of a *Wood & Walters* line).

For *Lucky Bag*, Victoria only added four new songs to her repertoire. 'Bastards' recycled a tune Victoria had used for an education programme. The song continued the messages of 'Good Fun' and 'Don't Do It' and seemed to articulate Victoria's own frustrations at her shyness and inability to speak up for herself in her early career. Make trouble with your gob, urged Victoria. Don't be a social liar, smiling, saying what others want to hear and never complaining. The conflict between being taken advantage of and taking advantage was a subject that Victoria would return to.

'Funny How Things Turn Out' was a cleverly crafted song based on the progress of three fictitious school friends. All three (the thin actress, the bohemian, the sports star) would have been real-life rivals to Victoria and with a certain relish she showed them failing to match their early potential. The actress fails her RADA audition, advertises cat food and ends up singing Lerner and Lowe to the mentally ill; the bohemian ends up marrying a man from ICI; the sports star ends up having a sex-change.

Her songs showed how Victoria was more at ease communicating on stage than she was in real life. The fact that she prefers to regard an audience as an indistinguishable mass suggests the comfort was derived from being in total control of a situation rather than any close bond with the public. Offstage she had a problem with shyness and found it difficult to voice her opinions, but in her songs she could be loud and outspoken, belting out the messages: 'It's one life and one chance'; 'Please enjoy what you are, ask me how? Live for now'; 'You just tell them what the hell you like'.

Although she was still described as a 'bulky blonde', 'rotund', 'reassuringly stocky' and 'roly-poly' the critics were taking the quality of her comedy and performance seriously. 'Miss Wood's new prowess as a stand-up comic is the great feature of the show,' wrote Robert Cushman in the *Observer*. 'She mocks a plastic world, but she does not rage at it; she even recognises that it is, in certain lights, fun. She is the poet of Tesco's, *Crossroads*, and the launderette down the street with one functioning tumble-dryer.'

In the *Financial Times* Martin Hoyle described her as 'The Betjeman of a slightly chipped enamel meritocracy in an increasingly plastic age.' *The Times's* Anthony Masters said: 'I think Ms Wood's most winning quality . . . is that so much of her harshest satire is not so much a clever sneer as an indignant cry for life and fun.'

Successful though the show had been, Victoria still suffered a gnawing discontent that manifested itself in some erratic and sweeping decisions. She decided to switch back to television, throw herself into 'normal' life in Silverdale and become fully vegetarian. 'I was just really up for doing some more television . . . I had loads of ideas and I had loads of energy,' she explained. The BBC, regarded as the natural home of Light Entertainment, commissioned a series from her and in the January of 1984 she began writing. Victoria was careful to learn from the mistakes of *Wood & Walters*. Quality control was paramount and she wrote double the amount of material needed. Judging by some of the sketches that did not make it onto the show but were included in the subsequent sketch book, it was evident that what Victoria rejected, other shows would have gladly snapped up. In effect, Victoria was competing against herself and therefore crafting a show of extremely high standards. Each sketch was a rival for another and only the best would make it to the studio.

Despite having 'bionic ears' (her own description) Victoria is not one of those writers who carefully eavesdrops for inspiration. On the odd occasion when she did jot down overheard nuggets they remained unused because she found it impossible to graft them onto her own words. Some of these *were* based on real life, but had to pass through what Victoria refers to as her 'barmy filter', which extracted the essence and added ridiculousness.

The writing process, once a great kick, became a hateful chore. She worked on the script from 9.30 a.m. until 7 p.m. every day, sitting at her desk, gazing out at the sheep and cows and 'just writing what comes into my head and hoping it's funny'. Organised as ever, she planned each individual show by arranging on the carpet index cards with brief details of each sketch. She admitted that being consistently funny was unnatural, it took hard work and time to create amusing lines. 'I would much prefer to be performing all the time. Writing is exhausting and can be lonely.'

She avoided using 'very rude' words, not because of any personal scruples but because her audience awareness told her they would leap out of the television into the sitting room and distract from the comedy. Apart from a throwaway dig at the then Social Services Secretary, Norman Fowler, politics were out too. Rightly, she considered political humour a fad. Like obscenities, it was something that jarred. This belief also applied to her stand-up work. 'I think it's patronising to try and change people when they've paid £6.50 to come and see you. You don't have the right.'

In light of her fondness for brand names it was highly appropriate that she should name the series after a phrase that signified the ultimate recommendation for products. *Victoria Wood As Seen On TV* was also a title that recognised the effect the medium had on her work. The shows were crammed with parodies of televisual genres: the advert; the documentary; the afternoon show for housewives; the children's programme; the soap opera; the period drama; the continuity announcer; the po-faced and humourless television play; the Sunday morning television schedule; public access and the late night Pause For Thought.

Work on the series was temporarily interrupted when *Lucky Bag* opened at the Ambassadors Theatre in February. Victoria was hailed as 'one of the best songwriters around', a 'nifty social satirist' and 'one of the funniest women in England'. The offending adjectives were still in the reviews – 'plump and homely', 'bulky' and 'chunky' – but, stood on the stage against a backcloth of seagulls over Morecambe Bay, Victoria was connecting more effectively than ever before. She had the knack of articulating the everyday absurdities of life and highlighting the gulf between image and reality. By turns sardonic, innocent, self-deprecating, precise, disarming, crushing, sly, warm and witty, she had total control of her audiences. Whether it was the throwaway literary criticisms – she flicked to the back of a Margaret Drabble just to see what didn't happen in the end – or the minute attention to detail, she made a tremendous impression during the twelve-night run. Even the programme was given due attention, with Victoria writing a hilarious introduction in the guise of The Woman Across The Road.

But there *were* some dissenting voices, most notably John Barber in the *Daily Telegraph*, who described *Lucky Bag* as 'a sub-standard music hall act which relies mainly on her old songs'. The use of brand names, once so quirky and amusing, was beginning to seem like an irritating tic. The almost shameless reliance on old songs was also detected by the *Sunday Telegraph*'s Francis King, who said they 'begin to seem a little narrow in range and monotonous in idiom as the evening progresses – particularly if one has heard them before.'

It was a mark of Victoria's growing celebrity at the time that she was roped into that showbusiness institution, the charity record. Victoria read the story of *Eric the Earwig* on a fundraising album for the Royal Alexandra Children's Hospital, Brighton. Other contributors included The Great Soprendo, Roy Kinnear, Melvyn Hayes and Ruth Madoc.

At this time Victoria's relationship with Julie entered its most tricky period. Contrary to popular belief, the two have never been 'best friends' and the friendship was severely tested when Julie began to reap the rewards of the film *Educating Rita*. It earned her a BAFTA and Variety Club Award for Best Film Actress, a Hollywood Golden Globe and an Oscar nomination. *Eric the Earwig* seemed slight by comparison. At that time Julie was being ferried around in Burt Reynolds' helicopter and being fêted by Hollywood.

'When she turned into a film star, I did become jealous,' admitted Victoria years later. 'It's not that I wanted to be a film star, really, and I was pleased for her. But I was very insecure at the time and I did have a pang about it, because although I was doing what I wanted to do, trying to build up a career as a stand-up, I felt I was being compared with her and being found wanting . . . I could never explain to people that I was not an actress and my career didn't lie in that direction.'

Julie, who furthered her stage career in 1984 by performing in *Fool For Love* at the National Theatre, was completely unaware of Victoria's jealousy. Attending the Oscars had been all very exciting but she remained grounded and agreed to be in Victoria's new series, as well as a film she had written about a seaside summer season. It was not a case of reluctantly obliging an old friend, working with Victoria was a very real pleasure. 'People can't understand why Julie bothers to be in a tacky little TV programme when she could be making a huge tacky film, but it's the acting equivalent of putting your feet up and having a fag and a good gossip,' said Victoria. 'It's great to be able to make yourself look awful in a show like mine – it's such a relief from all the Hollywood stuff.'

The film Victoria scripted never materialised, but Julie's show of loyalty, along with her relaxed attitude to stardom, enabled the friendship to endure.

'When she came back from Hollywood I was a bit scared of her, not because she'd changed but because the circumstances around her had changed. It made me nervous of bothering her, but we just carried on as we had, and she's worn it all very lightly,' said Victoria. Giving a rare insight into her own personality, she admitted: 'I think she is quite remarkable because if all her success and acclaim happened to me, I would be *unbearable*.'

Later Victoria became so comfortable with Julie's stardom that she was able to jokingly compare their two careers – where Julie was nominated for an Oscar, she disappointed a contestant on the Saturday tea-time game show *The Pyramid Game* by losing them a chance to win a toaster. At the time though Victoria did feel overshadowed and this may explain why she decided to try and integrate herself with her neighbours in Silverdale.

'I decided I would try to do really ordinary things. I used to visit their [her friends'] children at their playschool. Help them with their crayons, work at the jumble sales,' said Victoria. But the experiment failed, prompting Victoria to react: 'I hated it. I hated sitting in somebody else's house getting marmalade on my bottom. I suppose I had felt guilty because I had more money than they did.'

Around this time Victoria became a strict vegetarian. Characteristically she embraced the right-on attitude while simultaneously rejecting it: 'I'm all for killing animals and turning them into shoes and handbags, I just don't want to have to eat them.'

For *Victoria Wood As Seen On TV* Victoria needed a producer and director whom she could trust and Geoff Posner – the other Geoffrey in her life – filled both roles, as well as being a substitute for Peter Eckersley. Although relatively new to directing BBC entertainment programmes – his directorial career only began in 1982 – he already had a wealth of television experience, having directed *Top Of The Pops*, *Not The Nine O'Clock News*, *The Young Ones* and the pilot of *Blackadder*. In 1983 he won his first BAFTA for producing and directing *Carrott's Lib*. He would go on to work with Lenny Henry, Dawn French, Jennifer Saunders, Steve Coogan, Harry Enfield, Stephen Fry, Hugh Laurie and John Sessions.

Geoff Posner shared Victoria's drive and ambition, and had planned to be a director since the age of twelve. Just as importantly, he too worked within the same framework as Victoria and, like her, had slogged his way up, in his case from floor assistant.

Assessing Victoria's gifts he said: 'She manages to examine people talking and capture speech-patterns and subjects that are everyday, but hysterical at the same time . . . Victoria lifts up the stone and examines what's underneath . . . She always manages to be extraordinarily ordinary . . . The audience nods the whole time. It's quite unique to hold a mirror up to ordinary life and make it so special.'

Julie's place in the series was guaranteed but Victoria still had to find other actors who could be relied upon to deliver her words in the way she intended. In a sense, she set about creating her version of the Blue Door Theatre Company, forming a 'repertory' of key players. The recruits would have to understand her highly disciplined way of working. It was a comedy show but fluffed lines, unauthorised alterations to the script, in fact any hint of unprofessionalism would be frowned upon.

Since first becoming friends with Victoria in the early 1970s Celia Imrie had repeatedly told Victoria that she was a terrible actress, and Victoria took her at her word. She had worked in theatre and done bit-parts in various television programmes. Recognition of sorts had come from playing John Nettles's romantic interest, Marianne Bellshade, in *Bergerac*, but it was not until New Year's Eve 1981 that Victoria saw clearly the full range of Celia's talents. Sitting in bed watching a show by BBC Scotland called *Eighty-one Take Two* Victoria was highly impressed by Celia's performance, which was how she ended up being recruited for *As Seen On TV*.

Celia had a great deal in common with Victoria. She too came from a middle-class background and had been shaped by her siblings. 'I prefer to make my way by myself,' she said. 'Perhaps it is to do with being the fourth of five children. I have always wanted the approval of my brother, who was second-born, but feel that I've never got it, so there's an element of, "Right, I'll show him".' Celia had also faced blunt rejection – being told she was the wrong shape for ballet school – and her personal anxieties had also manifested themselves in her attitude to food. But whereas Victoria comfort ate, Celia starved herself, and suffered so badly from anorexia as a teenager that she was hospitalised.

Susie Blake had been spotted by Victoria in a musical at the King's Head Theatre. The LAMDA-trained actress was awarded the part of the acerbic community announcer. Susie, like Celia, had missed out on a ballet career for being the wrong shape.

Completing the core of the company was Duncan Preston, who turned down Shakespeare for Victoria. He had been offered the role of Hotspur in *Henry IV, Part One*, touring round the world for a year but, partly through the prospect of regular parts in *As Seen On TV*, and partly because he had just bought a house in Beaconsfield with his girlfriend, he turned it down. 'I was at a crossroads and I had the choice of going straight or going off at a tangent with Victoria,' said Duncan. 'I chose the latter and she changed my life.'

Other actors whom Victoria had worked with previously and felt she could trust were rewarded with smaller parts, namely Jim Broadbent, Peter Ellis, Meg Johnson and Sue Wallace. David Firman, the musical director of *Good Fun*, was also appointed the musical director for the series.

Rehearsals began in July and filming was done in August and September. At the studios Victoria boosted her energy levels by doing Jane Fonda's workout with Susie Blake.

The show was scheduled for a November broadcast and to capitalise on it Victoria arranged a short tour. The billboards read: VICTORIA WOOD AS SEEN ON TV, which backfired somewhat when the BBC decided to put back the series until January 1985.

The canny financial awareness Victoria was beginning to display was evident when she released an LP of a *Lucky Bag* show that had been performed at the Edinburgh Festival. In 1984 Methuen also published the *Lucky Bag* songbook, a collection of fourteen of her songs from the past six years, with an introduction culled from the theatre programme for *Lucky Bag*. Oddly, especially as Victoria had been upset by remarks about her weight in the past, Beryl Cooke was commissioned to paint a back view of her for the front cover, naked apart from a straining corset. That, along with her decision to surround herself with the petite and gamine Julie, Celia and Susie for the show, suggested that Victoria was beginning to overcome her hang-up about her weight. She had even taken to wearing sweatshirts with LARGE written across the front for interviews.

> *'Chipper' Patel arrived from New Delhi in 1962 with an artificial leg and five pounds in his pocket. He now controls a multi-million pound vinyl flooring empire. He didn't want to be filmed. So here's a tatty old comedy programme with some women in it.*

With that larky *Radio Times* listing, Victoria introduced *As Seen On TV* to the British public. The attention to detail – how many writers would pay such attention to a broadcast schedule? – showed just how committed Victoria was to the show.

The first *As Seen On TV* was broadcast at 9 p.m. on BBC2 on 11 January 1985 and the structure of the programme remained the same for the entire series. Victoria would dash on stage, dressed in blazer and loose tie with multicoloured highlights in her hair and treat the studio audience to five minutes of her old stand-up routine with the occasional variation. An 'advert' would follow, and then a fairly long sketch for Victoria and Julie or Celia. Susie Blake would pop up here and there dripping sarcasm and snobbery as the continuity presenter, brief traditional-style 'shortie' gags, a song from Victoria, various character monologues, an episode of 'Acorn Antiques', a parody of a televisual genre, and a documentary completed the main framework of each show.

The problem with discussing *As Seen On TV* in retrospect is that since it first appeared so many others have been influenced by Victoria's style. But back then her articulation of the everyday ludicrousness of life and her grasp of what was funny was truly unique.

Some of the 'documentaries' gave an insight into key areas of Victoria's troubled past and allowed a degree of purging through laughter. 'Swim The Channel' gave a frank message to Helen and Stanley Wood. Victoria played Chrissie, an innocent adolescent determined to swim the Channel. The humour stemmed from her naiveté and the rubber swimming cap which remained glued to her head, but it was the pathos that made the impact. The parents were totally disinterested in Chrissie and had even forgotten they had any children. In a scene reminiscent of the young Victoria's journeys to and from Bury Military Band, Chrissie is seen setting off for the coast alone while her parents head in the other direction, bound for London to catch an Andrew Lloyd-Webber. The last shot – after Chrissie has gone missing – is of her empty bedroom with her *Annie* posters and her bear, Mr Teddy.

The exorcism continued with 'To Be An Actress', in which Mary Jo Randle played Sarah Wells, a 24-year-old who has not had an acting job in the three years since leaving drama school. Randle had grown up not far from Victoria in Rochdale and had followed her to Birmingham in 1972, where she hated the drama course so much she switched to social sciences. In this documentary Victoria got her revenge on the auditioning pencil-thin identikit actresses, the pretentiousness of the profession, the casting couch, the self-obsession and the back-biting. The play which Sarah eventually wins a role in is not dissimilar to *Educating Rita* and featured Lill Roughley – an actress Victoria spotted working alongside Geoffrey in 1977 – as Mrs Mottershead.

'On Campus' was Victoria's take on the university experience, most noticeably the cruelty and bleakness of it. Victoria played Hilary, an overweight, slightly awkward undergraduate desperately seeking friendship. We see her sitting unhappily alone at the freshers ball and the target of a practical joke. When she attempts suicide her 'friend', Selina (Tilly Vosburgh) unsympathetically points out 'If you're fat and ugly with a hopeless personality, you're probably better off taking an overdose.'

Victoria turned her attention to Bury Grammar for 'Just An Ordinary School', in which she mocked the exclusivity and insularity of the public school system – the school featured has electronic gates and awards the Oswald Mosley prize for public speaking.

'A Fairly Ordinary Man' was set in a geographical replica of Bury and portrayed Victoria's North as a dismal, grim place, populated by dreary people. Jim punctuated his speech with 'erm' just as Mrs Starkey, a teacher at Bury Grammar, had.

Not all the documentaries in the series were of a biographical nature. 'Whither the Arts?' allowed Victoria to document the behind-the-scenes build-up to a musical based on Bessie Bunter in her own inimitable way, and 'The Divorce' had Maureen Lipman as the nervy, embittered Ruth recounting the horror of domestic disharmony.

Stand-out sketches included 'In The Office' and 'Shoe Shop' (shops and offices, along with libraries, were favourite comedic locations for Victoria). In the latter, which was one of Victoria's favourite sketches of the series, she took the absurd behaviour of unhelpful shop assistants to surreal heights. With 'In The Office' she expertly captured the truth that in everyday life it is the small things that loom largest (the characters Connie and Beattie discuss last night's television news but it is not world events that concern them, it is the newsreader's blouse).

Some sketches were not simply one-offs and the characters appeared throughout the series. This was the case with those doyennes of housewifely daytime television, Margery and Joan. If Joan (Victoria) was based on Judith Chalmers, then Margery (Julie) was a combination of Esther Rantzen and *Tomorrow's World*'s Judith Hann. Carl and Gail were regulars, discussing such weighty issues as guttering from their seat in the bus shelter, and Kitty often put in an appearance.

This Cheadle-based monster was played by Patricia Routledge (one of the pool of actresses, along with Thora Hird and Julie, shared by Victoria and Alan Bennett). Kitty could be seen as a relative of Dotty from *Wood & Walters*, both are Agony Aunts of sorts. Sitting in her chair she would hold forth with robust opinion on everything from lesbianism to mashed swede. But whereas Dotty was earthy, Kitty is more uptight and quicker to become indignant. To show her forthrightness, Victoria originally had Kitty introduce herself with 'I've had a boob off and I can't stomach whelks.' Whether it was BBC pressure or objections by Routledge herself, the mastectomy reference was changed to 'I've given gallons of blood.' It is difficult to imagine anyone other than Routledge delivering such lines as 'I've had my share of gynaecological gyp. I still can't polka without wincing but we're spunky in Cheadle, we totter on.'

Julie Walters was also given the opportunity for character monologue in 'Giving Notes', in which she played Alma, the director of the Piecrust Players' hysterically crass version of *Hamlet* ('if you dry just give us a bit of business with the shower cap'). It may have been light entertainment for the masses but Victoria was not afraid to throw in an esoteric joke here and there ('It's not like Pinter where you can more or less say what you like as long as you leave enough gaps.')

Self-deprecation was still present in *As Seen On TV*, with Victoria likening herself to a bale of hay with bosoms, and a horse box with highlights. Susie, as the continuity announcer complained of 'weak-willed, self-indulgent guzzlers' with 'enormous flabby arms' and the voice-over at the end of one show remarked flatly: 'There'll be more attempts at comedy from the overweight comedienne next week.'

A Northernness permeated the series, even down to the distinctive surnames used (Mottershead, Witherslack, Postlethwaite). Victoria highlighted London prejudice mainly through Susie's continuity announcer. She snootily made an apology to those living in the North ('it must be awful for them') and explained a plot for 'those of you living outside the London area who probably aren't very intelligent'. In 'To Be An Actress' Sarah is so desperate she is prepared to work anywhere, 'even the North'. But despite Victoria's apparent censure, she was not averse to patronising Northerners herself in some of the sketches, especially the 'slow-witted Northern pair' Carl and Gail in 'Young Love', who bordered on being retarded.

The songs, still regarded by some as a necessary evil, were written especially for the series. They tended to be about relationships, with Victoria as the abused partner ('All In The Game'); the appalled partner ('So Pissed Off With Love') or the disillusioned partner ('Go Away'). The latter was a serious, heartfelt reflection of a dead relationship, belonging in the same category as 'Don't Do It'.

There *was* a happy relationship in 'Big Brass Band', but the passion was for the band. Victoria made no concessions to those who still criticised her for being unfeminine and she sang the song in the narrative voice of 'a simple Northern lad' who is so shy he takes his brass band on honeymoon. This number gave Victoria the opportunity to realise a childhood ambition and be backed by a traditional brass band.

The series also included a Gospel song set in the cafe of a department store and sung by a sisterhood of shoppers bemoaning the tribulations of shopping, and a jokey farewell song ('Saying Goodbye Isn't Necessarily Depressing By Any Stretch Of The Imagination'). Perhaps the most bizarre song, 'I'm Gonna Knock, Knock, Knock, Knock, On Your Knocker', was performed by a trio. It was an absolutely straight 1950s-style number, which was even filmed in black and white. Completely unexpected – it was inserted during a supposed technical hitch – the only reason for its inclusion appears to have been Victoria's caprice. Perhaps she wanted to try a pastiche and this was the only way of letting it see the light of day.

For the soap-addicted Victoria a parody was inevitable, and she created 'Acorn Antiques', perhaps her greatest achievement in the eyes of many. The drama, set in a shop near Manchesterford, became an instant classic, as Victoria knew it would. 'I remember when I first wrote Acorn Antiques,' she recalled. 'Geoffrey said: "I don't think people will ever get that." I said "I think they will."'

The missed cues, the corpsing, the dropping out of character, the complete lack of talent, the poor improvisation when things went wrong, the wobbly sets, the unreliable props and the clumsy camera angles were all largely inspired by *Crossroads*. The hunchbacked charwoman, Mrs Overall (Julie Walters), was clearly based on *Crossroads'* Amy Turtle, and the dim handyman Derek (Kenny Ireland), was inspired by the Midland motel's Benny. Just as *Crossroads* tried to go upmarket and introduced a recreation centre, 'Acorn Antiques' branched out to offer sunbed and leisure facilities as well as Michelangelo's sculptures. Even the clumsy end credit sequence and the enigmatic cliffhanger ('Could you fetch my briefcase, Mrs Overall? I'd like to show Miss Babs my theodolite') were a steal from *Crossroads*.

The relationships between the characters were even more complicated and illogical than the plot. The unseen Kenneth is Babs's

(Celia Imrie) husband and, apparently, the father of her triplets. Babs also has an unseen son, Bobby, and a secret daughter – the troublesome Trixie (Rosie Collins) – who has a dalliance with Babs's cousin, Jerez (Peter Ellis), an affair with Derek, who could be the real father of Babs's triplets, and an evil twin cousin. It is not actually specified that Berta (Victoria) is the sister of Babs, she definitely does not share a father with her. Berta marries Clifford (Duncan Preston), an old flame of Babs's and it emerges she is the twin sister of Derek and the daughter of Mrs Overall. Clifford and Derek have a 'sordid' relationship.

It was even unclear who actually owned the shop. It is 'a family antiques business', not necessarily Miss Babs's. And although Miss Berta is the majority shareholder, it is Mrs Overall who is the sole beneficiary.

Paying as much attention to detail as ever, Victoria made sure she strictly observed the conventions of soap from the shock deaths (car crash, choking and electrocution by a household appliance) to convoluted intrigue, corruption and lack of continuity. Another soap staple, the quick-fix solution, was in plentiful supply. All it takes is a phone call from Babs and the Town Hall agrees to re-route the motorway through some poor people's houses; a quick word with the vicar means Trixie can marry her own brother; Berta is cured and released from intensive care when she tells her doctor that she has to help out in the shop; Mrs Overall's attempt at mass poisoning is glossed over as silly attention seeking; Trixie becomes a nun; Jerez becomes a kindly benefactor.

In an attempt to inject some glamour into proceedings foreign locations were referenced (a mysterious phone call from Kuwait, Clifford's return from Zurich; Derek and Trixie's plans to flee to Morocco and Cousin Jerez's arrival from Marbella).

There were also laughably heavy-handed attempts at authenticity and a desire to suggest the writers had done their research. 'Gainsborough's Blue Boy? Yes, I think we have it in mauve,' says Miss Babs in one of her many one-sided phone calls. And Miss Berta is perturbed to discover they have been charged for seven Laughing Cavaliers. One episode even credited an 'Antiques adviser'.

At the time that 'Acorn Antiques' was first seen, *EastEnders*, in an attempt to prove its gritty reality, was suffering from disease-of-the-week syndrome, which did not escape Victoria's sharp pen. So in 'Acorn Antiques' Berta has a bone marrow transplant, suffers from amnesia and is in intensive care for non-specified reasons. Babs has a fatal allergy to men's pyjamas, and spite and promiscuity could inflame Trixie's jaundice. It is little wonder that at one point Mrs Overall asks 'Have you got an incurable disease, or is it just the sterilised milk?'

Such was the impact of 'Acorn Antiques' that fans started a fanzine and held appreciation gatherings where they would dress like the characters and recite lines from the show. Its popularity led to the release of a video omnibus in 1993, and also contributed to *As Seen On TV* enjoying a word-of-mouth success that grew so that by the penultimate episode it was attracting 4.55 million viewers, making it the tenth most popular programme on BBC2.

CHAPTER 9

VICTORIA was not the only Northerner in the public eye in the mid-1980s. The complicated Manchester singer Morrissey, lead singer with The Smiths, had emerged as the spokesman for dispossessed Northern youth. Just as the press had compartmentalised Victoria as some jolly, down-to-earth comedienne, they had Morrissey labelled as a humourless depressive. To link the two Northern stars would have seemed ludicrous, yet they shared characteristics. Morrissey's sly sense of humour was usually overlooked in the same way that Victoria's darker side tended to be ignored. He 'hijacked' Victoria for the song 'Rusholme Ruffians', which appeared on the group's *Meat Is Murder* album. Morrissey borrowed the wistful and regretful lyrics of Victoria's 'Fourteen Again' and adapted them to give an even bleaker reading. Where Victoria wrote

> *The last night of the fair*
> *French Kissing as the kiosks shut*
> *Behind the generators with your coconut.*

Morrissey sang:

> *The last night of the fair*
> *by the big wheel generator*
> *a boy is stabbed and his money is grabbed.*

In 'Fourteen Again' there is the romantic 'The coloured lights reflected in the Brylcreem on his hair', whereas in 'Rusholme Ruffians' there is the more sexually urgent 'the grease in the hair of a speedway operator is all a tremulous heart requires'. Where Victoria is nostalgic ('When I was funny I was famous') Morrissey is scathing ('She is famous she is funny'). In both songs the protagonist turns to self-mutilation with a fountain pen.

Morrissey, known for his obsessive hero worship, added Victoria to his list of idols which also included Sandie Shaw and Pat Phoenix. He even joked about marrying her. Victoria responded by telling audiences: 'Morrissey and I have been married for eleven months, though due to touring commitments we have yet to meet.' The lightheartedness was all very well, but Morrissey liked to probe his heroines, which was something that the controlled and fiercely private Victoria could not countenance and she not surprisingly declined his dinner invitation.

A variety of projects helped keep Victoria's profile visible after *As Seen On TV* had ended. She was the subject of the BBC2 school programme, *Scene*, and helped present *Insight*, the educational programme for deaf children. In June (1985) she was surprised to be asked to perform a promotional song for Disney's *Return To Oz*, and that same month her first play for children, *Molly and the Seaweed Hypermarket*, was shown on BBC1. She was getting more work on the after-dinner speaking circuit and she was also attempting to write a screenplay, *The Natural Order*, for her and Julie, which called for a strict domestic regime.

'I know where everything is. I'm very, very orderly . . . I pare everything down to the bone so I can just get on with writing. If something can't go in the washing machine, I don't buy it,' she said. Obviously it would not sit well with her public persona if she mentioned the domestic help she employed, the latest accoutrement of fame.

Rising at 7 a.m. Victoria breakfasted on mashed banana on toast, or sometimes muesli and skimmed milk, washed down with herbal tea. A huge vat of vegetable soup would be prepared and then she would drive up to Kendal Leisure Centre to swim 40 lengths of front crawl – a healthy hangover from her *Nearly A Happy Ending* weight-loss regime. On returning home she would begin writing, breaking at around 12.30 for some soup and a walk. On the rare occasions when Geoffrey was not away on tour they would share supper at around 6 p.m. and Geoffrey would appraise her work. The writing would go on until around 8 p.m. and Victoria would unwind by tidying – which she listed as her recreation in her *Who's Who* entry. On one occasion she sat in the cellar until 1 a.m., sorting out the nuts and bolts that came with the house. Cleaning was another obsession, and in interviews she would rhapsodise about the joys of cleaning sinks, especially behind the taps.

Only a psychologist could give a reason for such compulsive behaviour, but it is probably safe to say that it displayed a rejection – or at least a distancing – by Victoria of her physically and emotionally messy childhood. That could not be tidied up, but her present could. As she said of cleaning: 'I see [it] as a way of imposing control on your surroundings.'

The November publication of *Up To You Porky*, a collection of sketches and monologues from *Lucky Bag*, *Wood & Walters* and *As Seen On TV* (dedicated to Peter Eckersley), demonstrated once again how Victoria was not averse to wringing every last financial opportunity from her work. She capitalised on the fact that lines from her sketches lent themselves to being performed. There was something immensely quotable about such nuggets as 'My God, if her bum were a bungalow she'd never get a mortgage on it.'

Despite her industry a sense of gloom prevailed. After months of working on her new play Victoria decided it was mediocre and threw it away. To add to her woes she also felt it had been a mistake to do *As Seen On TV*; 'I've been seeking to branch out but it hasn't happened,' she said. 'I wanted to do something different before I went back to TV.'

With a heavy heart and a bottle of Jif she followed Geoffrey down to Bristol for Christmas. While he was in pantomime she scrubbed the bath in their rented flat and began work on a film script. The script was abandoned in the new year for being 'too Alan Ayckbourn influenced', and instead she began working on the second series of *As Seen On TV*. With Bix Beiderbecke records and *The Archers* as her only company, Victoria aimed to complete eighteen minutes-worth of script a week. Fridays were left for rewriting, but this could also extend to Saturdays. It was a process she found hellish.

'It's a lonely existence – just me, my pen and the dreaded blank sheets of paper,' explained Victoria. 'I can't honestly believe anybody actually enjoys writing. It's an absolute agony . . . You pour everything you've got into one [sketch] and you don't ever want to write another – only you realise there are 59 more to go before you've enough for a series. It's torment. There's not a morning goes by when I'm writing that I don't panic and think there's not another idea left and my career is finished.'

This time round it was even more lonely as Geoffrey was touring extensively with The Krankies and away filming in Kenya. 'There are pressures, there's no denying that. You've just got to work that bit harder at it,' said Victoria. This involved writing and telephoning each other every day and arranging brief rendezvous whenever they could. She regretted the separations, but after years of unemployment they were reluctant to turn down work and she was philosophical: 'If you want to work then I suppose something has to go.' They were too busy to think about having children but were determined their partnership did not suffer. 'Our relationship comes first,' she stressed. 'We would never do anything that would endanger what we have.'

In all it took six months to write the series and the only 'break' Victoria had was for a tour, but before that came a triumphant interlude: she won the BAFTA award for Best Light Entertainment Performance. Victoria was genuinely shocked to beat Ronnie Barker, David Jason and Gordon Kaye, but the success did not end there and the show also earned the award for Best Light Entertainment Programme. The series went on to win the British Press Guild Broadcasting Award for Best Light Entertainment Programme.

Typically, the BAFTA euphoria was short-lived. 'I was very pleased to win but it really put pressure on me. I was already writing the new series and every time I looked at the award I kept thinking that people would be expecting so much more now and I just wouldn't be able to live up to it. In the end, I just had to put the thing away.'

For the tour which, with 22 dates in England and Scotland, was her biggest yet, Victoria debuted her tomboyish pudding basin haircut and what has become her most popular song, the mammoth, fifteen-versed 'Barry and Freda' better known as 'Let's Do It'. The saga of suburban lust had audiences roaring with laughter and remained Victoria's encore number for the following decade. What was refreshing about it was the way she took the clichéd comedy of a husband wanting sex and the wife refusing, and completely reversed it. So while Freda wants to wear nothing but stilettos and an oven glove, and roll in gay abandon on the tufted Wilton, Barry wants to lag the pipes and read a catalogue on vinyl flooring. As Freda's demands are given full vent ('Bend me over backwards on my hostess trolley', 'Smear an avocado on my lower portions', 'Beat me on the bottom with a *Woman's Weekly*'), Barry's excuses become more lame ('You know I pulled a muscle when I did that grouting', 'It's too chilly to go without a thermal vest'). Only Victoria could portray sado-masochism and kinky sex in such a funny, wholesome and inoffensive way. It is worth noting that her characteristic borrowing from earlier work was again evident here. Barry, like the boring Gail in *Good Fun* is a fan of The Spinners, and Freda's demand that Barry dangles from the wardrobe in his balaclava is not dissimilar from the reference to a businessman swinging from the pelmet in a rubber corset in *Nearly A Happy Ending*.

The tour, which commenced on 20 March also included songs from *As Seen On TV*, a mix of old and new stand-up routines and a new character monologue in the form of an usherette (another Margaret).

Because Victoria travelled light with few overheads, it was her most lucrative tour so far and saw her playing larger venues. Particular satisfaction was derived from appearing at Manchester's Palace Theatre, a childhood favourite. Her profile was also rising – at least people were mistaking her for Dawn French rather than Pam Ayres now – and with it her confidence, 'I know people like me or else they wouldn't pay to come and see me.' No longer did she allow herself to be manipulated into giving interviews on Morecambe pier or Trust House Forte hotels; now it was the Ritz and the Waldorf.

Despite moving into a higher league of celebrity, she was still at pains to keep herself rooted. 'You actually decide for yourself what level of normality you operate at. If you want to prance about being famous you can – but people will no longer identify with you because you have no normal life. But I still lead a very normal life. And I only get recognised 50 per cent of the time.' She was also wary of becoming a Much Loved British Institution. 'That's too much pressure,' she believed. 'Look what happened to Hancock. There's a line between doing what you want to do and being completely taken over.'

But like Hancock she was beginning to analyse comedy. She likened her role on stage to that of a shepherd, 'It's like rounding sheep up, you have to keep them all in the same place and attack them all at the same time.' For her, the joy of live performance was the sense of something special happening at that particular moment in time, and the secret of getting a laugh lay in the rhythm and timing. 'The content is very low down on the list. It's not as important as the way you say something and the syllables you choose and the consonants you choose to say it with. It's almost like if you could hear it, if you didn't speak English, you would still find it funny because that rhythm would just carry you along.' She also connected the comedian's skills with the musician's, 'It's very musical. It's all to do with rhythm and punctuation, and building up an expected pattern and then breaking it and catching people on the off-beat.'

Helping her in her analysis was Geoffrey. He would loiter at the back of the theatre and in the bar at intervals, eavesdropping on audience opinion and working out why certain parts of the act were better received than others. This information would then be relayed to Victoria who would adapt the act where she thought fit.

Somehow she managed to fit in a series of Asda adverts with Julie during this period. It was particularly apt that she agreed to promote a supermarket as so much of her act was concerned with branded goods and the housewives' lot. The commercials necessitated a mini-tour of Europe, filming on location in the Austrian Alps, France and Spain. Victoria and Julie pushed their shopping trolleys oblivious to their surroundings and more concerned with discussing such weighty matters as whether Nana Mouskouri could be classed as Country and Western. Whereas Julie went on to be the voice of Bisto, Typhoo and Sainsbury's, it took another thirteen years before Victoria made any more adverts. She could hardly mock dozens of products in her work and then appear on television endorsing them.

The day after completing the Asda ads she was in the BBC's rehearsal studios preparing for *As Seen On TV 2*. Additional commitments were the press interviews for the series, the release of *Up To You Porky* in paperback, and talks about a promotional tour of Australia where the first series of *As Seen On TV* was to be shown. By November Victoria and Geoffrey had spent only a hundred out of the last three hundred days together, and she had not been home for months.

The filming of As Seen On TV 2 meant Victoria had to spend the summer in London, a place she described to her local Lancashire paper as 'very boring'. She stayed at David Leland's Highgate flat (she would later buy her own) and Leland himself worked with Geoffrey that year on the critical and commercial hit film, Wish You Were Here. Leland wrote and directed the film based on the early life of notorious madame Cynthia Payne. Geoffrey played Harry Figgis, who gets Lynda (Emily Lloyd) a job at a bus company, and then fires her for titillating staff on the canteen table.

Filming of As Seen On TV 2 was not completed until the end of October, by which time Victoria had resolved to put an end to the show. 'It's not that I feel burnt out, but I believe in giving my best, and I think – so far as TV sketches go – I've given all I've got for a while. Now I need some fresh challenges,' she explained. She had grown frustrated by the hard work and limited format of sketch shows and wanted to move on in a similar direction as John Cleese after Fawlty Towers.

'I've done what I wanted to do and it's time to go while people still want more. I don't want to make the public sick of me,' she sensibly reasoned. But Victoria was careful to show her loyalty to the BBC, and did not rule out making Christmas specials and one-off shows for them.

For years she had kept her depressive side hidden from public view, but the burden of work began to make Victoria less cautious in some interviews. 'I take life much too seriously,' she admitted. 'People always thought Julie Walters was the intense one, but it's me all the time.'

Despite the plaudits her self-confidence had dropped: 'Sometimes I really do believe I have forgotten how to do it . . . There are days when I am sure I am not going to be able to deliver. I think I am a talentless little git and I should go off and be a waitress or load up the shelves in Woolworth's or something.'

There seemed to be something hollow about her quirkiness in other interviews of the time – raving about her excitement at spotting the cast of Howard's Way in the BBC canteen – almost as if she was on autopilot. Other interviews seemed to turn into self-therapy sessions:

One thing I do take seriously is miserable people. I see it happening. Very few people are living a rich life. People seem to live on a very shallow level, not because they want to. I feel lucky. I go to work. I have a lot of fun with people I like. Lots of different things happen and then I come home and weed the garden. I can do a million different things in the course of a day and they will all be good. And then I think, well, suppose I was in a house I didn't like with noise coming through the walls or I had a job where I couldn't talk to people and nothing happened. There would be all these strands missing out of the day.

The second series of *As Seen On TV* was first broadcast on 10 November 1986 and it was a measure of the BBC's optimism that it was shown on Mondays. The first series had been screened in the less-popular Friday slot. It was indicative of her growing stature that Victoria ditched the baggy blazers and lost the loose ties for more stylish jackets and brooches.

The first episode was watched by 7.15 million viewers, making it BBC2's third most popular programme. The second week it moved up to the number two placing with 8.30 million viewers. And by the third week, when repeats of *Fawlty Towers* ended, Victoria moved in to take the top spot with an audience of 8.55 million.

The old gang was reassembled, even Julie whose career was making more demands on her time (1986 saw her starring in *When I Was a Girl I Used To Scream and Shout* at the Whitehall Theatre and appearing in the film *Car Trouble*). And as well as the inner core there were once again parts for those Victoria had worked with before and trusted, including Eric Richards and Kathryn Apanowicz.

'Acorn Antiques' returned and Victoria continued to base a lot of the sketches on parodies of television and cinema genres such as the British war film, the Hollywood musical, local news programmes and 1970s' British thrillers.

New material began creeping into her opening monologues and one entire set was devoted to adolescence and schooldays. It showed how the adult Victoria could revisit her unhappiness and, using a comic's eye, turn the misery into mirth. In another monologue she demonstrated the growing sophistication of her comedy. It was a reworking of the train trip tale, first used in *Lucky Bag*. Again there was the woman eating an individual fruit pie by sucking out the filling through the hole in the centre. Originally the 'joke' was her picking her nose and saving her bogey to eat later. This easy laugh remained, but was now eclipsed by an additional gag which saw Victoria adroitly commenting on the psychology of the English: a couple make love on the train but nothing is said until they light a post-coital cigarette, making one woman shrilly point out that it is a non-smoking compartment.

In another sketch Victoria provided a wry social comment on the times by having Celia play a self-sufficient successful businesswoman who does not know what a pregnancy is.

The sketches 'Spaghetti' and 'No Gossip' best represented Victoria's unique style. In both she placed two lower-middle-class women – played by her and Julie – in an unremarkable environment (a restaurant and a tea room) and showed how the banalities of chat make for remarkable listening. The humour came from the juxtaposition of naturalistic intonation and delivery with content that took off at bizarre and sometimes surreal tangents.

This mismatched element was also used in 'Partly Political Broadcast', in which two housewives, Jean and Barbara, promote their newly formed party by prattling on about supermarkets.

But Victoria's favourite sketch of the series was a marked departure from her usual style, even though she did play yet another dim Northerner. 'The Trolley' could have been written by Spike Milligan. It is stripped of all Victoria's usual references and relies on the madness of her waitress for its humour. Her repeated question, 'Is it on the trolley?' and complete lack of comprehension is wedded to the physical humour of her whizzing on and off with a trolley while two totally straight businessmen become more and more frustrated by her barmy behaviour.

Those long afternoons staring out of the window at the sheep were doubtless the inspiration for one sketch in which Victoria played a woman driven insane by the boredom of country living ('We've got a barrel in the lounge and I like to look at that').

This time the only documentary with autobiographical content was

'A Very Funny Young Man Indeed', a look at comedian Baz Bennett's shot at fame. *New Faces* became 'Star Search', but the host for both was Derek Hobson. Perhaps Victoria got her revenge on her first manager by depicting him as the character who turned down Elvis. Through Baz's mercenary dream (to land an advert for microwaves) Victoria criticised the light entertainment Mafia. Her final comment on the *New Faces* experience was, tellingly, making a performing chimpanzee the winner.

Anne Reid – Peter Eckersley's widow – starred in the documentary 'Mr Right'. The part marked her return to television after a fifteen-year absence. She had last been seen as Ken Barlow's wife in *Coronation Street*. After leaving the show she devoted her time to bringing up her son. Victoria did not offer her a part in *As Seen On TV 2* as a thank you to Peter – sentiment never gets in the way of her professionalism – but because Anne was the perfect actress for Victoria's material. The 47-year-old spinster, Pamela Twill, is one of the RADA-trained actress's favourite roles, and she realised the part of the rueful suburbanite on the blind date trail so well that Victoria would later write a television playlet for her and make her part of her repertory company.

Margery and Joan were back, as was Kitty, and a new episodic character was introduced in the form of Kelly-Marie Tunstall. This over-the-top, Lancashire tart was played with relish by Victoria. Mouthing off at a bus-stop, this loud, common and uninhibited creature would have been familiar to Victoria from her childhood days waiting at Bury bus stops.

Just as Victoria pastiched television genres, she sometimes did the same with songs. With more than a nod to her namesake, Marie Lloyd, Victoria wrote 'Alice', a send-up of a *Good Old Days*-style song, performed by Julie in a music hall setting. The series also contained the 1950s-style 'Sitting On The Prom', with Victoria playing one of a trio of Radcliffe pensioners singing about the delights of Blackpool.

Elsewhere in the series there was 'Barry And Freda' and 'Count Your Blessings', which borrowed lyrically from the Ian Dury (one of the few lyricists Victoria admired) song 'What A Waste'. The poignant 'Crush' was a beautiful evocation of the yearning, insecurity and confusion of an eleven-year-old girl's first crush. The most interesting song, 'I Don't Care', is musically very similar to *Talent's* 'I Don't Know Why I'm Here'.

In it Victoria praises selfishness and unsympathy ('people's dreary lives are the biggest bore'). It shares 'Don't Do It's appeal for honest expression and 'Bastards'' message of self-liberation, but is much more defiant, with Victoria suggesting suicide as an alternative to supporting an old schoolmate. The song is significant in that it expressed Victoria's own real-life desire to be blunt while at the same time highlighting her isolationism and dislike of emotional expression ('cry away, away from me', 'don't come by anymore', 'keep my flat a tear-free zone') The lyric 'when people cry upon your shoulder you just get a soggy shirt' is close to *Good Fun's* 'Got mildewed shoulders from my sad friend's tears'.

The series received another good response, but Victoria's self-doubts remained. However, even her uncertainties could not fail to be temporarily lifted when an invite for the Royal Variety Performance arrived. Although no longer regarded as the ultimate accolade for an entertainer, an appearance on the bill was still quite prestigious. For Victoria, however, her appearance at the Theatre Royal, Drury Lane, represented a personal milestone. On the same bill was Peter Ustinov, the man from whom she had sought advice as a youngster.

Victoria began 1987 by attempting to write yet another play as a sort of insurance policy. Ever cautious when it came to personal popularity, she assumed that she had reached her peak as far as stand-up and sketch shows were concerned and feared the future could only bring decline. 'I'm probably at the peak of my popularity now, but the public will tire of me one day,' she predicted. 'I'm glad I'm doing work people like, and I'm lucky to have a chance to do it. But I don't want to start taking it too seriously because I'm not expecting it to last.'

It seemed the more plaudits she received the more she feared success would disappear. At the same time she was having to try to reconcile her status with her self-image. 'I lead the same sort of life that most people lead,' she said. 'When it's – quote – big stars, it's just a bit "them" and "us", isn't it? And I don't see myself as one of "them", that's all.' But the truth of the matter was that she was a big star, however much she tried to pretend she wasn't.

When she was Michael Parkinson's castaway on *Desert Island Discs*, she was careful to stress the downside of fame.

'It's not how you envisage it because it's a nuisance . . . when you want to go and buy your knickers and things it's just a bit of an irritation. People come up and poke you and things like that . . . mainly they want to know if you are who they think you are – which covers a large range of people from the woman who does the lip-reading on Sunday morning to Angela Rippon . . . What I mean is it's not what you imagine. It's not sort of swanning around in a fur coat. It's people saying "My wife's seen all your programmes and she hasn't liked any of them yet."'

Victoria's desert island luxury was a Wurlitzer organ and her musical choices consisted of numbers by Prokofiev, Fats Waller, Gershwin, Ian Dury and Noel Coward singing a version of 'Let's Do It' live in Las Vegas. 'He's obviously gone in to make a killing and make a few bob for his old age and he's playing the most unlikely audience,' said Victoria, who at the time was considering making a few low-key appearances in New York clubs. She said of the venture: 'That's a bit frightening, it's always easier to do the things that you know and stay here, but I feel I should try it.' She has yet to do so.

A further accolade came in March when the second series of *As Seen On TV* picked up the Best Light Entertainment Programme BAFTA, and both Victoria and Julie were nominated for the Best Light Entertainment Performance.

On the domestic front Victoria's massive success was in danger of becoming something of an embarrassment and she grew more defensive of Geoffrey, especially when interviewers assumed he was a kept man. 'There's no question of him being Mr Wood or anything,' she stressed. 'He's earning a packet – he's working so much he couldn't work more if he wanted to, and he's very happy about my success. Anyone in the business knows that he's at least as successful as I am, probably more so.'

There was a suggestion, however, that all was not well within the marriage during this period, prompting Victoria to be uncharacteristically open in interviews.

'I could survive if our marriage broke up,' she stated. 'I don't say I'd be thrilled at the prospect, but I would certainly survive. The quality of enjoyment of life is what's important, isn't it? And life would still be there for me if Geoff wasn't, in the same way that it would still be there for him if I wasn't. I don't think our relationship would be healthy otherwise.'

Her brother was also in the public eye in 1987, standing as the Liberal candidate for North West Durham in the General Election. Mindful of Victoria's displeasure when he had spoken to the press in the past, he made it clear that he did not expect any support from his youngest sister and was at pains to trot out the Wood Party line: 'She does not help anybody's campaign,' he told journalists. 'She prefers to take a private stance as far as politics are concerned. Her attitude is that she appears in public to perform and the rest of her life is private.'

Victoria did appear in public in 1987. Whenever life appeared to be treating her well she seemed to feel the need to test herself, which could explain why she decided to make another foray into what she considered the toughest arena – live theatre.

'I can do something on television and it might be really quite mediocre but because it's really well lit and it comes as part of something else you can get away with it. But if I come on stage and do something not very good then I instantly know and you really have to do your best because people have paid money to see you and it's their night out. And that's where you're really tested I think.'

Stand-up also enabled her to get dissatisfactions off her chest: 'There's no such thing as a comedy of approval where you write about things that strike you as right. You have got to see something wrong.'

The tour commenced in Ireland in October and would be her biggest yet. She drove herself from theatre to theatre and regarded her car as the most stability she had. Accommodation was either friends' flats or hotels (in Manchester she sniffily refused to stay at the Britannia because she thought it looked like a brothel).

For her, the joy of live performance was 'the feeling of communicating with all those people'. Elaborating on the point, she added: 'It's the *only* time I ever feel people are understanding what I'm saying.' In her opinion an expertly delivered routine to a warm audience was like flying – 'like' being the operative word, because however spontaneous and casual she wanted to appear to audiences, she was still tethered by her methodic approach.

'While one side of your head is performing the other half is thinking "Oh, that didn't go so well, I'm going to miss out the next bit" or "I'd better speed up, some quick laughs are needed!"' explained Victoria. 'You check what the audience is doing, what they're up to, deciding how you can get a better grip on proceedings.'

Earlier in the year she had criticised London for supplying the coldest audiences, but this opinion abruptly changed when she discovered her residency at the London Palladium had sold out. This was the venue where the *New Faces* Gala Final had been held, an event that she had missed out on. Now she would make it her own.

'Without brand-name funnies Victoria Wood's stand-up act would be fairly thin,' wrote the *Evening Standard*'s Nick Barker. 'In the first hour enough downmarket products were mentioned to clothe, furnish and feed a family of four for a fortnight.' A defensive Victoria remained in denial whenever the prickly subject cropped up. 'It's not all brand names, you know. Not by any stretch of the imagination.'

Victoria still showed signs of nervousness in her onstage body language (hands in pockets; pushing up her sleeves; batting her hair forward), but she also began to use physicality to add to the comedy of her performance, such as in an impression of a punctured inflatable doll, and the comic stance of a market researcher and make-up demonstrator.

The self-deprecation was diluted – Victoria described herself as a compulsive eater and made out she had to vacuum the theatre beforehand – but the show marked a shift from getting laughs from her own inadequacies to getting them from other people, sometimes viciously so, particularly where the elderly were concerned.

There were no groundbreaking new takes on life or edgy comedy in the show. Instead Victoria contented herself with musings on motorway life; the misery of family Christmases (first visited in *Happy Since I Met You*); the horrors of a stay in hospital; a holiday to Spain; the direness of English farce; and a case of mistaken identity which enabled her to take an extended stroll along the contemporary British high street.

It was nothing radical, which was how Victoria liked it. As she remarked at the time: 'These bloody barriers. What are they? Why do we have to push them back?'

She was at pains to align herself with her audience. For instance, she gets a *chartered* flight to the accessible Spain in the holiday routine, and in the part of the act which deals with her stay in hospital the grim conditions make it clear she is an NHS patient. Yet at the same time there was a certain degree of snobbishness. Her fellow holidaymakers are portrayed as sex-crazed sluts and the artistic tastes of the lower classes are mocked (the 'lovely' painting of white horses running in the surf in the moonlight). Bizarrely, it seemed the very people she was attacking for what she deemed as poor taste were the same people sitting in the theatre having hysterics. She embraced her audience, while at the same time holding them at a distance.

Victoria also expanded the scope of her targets, incorporating into her act a mocking affection for the British aversion to anything that might trigger a pulse. She wondered if couples who drive to beauty spots and sit in the car looking out would be unable to fully appreciate the sight of the Taj Mahal unless there was a tax disk and windscreen wiper in vision. And she compared the Indian practice of suttee (where the widow throws herself on her husband's funeral pyre) to its English counterpart: an English widow and her friend deciding who is to slice the baps and who is to spread the butter. She zeroed in on the sudden suburban upfront attitude about safe sex (crowds of shoppers calling out their Durex orders in loud jolly voices), and touched upon NHS underfunding (her doctor has to double-up as a cab driver).

There were only two new songs for the show: 'It Would Never Have Worked' and 'Litter Bin'. The former was yet another song about incompatible lovers and dissatisfaction with a relationship, but its lighthearted approach allied it more to 'Thinking Of You' than 'Don't Do It'. The song's denouement – 'his' basic homosexuality – had also occurred in one of Victoria's earlier songs, 'Song of the Lonely Girl'. 'Litter Bin', which gave full vent to Victoria's bleak and pessimistic streak, created confusion and embarrassment for an audience not used to straight sentiment from her. It is a lament on the bleakness of modern life, where babies are abandoned and innocent lives are blown away or crushed beneath the tyre of a drunken driver. 'If something sounds cruel and pointless/Chances are it's true' sang Victoria. The song, which closed the first half of the show, ends with a glimmer of hope in the chorus, 'We have to light tiny bonfires/That can pierce the dark' but by that time most audience members were tittering uncomfortably or waiting for a punchline. As far as Victoria was concerned, the song had its place in the show no matter what the reaction was.

'It always felt like a challenge to shut them up . . . to halt the gigglers. I quite enjoyed seeing how soon I could shut them all up . . . it shows another side I suppose. It's mainly for theatrical effect. And it gets you off in a black-out. Throw them a shocking last line, and then out goes the spotlight! By the time they realise what's happened, zap, you've disappeared. Gone in a blaze of glory; nowhere to be seen. They're still there, feeling disturbed, and you're in the dressing room with the kettle on.'

The character monologue had become an expected component of Victoria's act by this time and we were introduced to three new ladies. Deirdre was the nervous, tongue-tied market researcher attempting to way-lay passers-by with a hidden agenda. It was a creation worthy of Joyce Grenfell. Madeline was equally superb. An in-store representative for Cacharel, it was her job to encourage customers to try out the new autumn range of cosmetics and skincare preparations. As with Deirdre, it was yet another example of the non-professional public speaker. Over the tannoy Madeline launches into a sales routine littered with nasal tones, malapropisms, strangulated vowels, rising and falling intonation and elongated words. The jargon she uses is very similar to *Good Fun's* Betty and the overall effect is one of a failed attempt at sophistication. As she grows increasingly exasperated by the lack of response, Madeline begins to drop the pretension along with the aitches. Her Northernness comes through and her language grows less flowery as her desperation mounts. The mask is dropped and she reveals her true self.

The third character, and one which has enjoyed an extended life, is the nameless Friend of Kimberley. Another Northern borderline retard, she is never seen without a brightly coloured beret (a covert reference to her creator's home town?) and works in a supermarket. It is the wide-eyed innocence Victoria invests in the creation that makes her so appealing. Kimberley's extreme drunken exploits are relayed without censure and the character is totally without malice. Although she shares some characteristics with two of Victoria's earlier creations, Gail and Kelly Marie Tunstall, she stands out as the most endearing, largely due to the underlying pathos of the character. She is the ultimate in the line of non-professional public 'performers', wandering on stage in the belief that she's in a Wimpy. She was also a vessel for Victoria's only attempt at employing a catchphrase: 'I'm lookin' for my fwend' – a line that now draws applause from audiences.

The critics were united in their praise for Victoria, noticing not only her increased confidence, but also a vein of viciousness and cruelty in her material, suggesting some repressed English desire for rebellion and violence bubbling under the surface. True, there was an almost audible sigh of relief at her weight loss, but she was no longer being described as some cosy, cuddly and harmless light entertainer. However, Victoria's stance remained elusive, and she was described variously as middle class, appealing to the common man, Northern, typically British, the most completely English performer around, guileless, and snobbish. It was impossible to compartmentalise her and, consequently, it was impossible to limit her.

CHAPTER 10

THE end of the tour in late November segued nicely into the publication of *Barmy*, another money-making collection of sketches, culled this time from the second series of *As Seen On TV*. Victoria was also given a 40-minute *As Seen On TV* Christmas special, which aired on 18 December.

Wisely, she decided it was to be her last sketch show. 'I love television, and if it was possible for me to work in it more, then I would; but because of the position I've put myself in of being the only writer on the show, I can't physically work in it that often,' she explained. 'I've just had it with sketch shows for a bit – people have liked it, and I want to stop while they still like it.'

Dour as ever, she defined the 'special' as 'ten minutes longer than usual and I've splashed out on a new bra'. *Gardeners' World* had not wanted the extra ten minutes created by someone turning the oven up too high on a cookery programme, she explained in her opening monologue, so BBC2 had dumped them on her.

Julie Walters, Celia Imrie, *et al.* were obviously included in the cast and Victoria once again allotted other parts to such colleagues as Kay Adshead, Georgia Allen, Nicholas Barnes, Jim Broadbent, Deborah Grant, Meg Johnson, Sam Kelly, Maggie Steed, Sue Wallace and Sandra Voe, all of whom she had worked with previously.

Her fascination with television was more apparent than ever with a *Doctor Who* parody, a mickey take of Sunday television, the money-saving advice show 'McOnomy' (with Celia Imrie and Molly Weir playing a Scottish version of Margery and Joan), a badly dubbed foreign advert for men's bras, a *Right To Reply* slot, a *Coronation Street* parody, a documentary, and a sketch in which Julie and Celia conversed solely in advertising speak, reeling off a string of credible products and slogans. Television programmes in general and soaps in particular formed the main topic of discussion in Victoria's opening monologue.

'Self Service' saw Julie and Victoria as Enid and Wyn queuing for a snack and creating a vivid world of suburban madness with the most casual of gossip. The only other non-television-based sketch saw Julie and Victoria as unhelpful hotel receptionists, inspired by Victoria's experiences during her tours.

Song-wise there was 'High Risk Area', which, because it was a special, was shown in wide-screen film rather than cheaper video. Yet again it was another number about the dangers of relationships and the preference for insularity. In it Victoria sang how she had a degree and O-level Maths. This habit of justifying oneself through academic qualifications had previously been used in *Good Fun* and *As Seen On TV* and was, perhaps, a hangover from the Bury Grammar philosophy of academic excellence at all costs.

The special also included an ensemble song, 'The Chippy', which applied *West Side Story* staging to a gaudy celebration of working-class pleasure.

The affection of her *Coronation Street* 'tribute' earned praise from none other than Doris Speed (the soap's Annie Walker), who ended her days in a Bury care home. Victoria expertly captured the early years of the soap with her, Lill Roughley and Julie playing Ena Sharples, Minnie Caldwell and Martha Longhurst in the snug of the Rovers' Return. Shot in black and white it was a brilliant recreation of the show's glory years with knowing predictions and a brilliant send-up of style. There was even a jokey allusion to the demise of Anne Reid's Valerie Barlow.

One sketch had Victoria as a humourless feminist with lesbian tendencies. Plonked on a chair staring austerely at the camera, in spectacles identical to her mother's, she condemned the previous sketch. Any militants who saw Victoria as a figurehead may have found themselves revising their opinion.

There was also a brilliant documentary about the making of Acorn Antiques, inspired by the BBC's recent *Just Another Day* documentary on *EastEnders*. Maggie Steed played the much-feared executive producer Marion Clune, an obvious imitation of *EastEnders'* intimidating Julia Smith. The complete lack of chemistry between the actors, the arrogance, the egos, the bitching and the cliques all helped to make it an unforgettable experience.

While Victoria maintained her usual practice of name dropping (Eva Braun, Phyllis Calvert, Maurice Chevalier, Alma Cogan, Lord

Delfont, Janet Ellis, Fergie, George Formby, Princess Margaret and Wincey Willis), the recurrent character names of Pam, Pat and Renee, and afflictions (gyppy kidney, diabetes, whitlows, blindness, athlete's foot and haemorrhoids), she was unusually sparing with High Street/brand names (*Woman's Weekly*, *Daily Telegraph*, *Daily Mirror* and Oxo). Likewise, the only garments she mentioned were support stockings and a side-winding thermal body belt.

Whereas 1988 saw Julie Walters score a much-needed cinematic success with *Buster*, Victoria's chance to make a film was frustratingly snatched away. She had been approached to adapt Jill Tweedie's 1986 comic novel, *Internal Affairs*, for the screen. Paul Hogan was set to play the Adonis-like photographer, Kelly, with Victoria herself co-starring in the film. She was cast to play Charlotte Macanally, 'a large, white mound' of a woman who lives in Kentish Town. The luckless 37-year-old is in a floundering marriage and works at a fertility counselling clinic in Clerkenwell, but has an aversion to the smell of thawing semen. She finds herself going in an advisory role to a South-East Asian island. There she meets freelance photographer Kelly, who helps her become self-assured and carefree, before, ironically, returning home pregnant.

It was the sort of vehicle that could have enabled Victoria to make the transition to international stardom, but the project crumbled when Hogan's salary demands became too high.

International success would most likely have meant leaving Silverdale. At that time Victoria was still trying to justify living in rural isolation on practical grounds. 'I think it's nice to be where everyone else isn't,' she said. 'I do like to keep away from other comics. I don't want to end up doing the same as everybody else and also I can get a lot more work done if I'm living in a place where there's not people ringing up and knocking on the door every two minutes.'

In fact Victoria and Geoffrey did move from Stankelt Road, but only five minutes away to the other side of the village. Cove Lea was tucked away in the cul-de-sac of Cove Road. The house had originally been several eighteenth-century cottages, which accounted for its higgedly piggedly interior. It boasted six bedrooms and two open fireplaces. It had its own orchard on the other side of the road and beyond the fruit trees and daffodils lay buttercup meadows. The huge rear garden was park-like in proportion, and the property had a barbed-wire protected perimeter path affording spectacular views over the bay.

Despite feeling more comfortable in her isolation, Victoria was roped in to take part in the first studio-based Comic Relief night on BBC1 in February 1988. She and Julie performed a short Margery and Joan sketch in which they demonstrated how to turn a leather jacket into a bookmark. The event raised more than £13 million, and in the coming years Victoria's involvement would grow stronger.

For the third year running she picked up a BAFTA award, this time the Best Light Entertainment Programme for the *As Seen On TV Special*. She was also named BBC TV Personality of the Year by the Variety Club of Great Britain. Her droll sense of humour caused those attending the Hilton Hotel ceremony to erupt with laughter when she reminded them just how irritating it was to be stuck behind a Variety Club coach on the motorway.

With her career successfully established, Victoria's mind turned to motherhood. The pregnancies of Julie Walters and other friends helped encourage her and Geoffrey to try for a family of their own. 'I feel like a clock is ticking away and that time is running out,' she explained. After 20 years of 'doing exactly what I'd wanted' Victoria had a yearning to be responsible for somebody else. 'I had to make sure I had done what I wanted to do in my career just in case having a baby meant I couldn't carry on working,' she said. 'I don't think I would have handled it so well any earlier. You just know in yourself what would be a good time for you.'

She did not want to be newly pregnant on the April leg of the tour which she had resurrected from 1987, nor did she want to be too pregnant. Conceiving the baby was arranged with a military precision that owed more to efficiency than romance. It meant Victoria had to fly back from Dublin and make a midnight drive from Heathrow to rendezvous with Geoffrey, who had been touring the country as The Great Soprendo.

London Weekend Television's *Audience With* . . . shows are extremely pressurised occasions for the honoured celebrity, yet Victoria was six months pregnant when she stood before her peers in August 1988. Amazingly, she gave a 90-minute performance of her stage show without a single fluff or recording break. After weeks of touring the show she was well prepared, the material was primed and all she had to do was deliver it.

'It was very nerve-wracking because I could see their faces all lit up, with the cameras on *them*,' she recalled. 'They were a very friendly audience but not a normal one, so I was trying to play to the normal audience behind them and to ignore the celebrities. Thank God they put Julie in the front row, so I could see a friendly face.' She described it as a hellish experience:

'Not only are they who they are but they're all lit up so you can see them, whereas in the theatre you can't see anything except the exit signs. You're trying to concentrate, but when you look out, you can see all the horrible little blank faces staring back at you and you don't know what to expect. And, on top of that, they're all hyped up because they know they're on camera, too.'

Victoria had a say on who was featured on the guest list, which included Judi Dench, Dave Allen, Joan Bakewell, Dawn French and Michael Grade. Wisely, she acknowledged the artificiality of the situation, remarking:

'We've not done bad here tonight. Who have we got? Some friends of Wincey Willis and some people from Guildford. They're all up there – the people from Guildford. We don't show them because they're not famous.'

The staged questions of *Audiences With* can be embarrassing, but Victoria saw to that by ripping into her interrogators, making a mockery of the contrived situation. Julie Walters was 'star of *Educating Rita* and *Typhoo One Cup* – and she only got that because Meryl Streep turned it down', Celia Imrie was described as someone who needed exposure, and when Joan Bakewell asked a question about big bosoms, Victoria mocked: 'She's slumming it really tonight, Joan, isn't she really? I suppose MENSA was shut was it? Having a new billiard table put in, is that it?'

After the recording of *An Audience With* Victoria told a few trusted friends like Julie, Dawn French and Jennifer Saunders about her pregnancy, but it was still a closely guarded secret – helped no doubt by the fact that she actually began to lose weight. 'I felt it was nobody's business,' she said about the confidentiality. 'And that if anything went wrong I'd have to deal with the publicity as well as the actual happening.'

The hush-hush pregnancy became public when royal reporters spotted Victoria attending an ante-natal class at the exclusive £500-a-night Portland Hospital in London, where the Duchess of York gave birth to Princess Beatrice. Victoria's reason for going upmarket was, she said, for privacy. She imagined autograph hunters would plague her if she had gone to a Morecambe hospital. A member of staff confirmed Victoria's pregnancy to a tabloid journalist, but Victoria still managed some subterfuge by pretending the baby was due in November rather than October. 'I was determined to get to know my daughter properly without any interference from outside . . . She belongs to a part of my life which is Geoff's and mine.'

A brief holiday in August and a switch to Jane Fonda pregnancy workout tapes were the only concessions Victoria made to her condition. Work was still at the forefront of her mind and an idea was germinating that would have made for a very revealing insight into her life had it come to fruition. The play she was working on was set in 1969, about adolescence, and based on herself and events in her life.

Grace Durham was born on 1 October 1988 and was given the middle name Eleanor after Victoria's paternal grandmother. Victoria went into hospital at 3 a.m. to be induced, but the delivery rooms were all in use. Throughout the night she and Geoffrey watched the synchronised Olympics swimming and when that finished Geoffrey popped out for a drink, returning just in time for the birth. Victoria had wanted natural childbirth but in the event had an epidural. The placenta was dropped on the floor and the nurse was mortified when Victoria pretended she had wanted to eat it. It wasn't the only gag; Fergie had given birth at the same hospital just two months before, prompting Victoria to remark 'I knew it was the VIP suite, I found a couple of long ginger hairs under the pillow.'

An Audience With Victoria Wood was given a prime time 9.05 p.m. Saturday night slot on 10 December, earning Victoria two more BAFTA awards for Best Light Entertainment Programme and Best Light Entertainment Performance. It also earned her the *TV Times* Favourite Female Comedy Performer award.

The villagers of Silverdale were unlikely to pay to see Victoria on stage, but they could not escape seeing her on TV. Part of the routine included a swipe at Silverdale. ('I live in the dullest place on God's Earth with the most stupid, thick people'). It was hardly surprising that the residents refused to speak to her after hearing such lines. As village elder Cyril Farrer said: 'If you kick one we all limp.'

Victoria's actual verdict on her neighbours was ambivalent and vaguely patronising: 'I do like the people. I'm not saying they're better people than others, but I feel much more comfortable with Northerners. I just love the way they talk. The way they use language . . . But I do like to get away from them . . . fairly often.'

Shortly after *An Audience With Victoria Wood* was televised Victoria released an album (*Victoria Wood Live*) of the stage show just in time for Christmas. It was recorded at The Dome in Brighton and produced by Geoffrey. It revealed just how financially astute she was – the same material had been used on stage, on television, released as an LP and, later, as a video. She was also making money from the publication of *Talent* and *Good Fun* by Methuen.

Such exposure did not extend to her new baby and Victoria would not permit photographs of her for anything but the family album. It was indicative of her utter obsession for Grace and parenthood. 'I don't think I ever had a normal life until she was born,' she declared. But, punitively, she felt there had to be no dropping of standards. So scared was she of becoming the kind of mother who 'sat around for nine months covered in sick' that she got up at 4.50 a.m. to dress and do the housework. 'I never slobbed about at home, the house was always spotless and I was never late for an appointment,' she revealed years later. 'I was totally ridiculous really.' Providing further insight into her state of mind at that time, she added:

'I was very manic – I'm compulsive and did it to the detriment of everything else. I did the ironing in the middle of the night. I'd never done the ironing before, but my big failing as a person is that I have to do everything perfectly. I don't think I spoke to Geoff for the first three months.'

By Victoria's own admission, Geoffrey was not a natural father, preferring to do the shopping and cooking instead. This suited her as it meant she was the one who had total involvement with the baby. With the adolescence-based play completed, Victoria spent the weeks leading up to Christmas getting to know Grace in their recently acquired North London flat while Geoffrey was appearing in yet another pantomime.

Bored by the television sketch show format and frustrated at not being able to recapture her earlier successes at writing plays, a series of six individual half-hour playlets – or 'playdolinos' as she referred to them – was the perfect compromise. It allowed Victoria to try and sustain characters and material without asking to be judged as a fully blown dramatist, and work commenced in January 1989.

As always the hardest part was beginning and Victoria came up with a number of ways to avoid starting. These included writing letters and chatting to Geoffrey over the intercom. He was busy preparing for a new Thames Television series, *The Best of Magic*, in his office at the other end of the house. Exercise was another good delaying tactic and, combined with Victoria's abandonment of junk food in favour of fruit, she lost two stones. Grace provided an additional distraction, although it was strictly on Victoria's terms. Within three months of giving birth she acquired a nanny.

'It was hard to get going at first, I wasn't exactly sure what I was doing,' said Victoria of the new series. 'What appears on paper is usually very bad, not funny, *terrible* even, at first – but at least I've started . . . I get miserable when I think the writing isn't going well. Every time I've ever written anything, the first months or so have been *just awful*. Even though I know it'll finally sort itself out, I get miserable. But it has to be gone through.'

Of the creative process, she said: 'I don't write things that are based on funny things that happened to me. I just can't write about the way I live. It wouldn't be interesting. I get up every day and I write and that's it.' She did not aim for topicality because of the gap between writing the material and performing it, and she never used jokes as such.

'What I've learned is to work instinctively within the limits of what I can use, what I personally find funny,' she explained.

'I have certain characters I like and others I don't like *so much*. The ones I like I often get it right – certainly that's the direction I'm going more now. You create sympathy for one character and direct laughter at the other.'

The parts for the series were written with specific actresses in mind, but in a marked departure, Victoria decided to play a version of herself. 'I want people to like me and the people who play my friends, and not everybody else,' she said. Fiction allowed her to rewrite her own childhood. The scripts were completed by July, one play was even written in just two days.

Much as Victoria liked to make out she was disconnected from the baggage which showbusiness brought, it was simply not true. In August she travelled to Edinburgh to lecture on soap operas at Melvyn Bragg's behest and 1989 also saw her lend her name to that cliché, the Celebrity Cause. She was one of several celebrity mothers to join Pamela Stephenson's Parents for Safe Food Campaign and was given special responsibility for Labelling. Typically she used her simple, Northern mum-who-just-happens-to-be-a-star persona to try and distance herself from such backslapping worthiness. Of a dinner party at Pamela Stephenson's she said she was so overawed by the glamour of it all that she sat and said nothing all night.

It had been nine years since Victoria had given a sustained acting performance so the prospect of the playlets may have caused some trepidation. She eased her way around any nervousness by opting to play 'herself'. She was 'Miss Wood'; she is 'in television'; she could have used the VIP lounge at an airport; she is au fait with television; she is 'a much loved and irreplaceable entertainer'; she is a 'comedienne'. It was an unusual concept for British television – even Tony Hancock, while playing 'Tony Hancock' never acknowledged that the character was a television celebrity. But Victoria's decision may have confused the audience. She was 'Victoria Wood', Una Stubbs was 'Una' and Lill Roughley was 'Lill', yet the likes of Celia Imrie and Julie Walters went under a variety of guises. The theme of identification recurred throughout the series. Victoria would be mistaken for a travel representative, a carol singer and Dawn French, but she also deliberately assumed the identity of an exotic dancer called Sapphire, the old bag Marjorie Witherstrop, Lorraine – an update on Kelly-Marie Tunstall, adventurer Miss Elizabeth Gough and a wealthy brainless bore. Even when she is introduced as 'the comedienne' at a cocktail party, the host's assumption that the act can simply be turned on was Victoria's way of showing that she was a person first and a performer second.

The series was also unusual in Victoria's use of straight-to-camera asides, explanations and confessions. Stand-up was her forte and perhaps the to-camera incidents were a way of securing the comfort direct audience contact gave her.

She observed comedic conventions with the frequent appearance of an authority figure and it was in her treatment of them that she revealed a personal development. Whereas in the past she played the victim, in the playlets she was usually the one who mocked/stood up to/outwitted the authority figures. In *Mens Sana In Thingummy Doodah* it is Judy the efficient keep-fit instructor ('she's worked by a computer in Milford Haven'); in *The Library* it is the gorgon Madge ('awfully narrow-minded, makes Mary Whitehouse look like a topless waitress'); in *Over To Pam* it is the dreadful daytime television star Pam ('patronising old cow'); in *Val de Ree* it is the batty Youth Hostel owner, Susan.

Along with identity, choice figures prominently in the playlets. Who should Sheila date?; should Lill embrace the diet industry?; should Victoria go on holiday?; should she masquerade as Elizabeth Gouch?; should she sacrifice her own pleasure for that of a friend?

The targets were predictable: the diet industry, airport delays, daytime television, country living, pretentiousness and superficiality. But Victoria was able to weave unpredictable, offbeat and very funny characters, incidents and dialogue into the most simple of plotlines.

The series kicked off with *Mens Sana in Thingummy Doodah*. Victoria's hatred of the diet industry was no secret, as far back as 1980 she had taken a swipe at it in *Nearly A Happy Ending*. But now she extended her attack by setting the entire playlet in Pinkney's Hydro, a health farm. Victoria, who had only been to a health farm once, reluctantly accompanied her friend, Lill (Lill Roughley), who believes that losing weight will encourage her boyfriend to leave his wife for her. Throughout the playlet Victoria mocks the whole regime, from the masseur who tells Lill that underneath her fat she's actually very slim, to such weight-based afflictions as underarm swoop and runaway midriff. The empty-headed model Sallyanne (Georgia Allen) is held up to ridicule for believing that eating a hard-boiled egg before every meal means the egg will eat some of the meal for you, in much the same way that the unhappy teenaged Victoria believed grapefruit had the same magical ability.

More serious is Lill's growing neurosis about her weight; she has lost all self-belief and has been brainwashed by the diet industry and a callous lover. The guilt of eating one chocolate-covered raisin is enough to convince Lill that she will have to be wheeled around. It is down to Victoria to step in and convince Lill that her weight does not matter and has nothing to do with her value as a person. The playlet ends with her and her cronies sneaking out to the cafe and treating themselves to a greasy fry up complete with additives and germs.

The Library saw Anne Reid reprise another anxious spinster in the same mould as *As Seen On TV*'s Pamela Twill. Like Pamela, Sheila was entering the dating game, though she opted for video rather than computer dating. The extended format allowed Victoria to create a full character for Anne, who gave a brilliant performance. It was a perfect marriage of writer and performer. 'I was the same with Sacha Distel in Boots' explains a panic-stricken Sheila as a prospective date approaches. 'The times I've been saddled with an unrequested bilberry yoghurt' she complains of a liberty-taking milkman. Her funniest moments occur on her dates. First there is the humourless pedant Keith (Philip Lowrie) who dominates conversation. Sheila tries to converse but is reduced to making jarring irrelevancies ('I see in the paper today Mrs Thatcher's sporting a new brooch.'). She fares even worse with the cultured Richard (David Henry). To her the Great Painters are a set of table mats. Serendipity sees her linking up with John the librarian (Richard Kane). Victoria, acting as her chaperone, disguises herself as Northern bag Marjorie Witherstrop, but her cleverness backfires when she spends the evening getting chatted-up in the kitchen by Ted (Danny O Dea), the randy old man.

We'd Quite Like To Apologise sees Victoria setting off on a holiday abroad. As with the 1987 stage show, the need for audience identification meant it was a chartered flight to that most lower class of destinations – Alicante. She is one of us even though, as she admits, she could have gone in the VIP lounge at the airport. The inevitable airport delay enables her to interact with very recognisable types – the hypochondriac (Una Stubbs), the sickeningly lovey-dovey young couple (Jane Horrocks and Richard Hope), the professional slut (Julie Walters) and the unhappily married couple (Lill Roughley and Philip Lowrie), who all want a piece of her. These 'upsetting misfits' are stock characters, but with Victoria's handling they each bring off-the-wall humour to proceedings. The set up also enabled Victoria to examine the English characteristics that most irritate her: inefficiency, bad manners, insularity and indecisiveness.

'Television does funny things to people,' warns Victoria at one point in *Over To Pam*, and uses the 28 minutes to prove her point.

When Victoria collects her friend Lorraine (Kay Adshead) to take her to the television studios, she is in effect taking the viewer on a behind-the-scenes tour of the world of television in which disillusionment is inevitable. Victoria may be 'in' television, but her loyalties lie with Lorraine/the viewer. An insider more at home with the outsider is the image she tries to portray.

Victoria narrowed her focus on daytime television, something that she saw an awful lot of while at home with Grace. 'It's so cheap and nasty. It's such an easy formula to get women in the studio and pay them virtually nothing to say a few words. We should instead put up a caption saying "We have no TV worth showing", and then leave the screen blank,' she suggested to the *Observer*. Seven years later she softened considerably and told the *Daily Telegraph*: 'I'm not a snob about what's on in the daytime. People with important, exciting jobs and wonderful family lives forget that television is an important part of people's lives. Most people in this country can't get out and go to the theatre and do exciting things. They are in their houses, and they want cosy, friendly people. They don't need educating every minute of the day.'

To anyone who has ever been inside a television studio, the staff at Victoria's *Console TV* are immediately recognisable types: the superior receptionist who aligns herself with the stars, the patronising researcher, the camp, neurotic assistant stage manager, the tactless make-up girl.

The condescension doled out to Northern Lorraine is exactly the sort of treatment Victoria received in her early days when it seemed to her that television was run by mad Southerners. Indeed, the playlet could be seen as the more self-assured 1989 Victoria leading, protecting and advising her vulnerable and naive younger self. It was another example of her tackling and cancelling out the negatives of her own past. It is Victoria who stands up to the make-up girl, the researcher, the wardrobe department and, most triumphantly, the egocentric star of daytime television, Pam. This gloriously horrible creation was played by Julie Walters, and was an early incarnation of Pat Bedford in Victoria's film, *Pat and Margaret*. Pam's downfall is brought about by Victoria's taking Lorraine's place in the interview and giving her exactly the sort of interviewee she likes to exploit. Victoria's impostor Lorraine was yet another thick Northern tart and, in a way, the real-life Victoria was exploiting the stereotype for laughs but disguising it as an attack against condescension. She confesses to a gleeful Pam that she had seven kids before she was eighteen but was so stupid she kept leaving them in skips. She goes on to give biographical details which are the mainstay of 'Live With Pam'-type programmes; sexual abuse, tranquilliser addiction, alcoholism. The climax comes when Victoria whips off the blonde wig to reveal her true self and unmasks Pam as 'the most patronising old cow to hit the airwaves since Mrs Bridges caught Ruby with her corsets on back to front'. Pam, who is a borderline hypoglycaemic, collapses and her show is axed. The day has been a learning experience for Lorraine. She had ended up on *Chuck a Sausage* hosted by Geoffrey Paige, who she is nuts about until she discovers he wears a toupee.

As a country-dweller herself Victoria knew the gap between rural idyll and actually living there, and she exploited it in *Val de Ree*. In this playlet she and Celia Imrie play two pals on a walking and camping holiday on the Yorkshire Moors. They soon learn the countryside is inhabited by yuppies and batty old women, not 'loveable old farmers' wives'. Bleak weather, disorientation and bickering add to the reality, and the complacent assumption that youth hostels have changed and are run more like hotels is soon discovered to be a myth. A stickler for realism, Victoria bought a tent when writing the script to make sure she named the parts correctly and could describe assembly instructions accurately.

While out in the wilds she and Jackie (Celia) meet an elderly duo – another typical Victoria device – Mim (a relative of *Good Fun*'s Betty) and Daddy. Daddy has 'terrorised the cardboard box business for 40 years' a suburban boast akin to *Happy Since I Met You*'s Dennis ('reasonably well-thought of in chemical engineering'), *As Seen On TV*'s Nick who is 'very high up in sewage', and the husband in *Lucky Bag* who is 'well thought of in the curtain-track world'.

Victoria and Jackie trick their way into the youth hostel by pretending to be that night's guest lecturers and it is only when they are congratulating themselves that they realise they will have to give a speech. The cleverer they think they are, the more things backfire on them.

The opening of *Staying In* made it blatantly clear who Victoria wanted to be identified with. She is sitting on the sofa watching some mindless comedy film of old. She is in fact mirroring the viewer at home; both are facing each other through the prism of a television. Within seconds she gets the audience on her side with her irritation at having her viewing interrupted by a phone call. The call comes from her bossy friend, Jane (Deborah Grant), who asks Victoria to accompany her to a party.

Victoria's abhorrence of parties in real life – some aspects of shyness have never seemed to leave her – had made its way into her stand-up monologues. She would describe dire suburban dos where she found herself in a kitchen full of women yapping about cystitis, or stuck with a couple who had done their own conveyancing. Her elevated place in the television firmament saw her being invited to the sort of swanky London parties satirised here. Despite her changed circumstances, Victoria cleverly manages to remain 'one of us' by undermining the event.

The hostess is the upper-class Moira – the self-crowned most successful hostess in London Society – played by Patricia Hodge who was cast after Victoria heard an interview in which she revealed she would like to do more comedy. Moira is this playlet's authority figure, ushering guests and introducing them to one another with a breezy confidence.

The guests themselves are brainless, affluent movers and shakers. They are patronising, chauvinistic, even racist to a degree. Again, Victoria seems to be reassuring the viewer that 'we are better than them'. It soon becomes clear that Victoria The Comedienne, Kevin The Rock Star (Richard Lintern) and Jim The Artist (Brian Burdon) – none of whom fulfil pre-conceived expectations – have been invited as party novelties. Needless to say it is Victoria who refuses to be compartmentalised and used in this way and who leads the other 'goodies' to the kitchen for good, simple Shepherd's Pie. There she bonds with the young Scottish housekeeper Aisla, expressing a genuine interest in how she coped as a homeless person. When Moira discovers them it is Victoria who stands up to her and, on behalf of the others, informs her that they have no wish to perform. The personification of the chattering classes is reduced to tears and her confidence is shown to be a veneer of insecurity caused by the brittleness of her circle. Unpretentious and natural Victoria saves the party with a good old-fashioned game of musical chairs.

Triumphing over Society was not enough for Victoria, she also had to defend herself against fellow comedians, serious playwrights and other Northerners. Setting herself above her contemporaries Victoria includes the detail that a 'raunchy, anarchic, foul-mouthed, alternative comedienne' had to drop out of the party because she was playing Dick Whittington in Windsor. Playwright Alan Hammond (Jim Broadbent) is held up to ridicule for being a Professional Northerner. Through this character, Victoria may also have been having a private dig at her old boyfriend. Bob Mason wrote Northern plays and, like Alan Hammond, lived in Chiswick.

Predictably, the series of playlets contained many namechecks, textile/garment mentions, afflictions and High Street/brand names. As was only to be expected, there were references to Raffia,

Tupperware, shoplifting, and nuns in the guise of a Mother Superior. Limited gynaecological references made way for word play. Victoria also made more use of surrealism: the calorific value of a pillowcase; assuming someone is wearing a tie neck blouse from the sound of their voice; mistaking a terrapin for an indoor plant; someone having a tweed sofa inserted in their mouth at a party in Brighton; the idea of faxing milk.

The series saw Victoria's love of language being given more of an outlet. Aside from the usual use of extraneous dates, many of the characters Victoria encountered in the playlets had an idiosyncratic way of speaking, the oddness and humour heightened by the contrast with Victoria's own realistic manner of speech.

The tongue-tied malapropisms of Nicola in *Mens Sana in Thingummy Doodah* are a joy, as are the incongruous and unexpected utterances of Connie and Enid. The peculiar jargon of airport check-in staff is neatly captured in *We'd Quite Like To Apologise* and the over-use of figurative language is equally amusing. Keith in *The Library* has a distinctive precision to his utterances, and Mim's refined and unexpected vocabulary in *Val de Ree* is every bit as comic. In the same playlet Joan Sims made the most of Susan's strange speech.

Sly little in-jokes, such as the awful video at the health farm being an 'Acorn Enterprises' production, and Anne Reid (*Coronation Street*'s Valerie Barlow) going on a blind date with Philip Lowrie (*Coronation Street*'s Dennis Tanner) crept in, along with another mocking remark about Celia Imrie's nostrils.

Victoria's favourite names (Connie, Enid, Madge, Marge, Pam) featured in the series, as did typically Northern surnames such as Witherstrop, Wythenshawe and Mottershead. We also saw more of her fondness for toying with the most plain names – conjoining two to create an unusual and therefore funny result, such as Shulie, Saundra and Joyanne.

Serious topical events such as Chernobyl, passive smoking, the ozone layer and global warming were reduced, with Victoria once again showing how to her characters – and most people – it is the smaller issues that matter. So for instance, when mention is made of the polar ice caps melting, Victoria remarks that some tropical islands will be completely submerged but she personally stands to lose a bit of a privet and a bird table. Similarly, in *Mens Sana in Thingummy Doodah* Lill's declaration that today is the first day of the rest of her life jolts Connie into remembering that it is the first day of Lewis's sale.

CHAPTER 11

THE *Victoria Wood* series marked a deliberate step towards mass appeal for Victoria. For the first time her work was to be shown on BBC1 at the viewer-friendly time of 8.30 p.m. In light of her past successes, expectations were high and Victoria was described in the press as one of the 'First Ladies' of British television. But it might have irked her that some of her thunder was stolen. Ten days before *Victoria Wood* started in November, ITV began broadcasting *About Face*, a series of six half-hour comedy plays starring Maureen Lipman. And an hour after the first episode of *Victoria Wood* ended, Mel Smith and Griff Rhys Jones popped up in a new series of extended sketches. To have her originality questioned was irritating, but Victoria's pride was further dented by the lack of customary praise by the critics. The *Daily Express* described the show as 'tiresome stuff' and the *Daily Mirror* said her targets were predictable and snobbish. The biggest fault with the playlets was their weak endings. It was a shortcoming that had always dogged Victoria's sketches and monologues. The quality of what came before was of such high calibre that most critics tended to overlook the clumsy 'punchlines', but not any more.

There had been high expectations for the series and the first playlet attracted 13.16 million viewers, making it the 14th most popular programme in the country that week. The public were obviously disappointed with what they saw, because by the next week viewing figures had dropped to 11.03 million and the show slipped to number 29 in the ratings.

Victoria had had some concerns during the filming of the series, not least the decision not to film it before a live audience. The instant gratification was absent, even though the finished tapes were later screened before an audience, and she described the recording as a 'boring, diabolical and awful' experience. Another change from the usual method of working concerned Geoffrey Posner. He still produced the series but only directed two of the playlets: Kevin Bishop had responsibility for the rest. The sense of continuity remained with the music, however, and David Firman was once again the musical director.

Victoria accepted some of the blame for the disappointing reaction to the series herself: 'It wasn't as well written by me as it could have been, and I shouldn't have been in all of the sketches.' But like the boxer she had once wished to be, when she was in a corner she came out fighting. During the making of the shows she was not afraid of voicing her opinions. 'It's often the only way to get things done properly,' she said. 'It's not easy to do without hurting people's feelings. I think life is too short not to ask for what you want.' This attitude was in dramatic contrast to the Victoria of old who would have smiled, kept her mouth shut and hated herself afterwards.

'There's a limit to your quest for popularity,' she realised. 'You have to say: "Well, I don't care if people think I'm an old ratbag. I'm going to ask and get this right, whatever it is." Years ago I would put up with things just to appear to be a nice person. Now I think "I want it done properly", and I don't care what they think of me.'

The year had begun with Victoria in the witness box at Lewes Crown Court. A 33-year-old man was being prosecuted for stealing £20 from her shoulder bag which she left in a changing room while she popped to the toilet in a Brighton theatre during her last tour. He received a nine-month suspended sentence and was ordered to repay the £20 he stole. A more welcome public appearance came at the end of the year when Victoria was presented with an honorary degree by Lancaster University for her contribution to the arts (earlier in the year she had picked up another award, the *TV Times* Favourite Female Comedy Performer). She received her degree from the university chancellor Princess Alexandra. The university had given an honorary degree to Eric Morecambe in the 1970s and Victoria was thrilled at sharing the distinction.

Her relationship with her parents had obviously improved, as she invited them to the ceremony. And her relationship with Geoffrey had also grown stronger, thanks largely to their mutual adoration of baby Grace. The normally controlled couple aired fulsome public praise for each other. 'I'm her greatest fan. Nothing could give me more pleasure than her success. I can't understand people who are jealous of their partner. And it hasn't changed her at all. She's exactly the same as she always was,' gushed Geoffrey. Victoria reciprocated, but focused more on the career benefits: 'Geoff means everything to me; he writes none of it, thinks of none of the ideas, but if he didn't like it I wouldn't care to carry on. His enthusiasm is such a charge. Without it I would get very cold about what I'm doing. I'd very quickly decide "It's no good, I'm going to stop doing it." I wouldn't be able to gather myself up to write. It would go dead on me.'

Geoffrey's growing security and fulfilment was demonstrated by his decision to kill off The Great Soprendo. 'There are just things that I want to do that I could not do as Soprendo and tricks I wanted to perform that I could not, pretending to be Spanish,' he explained. 'I'm not going to stop doing magic, but I'm moving on, performing better and "impossible" tricks which I think I'll be able to do more successfully as Geoffrey Durham than The Great Soprendo. I'll open myself up and say, "This is me." I used to enjoy dressing up – there was an element of hiding behind a character.'

The unexpected weight loss since pregnancy, and the discovery that she was allergic to sugar and its subsequent banishment from her diet, meant it was a new, streamlined Victoria who embarked on a 60-date tour in 1990.

A lengthier hairstyle added to her attractiveness and the overall effect seemed to have boosted her confidence, although she still hid behind a stand mike on stage. The critics certainly noticed this sexy assuredness.

'It is hard to square the glowingly self-confident woman on stage with the diffident fattie who cut her comic teeth in the cramped surroundings of the King's Head in the early Eighties,' wrote Charles Spencer in the Daily Telegraph. In The Times Alan Coren said: 'The Lancashire duckling is [now] this slim and pretty superswan', and Colin Donald wrote: 'The chubby, ultra-audience-friendly character with the Alan Bennett-like Northern cosiness has been superseded by a leaner, more confident voice.'

Interestingly, it was only when she had slimmed down that Victoria became more caustic about the thin. When she had been larger she was as average as her audience and perhaps it was concern at losing this bond that made her go on the attack by negating the slim. Her 'thin, neurotic, body-conscious friends' are always on a diet, while her 'massive jolly friends' amuse themselves by watching aerobics videos over bottles of wine and criticising the leotards. The slimming industry is witheringly dispatched with Victoria's description of Weightwatchers' Quick Start programme ('You run in, they shout "You're too fat". You run out again'). There was only one disparaging – and patently untrue – remark she made about her own figure, probably to inspire affection and identification. She did not have a waist, she said, more of an unmarked level crossing.

It was typical of Victoria's perfectionism that even the tour programme was carefully crafted. She wrote a parody of a *Hello!* interview (*Ooh Hello!*). It was gloriously out of touch, full of ludicrous inaccuracies and condescension to Victoria's Northern origins, with 'oop't 't' North' and 'Ee by Goom' inserted indiscriminately.

As well as the obligatory mentions of nuns, Tupperware, shoplifting and unsatisfactory sex the routine covered her week, hotel life, the Bury Grammar School reunion and her efforts to conceive. For a wife-swapping routine she created a verbal mini farce in which she played the two couples (including the ubiquitous Pam) applying surburban sensibilities to a swingers' party.

She was particularly good on the English character ('We don't like to be happy'), giving brilliantly perceptive insights on the personality of the country. If we had the Ceausescus here, she said, we wouldn't have executed them, we would have written funny letters about them to *Points of View*. And only a ban on car boot sales and caravanning could inspire an uprising.

More and more physical comedy was creeping into the act, from an exaggerated impression of *Coronation Street*'s Deirdre to a graphic mime of the insertion of a tampon. The innuendo was more unsubtle than usual too, and Victoria lazily relied on easy laughs from jokes about hanging a sign on a knob and a man sitting on an enormous organ.

The antipathy the villagers of Silverdale felt towards Victoria after the remarks she made about them in her last tour seemed to provoke rather than restrain her. Now she described them as making Dustin

Hoffman in *Rainman* seem outgoing and vivacious, and that because they do not have any money their idea of celebrating is to book a window table at Kentucky Fried Chicken. The song, 'Saturday Night', also displayed a cold superiority to the North with Victoria depicting the exploits of two gormless Northern tarts, Tracey Clegg and Nicola Battersby.

Politics appeared in the act, but as usual Victoria dealt with it in workaday terms. She attributed the mortar attack on Downing Street to an attempt by Margaret Thatcher to get her curtains back, and Douglas Hurd was said to look like 'someone very high up in the carpet department at Selfridges'.

In the character monologue slots, Friend of Kimberley made a return and was celebrating the fact that she had caught the right bus. There was also Susan, Victoria's 16-stone roadie ('Like Desperate Dan only not quite so effeminate'). For the song 'Saturday Night' Victoria borrowed the tune from 'Oh Dear What Can The Matter Be' and another song in the act was strongly reminiscent of 'In The Bleak Midwinter'. It was about another unhappy relationship, but whereas in the past Victoria had tended to have the downtrodden and abused female accepting her treatment and, later, progressed to having her accept the relationship was over, here 'she' is pro-active, and electrocutes the offending man by dropping a heater in the bath.

In *Lucky Bag* Victoria had sung about her relief at not being a celebrity in the song 'Dear God'. In 1990's 'Reincarnation', however, she wishes she could sample the life of what she believes is an ordinary person. Both songs suggest she is in an isolated position, but 'Reincarnation', although seemingly affectionate on the surface, contains an element of snobbery. Her concept of 'ordinary' people includes a suburban housewife obsessed by the paraphernalia of domesticity, a yuppie mobile phone salesman, the spinisterish invoice clerk, the vulgar good-time woman, and the suffocating mother. Victoria expressed a desire to be them all but the reality was she would cross the road to avoid such specimens.

The explicit tampon mime, in which Victoria demonstrated the insertion instructions, suggested that she was trying to break out of her 'cosy' straightjacket, but it was at the end of the show that she really allowed her more subversive and mischievous side to show. Announcing how she didn't normally do this sort of thing, she explained how she'd got a nice letter backstage before the show from a lady whose name she forgot (but who is sitting in the circle) saying that her husband was supposed to be there but he's in Stoke Mandeville Hospital. She has asked Victoria, on her behalf, to thank the nurses who've helped her husband learn to drive, get dressed and cook. Demonstrating a superb acting ability Victoria was totally sincere and believable. Just when the audience grew cowed and respectful Victoria took a beat and said: 'He's not paralysed, he's just a pillock.'

A short family holiday in Ireland allowed Victoria to rest before she commenced a ten-week run of the show at the Strand Theatre in September. By this time she was being hailed as a national institution and a survey by market researchers Mintel found that most working women would like to be seen more like her than Margaret Thatcher, Anita Roddick, Claire Rayner, Marilyn Monroe, Kylie Minogue or Raisa Gorbachev.

For the London run the show was titled *Victoria Wood Up West*, a title which suggests a night out and a night off from ordinary suburbia; a temporary escape into a nicer world. It also neatly encapsulated Victoria's duality; she was both the audience and the attraction; the struggling victim who had to negotiate the pitfalls of everyday life and the star of the show who had triumphed over suburban gaucheness.

Rather than ignore the fact that the down to earth, 'ordinary' Victoria Wood was appearing on the West End stage, Victoria incorporated the incongruity into her act in a further bid to align herself with the audience. Joan Collins was appearing in *Private Lives* at the nearby Aldwych Theatre, prompting Victoria to tell the audience: 'Don't clap, it does annoy Joan.' There were gales of laughter when Victoria confided she had spotted the star popping out for a packet of cigarettes, the joke being that an act that would be normal for Victoria and her audience, was totally unthinkable for a star. Victoria may have made out that she, like her audience, read *Hello* and shopped at Argos, but in actual fact she was the real star; *Up West* had sold out, but *Private Lives* had not.

In *Talent* Julie Walters, as the desperate Julie, struggled to remember the lyrics to 'Cabaret', but in 1991 she found herself starring alongside cinema's Sally Bowles in the film of Richard Harris's stage play, *Stepping Out*. Even with the presence of Liza Minnelli, the film failed to attract vast audiences and was yet another flop for Julie. Her failure to be a box office draw, however, was the least of her concerns, because it was during the filming that her two-year-old daughter was diagnosed with leukaemia, a battle that would take three years to win.

On learning of the terrible news Victoria wrote Julie a supportive letter and sympathised on the phone.

'Of course, there's nothing anyone else can do and often it's intrusive to be too sympathetic or make too many inquiries, because that can drain what energy they have got that they need for dealing with the situation,' she reasoned. 'So I did back off while the worst was going on. Sometimes it's better to keep away, and that's how I felt, rightly or wrongly,' she explained.

Even if she had wanted to be with Julie it would have been impossible because Victoria, flushed with the success of her 1990 show, took it on the road for a six-week sell-out tour in the March of 1991. It coincided with her, technically at least, having a number one hit in the record charts. As a guest on a Saturday morning children's television programme, filmed for some bizarre reason on a cross-Channel ferry, Victoria expressed a desire to do a Comic Relief song with the Pet Shop Boys. The Northern duo shared her sly humour and drollness, and a collaboration may have yielded a song more sophisticated and intelligent than the standard charity single. The Pet Shop Boys failed to take up Victoria's bait and so in early 1991 she went ahead and wrote 'The Smile Song' for herself. The song, the flip side to the Hale and Pace song 'The Stomp', which received the air play, allowed Victoria to display her rarely seen talent for mimicry. She turned in highly credible vocal and physical impersonations of Kylie Minogue, Janet Jackson, a rapper and Jessie Matthews. Straddling a throbbing motorcycle in thigh-length leather boots helped effect her transformation into the lead singer of the female rock group, Heart, and there was even a send-up of the Pet Shop Boys.

The song itself was another of her lists of life's nasties. As a song for

Comic Relief it might have been expected that famine or flood would have featured among life's negatives, but Victoria remained true to her pet hates, so there was a plea for no more Kylie and Jason, stopcocks, instant mashed potato, pink acrylic knitting, rainhoods, tartan shopping trollies, ranch-style new houses, sex scenes with Ken Barlow and see-through tie-neck blouses. Mindful of her public image she even put Hampstead on the abolition list and, mischievously, 'dreadful charity singles'.

The money Victoria made from her latest tour was supplemented by the £22,000 she received for a 30-minute show in Nassau that May. The idea of performing her brand of comedy at the luxurious Bahamian Merv Griffin Paradise Island complex at first seems incongruous, but the booking was made by the Derby-based boiler installation firm Gloworm, which was much more Victoria's territory. As a struggling stand-up she was prepared to travel the length of the country for an engagement, so flying across the Atlantic for a 48-hour stay was a small price to pay for such a huge fee. She was booked to round off the company's annual five-day conference and the fee included her then basic £15,000 charge, two £2,500 club class BA tickets for her and a friend, two nights accommodation at the complex, food, drink and other expenses. Gloworm spokesman Roger Wilson said: 'She was worth every penny ... We wanted something special to thank the employees and we got it.'

Victoria's bank balance was further increased by sales of *Mens Sana in Thingummy Doodah* – a book of the *Victoria Wood* scripts – and the release of *Victoria Wood – Sold Out*, an hour-long version of her most recent tour filmed at Southampton's Mayflower Theatre. A Good Fun product, it was produced and directed by Marcus Mortimer with Geoffrey as executive producer. It generated even more profit when ITV paid to broadcast it the following year.

'I'm very puritanical about spending money. I have a real problem spending it on myself,' Victoria told the *Daily Mail*. Amassing a fortune was presumably awkward for someone with such a modest approach to finance, so perhaps the multi-million pound mansion she bought in Highgate was simply an investment.

'The quality of life is much better where we are. If we moved any nearer to London it would only be to somewhere like Sheffield and that would be close enough,' Geoffrey said in 1990. So averse was he to the capital that he refused to read the Sunday papers, feeling they were too London orientated. The fact that they did uproot themselves in 1991 and made a permanent home in London may suggest something about Victoria's career and their changing attitude to its necessities.

At the time she attributed the move to purely practical reasons. Work and business meetings meant making a 200-mile journey, leaving home in the early hours and returning in the middle of the night. Victoria also professed a concern for Grace's well-being, anticipating problems for her daughter if she grew up in a quiet village as the only child of a celebrity. Grace was nearing nursery age so if they were to move, then was the time. But fundamentally, the real reason was not so much practical as mental. 'I could feel on some very very basic level that I should not live in that isolated way . . . at the bottom line I wanted to join the human race and that's what I did,' Victoria confessed seven years later.

In their first year down South they lived in two flats before investing in the huge house on Highgate West Hill. That Victoria, seen by many as the epitome of Northernness, chose such a clichéd celebrity enclave as her new home surprised some. It should not have. Her personal wealth and cultured tastes meant she blended in perfectly to Highgate life. And Grace would be socialising with the children of neighbours like Annie Lennox and Jonathan Pryce, meaning she would not be regarded as an oddity.

Victoria missed the space and the countryside around Silverdale – on the day she moved she made a poignant walk across Morecambe Bay – but she found Highgate liberating. By extracting herself from a Northern village of 'ordinary' people she obtained a comparative anonymity, camouflaged by her fellow celebrities. 'What I like is the acceptance,' she said. 'People are caught up in their own concerns. It feels very open, that anything is permitted.' This new-found enthusiasm for life even extended to her family and her niece, Rebecca, one of Chris Foote Wood's three children from his first marriage, was invited to move in with them and stayed for three years.

Victoria entered into London life with gusto, attending book launches, gallery and exhibition openings, first nights and concerts. She acquired a secretary and there would be occasional trips to the Groucho Club and thrice-weekly visits to plush gyms. 'I can't be put in a box' was her response to those who questioned the ease at which she embraced such a lifestyle.

Victoria's fifth attempt at a screenplay coincided with a period of reassessment. Uprooting herself from the North was the catalyst. Her need for order and neatness meant she could not simply extract herself from the scene of so much personal mess and unhappiness and start afresh. It had to be dealt with and her new lifestyle forced her to confront the journey she had made. The way her career had accelerated so rapidly had left no real opportunity to take stock or properly orientate herself. Counselling sessions were imminent, but her new project may have been a form of therapy in itself.

Not surprisingly, the inspiration for it came from television. 'I must have seen something like *Surprise, Surprise*. I remember wondering what happened at the end . . . I was interested in the idea of people being divorced from their pasts. Even if you invent a persona for yourself, in the end you have to face what's inside,' she explained.

The vehicle she used for her idea was the reunion of two sisters; one living in the working-class North, one a famous Hollywood actress. Victoria was interested in exploring the nature of fame and celebrity and the clash when someone who believes their own publicity is forced to confront their past and their family. She acknowledged that it came at a time in her life when she had begun to re-examine her own youth and the changes she had undergone.

Attuned to her fans, she said she found it easier to identify with the anonymous working-class sister of the piece. 'I was interested to write about people who have no control over their own destiny. Most people don't have access to influence or power or money and are virtually stuck where they were born and have to make the best of it,' she explained.

'It was as if it was always there waiting to be said. I was looking back to my own childhood and my relationships with the people I knew. I mean, what would have happened to me if I hadn't gone into showbusiness? I could have just been a nice person, with no possessions and no security and unable to move from the position I was in. If I have a different lifestyle, does that make yours any less worth living? I don't think so. That's the story.'

Victoria conceived the idea at around the same time that she became pregnant again. She had hoped for another girl and was initially rather disappointed when she found out it was to be a boy. As with her first pregnancy she did not reduce her workload. Besides writing the film script she helped prepare the revised and expanded *Lucky Bag Songbook* (six of the fourteen songs were from the original, and the introduction was lifted from her 1990 tour programme), and was the main contributor to the LWT Special, *Julie Walters and Friends*.

The show, broadcast on 29 December 1991, was nominated for a BAFTA, and won the Writers' Guild Award for Best Light Entertainment Script. Six of the nine sketches and the one song were written by Victoria, proving that she could more than hold her own in the company of England's greatest contemporary playwrights (Alan Bleasdale, Willy Russell and Alan Bennett also contributed material). Television sketches were her medium so she had the advantage. Such experience worked in her favour and her material was the most original. Bennett basically wrote an extension of the Lesley character Julie had played in *Talking Heads*, Bleasdale penned a mini sequel for the character Mrs Murray which she played in *GBH*, and Russell wrote a lamentable piece in which the arts were mocked in rhyme.

Victoria appeared in four of the sketches with Julie. In the first delightfully observed and performed one they played two young Northern girls in the 1960s. They aged up to become Southern pensioners for a sketch set at a funeral reception and, as in her 1987 stage show, it was another piece which hinted at her dislike of the elderly. Julie changed sex to become the blazer-wearing, incontinent, namedropping, culinary xenophobic chauvinist with all the lines, but it was the grey, permed Victoria who got most of the laughs with her 'dancing'.

Another sketch revolved around the seating arrangements for a gathering of family and friends. It gave Victoria free rein to cram in references to such suburban necessities as, breakfast bars, foldaways, tumptys, tip-ups and such textiles as velour and one-way plush. Bizarre afflictions also featured heavily.

In another sketch Julie played the forthright Rhona receiving a manicure from Victoria's Jewish lesbian. Rhona loves the sound of her own voice and has gloriously off-kilter opinions on Apartheid, the collapse of the Berlin Wall and Israel. Like so many of Victoria's characters the humour comes through her use of extraneous detail, unique phraseology and the admittance of having had 'female surgery'.

Victoria wrote solo sketches for Julie which saw her as a loopy Barbara Cartland figure and the 53-year-old Mary Brazzle, a serene woman filming an advertisement for her relaxation routine who becomes increasingly stressed after every retake.

The song Victoria wrote for Julie charted a relationship from the excitement and nervous preparations for a first date to the disenchantment with marriage, combining elements of the earlier songs 'Go Away' and 'Living Together'. Unusually it ended optimistically ('He says let's stick with this it has to come right . . . and the sun shines cos love can struggle up between the lines').

Inserted into the programme were surprise tributes from the contributors. Whereas the other three leaned towards affectionate praise there was no sentimentality from Victoria, who had fun playing with her Northern image.

Shortly before Victoria's 39th birthday Marcus Plantin, director of programmes for London Weekend Television, announced that her still-untitled screenplay would be made into a £6 million two-hour cinema film. Negotiations had already started to ensure it would be going into production in 1993.

Victoria was delighted. Breaking into cinema was a long-held ambition and she was convinced that having Julie on board would open up the American market to her. The gestation of the film, however, was much more troubled than that of Victoria and Geoffrey's second child, who was born on 2 May. Like his sister, Henry William Durham was born at the Portland Hospital. It was one of those rare occasions when Victoria's careful plans went awry and she panicked. For once the circumstances mirrored the sort of domestically farcical situations that Victoria spoke about on stage. Because they could not get a taxi, she insisted on going to the hospital by Tube. This meant a ten-minute walk to the station laden down with two enormous bags, and when they did get on the train it was rush hour and they had to stand all the way. This time round though, she got her wish and had natural childbirth.

'Because I had a distant relationship with my mother . . . I'm closer to my children than she was to me,' said Victoria with familiar understatement. The strength of feeling she had for her children was sometimes exclusive of Geoffrey. 'I think I pushed him out for a while. They became the focus of my life,' she later admitted. Victoria hoped to have four children, but in light of her all-consuming love for them, Geoffrey, who had not been keen on having *any* children, put his foot down – and got his own way for a change.

Even though she had staff, the demands of being a mother to two small children forced Victoria to make changes. 'You'd think it would be easier with your second child but, if anything, it's harder,' she said. 'You seem to have four times as many things to do. You think you're prepared but you're not. Your hormones are still whizzing round in your brain and you're just as batty the second time round.'

Rather than a set working routine she now had to do as much as she could when she could, cutting out any time wasting. Another baby also meant less time for internalising and negativity. 'I used to be very negative, very apprehensive, a bit precious about it all. Now I just do the best I can,' she said. 'I used to be very shy but after a certain age it becomes a bit of an affectation . . . Shy people are very self-obsessed.'

A nanny helped, but even she could not breastfeed the baby every 90 minutes. It was through her maternal obligations that Victoria got the idea for her next television show. Staying at home with Henry meant she was watching more television than usual and was able to examine daytime television in particular. 'It doesn't take long to realise that everything that comes on from breakfast time to teatime is actually the same thing – it's all social conscience and ovaries, really,' she said. The programme that most caught her attention was *This Morning* and it was this format she chose for her new show.

Victoria Wood's All Day Breakfast was broadcast on Christmas Day in the spot once taken by *Morecambe and Wise* and *The Two Ronnies*. Directed and produced by Geoff Posner in association with Good Fun, it won the Royal Television Society's Best Light Entertainment Programme Award and the Writers' Guild Award.

It was unquestionably a parody of *This Morning*, from the Albert Docks backdrop to Victoria's and Duncan Preston's winning impression of Judy Finnigan and Richard Madeley, here called Sally Cumbernauld and Martin Crossthwaite. They interrupt and hurry their guests, switch subjects abruptly, are glib, insensitive and drop nuggets of their domestic life into conversation. Susie Blake popped up as Jolly Polly, the right-wing aerobics instructor giving unsolicited advice, and there was even a brief guest appearance by Alan Rickman playing himself. It was the first time he and Victoria had performed together since 1976 when he was Big Chief Blackmoon to her Wild Wilhelmina Fifty Fingers in *Gunslinger* at Leicester.

As always, other famous figures were named but not seen, from Hollywood stars, to opera divas, to old soap favourites. The daytime TV format was a perfect opportunity for Victoria to get gynaecological, with mention made of 'faulty fallopians' and 'wonky wombs'. Brand names were remarkably thin on the ground but Victoria was able to show her obsession with them via three adverts in which she tried to sell Sonara – the slimline sanitary towel with last number re-dial – Acton Liquid Detergent and Romany Roast Fine Blend Coffee. The adverts themselves were sharp parodies of existing advertising techniques; the blue ink on the sanitary towel, the Green sell for the detergent packaging ('Because we care about the environment we'd like it to be in a green box') and the ludicrous sexual element deemed so necessary for coffee adverts.

Inserted into the daytime television format were unrelated sketches, the first of which followed the familiar formula. Set in a knitwear shop – which allowed Victoria to reference such favourites as a cerise batwing, sling backs, angora roll-neck and crinoline – it had Julie as shop owner Saundra and Victoria as the lumpen assistant, Petrina. Saundra was another of those opinionated outspoken middle-aged figures so beloved of Victoria, while Petrina was the familiar thick Northern girl. The dynamic of the relationship was very similar to the manicure sketch in *Julie Walters and Friends* in that the older character dominated a younger, more subservient character. Julie was the exponent of Victoria's usual idiosyncratic figurative language ('body odour that could strip pine', 'sitting round waiting for something to happen like an undescended testicle') and was the vessel by which the weighty was transferred into the trivial ('Chernobyl, I worried for weeks about that . . . the night that it occurred we'd had our garden furniture out').

Victoria portrayed yet another limited Northerner (Alison Smedley) in a sketch with Susie Blake. She was a 38-year-old woman who, for some undisclosed reason, still attends 'a very well-respected grammar school'. Susie is the disciplinarian teacher demanding an explanation for increasingly extreme schoolgirl misdemeanours.

Victoria's underlying dislike of the old was given vent in a sketch in which Julie Walters played the cronish old mother trying her utmost to make her daughter (Lill Roughley) feel guilty and uncaring ('When I go I don't suppose anybody will find me for several days . . . can't see much end for me but an eternal, black nothingness'). It was another negative portrayal of the mother–daughter relationship that cropped up time and time again in Victoria's work. Victoria's mothers are either suffocating, uncaring or manipulative.

The final sketch allowed Victoria to take a timely poke at political correctness. She played the tidy Nicola on a first date with Sean in the pub. Nicola collects pictures of Mrs Bridges from *Upstairs, Downstairs* and approves of the idea of men knocking women out with a club and dragging them back to their cave. As she says: 'The man is lord and master . . . what he says goes.' She manages to get an initially surprised Sean to agree before blowing her whistle and revealing that she is an undercover member of the politically correct police; a p.c. PC.

For fans who were still trying to come to terms with the demise of 'Acorn Antiques', there was a treat. Victoria created 'The Mall', a parody of the ill-fated BBC soap, *Eldorado*, of which she had been a fan and had even donated money to the *Save Eldorado* campaign fund. Although it was difficult to achieve, the production values were even poorer than on *Acorn Antiques*. In the dramatic climax Mrs Overall, last seen choking to death on her own macaroon, made a surprise reappearance.

She revealed Miss Babs, Miss Berta and the other principals had been killed in a mysterious food poisoning accident on the M42, leaving everything to her. She brings the curse of *Acorn Antiques* to *The Mall*. As soon as she appears, the Mall's fountain breaks, cameras zoom into view and lines are fluffed and forgotten. The soap ended with Mrs Overall unveiling a new Acorn Antiques.

Victoria concluded the programme with a short stand-up routine. The brevity meant she was sharper than usual – professional autograph hunters were dispatched with the withering description of them being like trainspotters but with more body odour. Her habit of date specification was still evident ('I'd just blown my nose on my husband's dinner jacket to pay him out for something that had happened in 1979') as was her self-deprecation, only here the humour eclipsed the self-cruelty. Victoria explained how she used to have a self-help manual that advised stripping naked, looking at oneself in the mirror, picking out your best feature and saying it out loud. 'You have Latin O level' Victoria told her reflection.

The show finished with a new song and David Firman was once again the musical director. 'Real Life' highlighted the discrepancy between the ideal and the reality. Life, Victoria proclaimed, is badly designed, under-rehearsed, not a nice address, a knee in the groin, a windowless room in the Hotel Belle Vue. We live in real life, blundering around the shops, squinting at lists and dropping our specs. We are not allowed to swap our lives for ones with more plot and sex. Life is a fan club and Victoria is not a fan.

CHAPTER 12

THE concept of the troubled clown is far too clichéd for Victoria to ever associate herself with. Similarly, she would not admit to the traditional mid-life crisis on the approach to a 40th birthday. But in 1993 Victoria, who portrayed herself as a Northern beacon of common sense with no time for introspection, began therapy. The sessions would last on and off for the next two years and at one point – orderly as ever – she was seeing two therapists simultaneously about different things.

She threw out a whole shoal of red herrings about why she required therapy, including the fear of career failure, heavy workloads, her belief that it was better for things to be difficult, her shyness, her feeling that everyone else had a better grip on life than her, a puritanical streak which prevented her from treating herself, and a lack of assertiveness and confidence offstage. She even joked that it was 'something to do of a Tuesday'.

'It is just too personal a thing,' she later admitted, when pushed to explain the *real* reason for therapy. There were some strong hints, however. 'I did go through a lot of childhood stuff which was useful because it was an area I had never gone into before,' Victoria explained. 'Counselling helped me to clear up things that might have been bothering me from my past. And afterwards, I realised it is possible to make changes to your life . . . I wanted to get the problems from my past out in the open . . . When you do that, they lose their power over you – it's very releasing.'

Victoria had been so troubled by her history that she actually tried to physically expunge the past by purging herself through colonic irrigation. 'I was in the last throes of punishing myself. It was the same as scrubbing with bristle brushes to get the toxins out but you do it really because it hurts,' she said.

All the evidence suggests that it was Victoria's relationship with her mother that lay at the heart of her troubles. It was distant even when they lived in the same house and had not improved over the years. Helen had never encouraged Victoria and was reluctant to acknowledge her success. 'She would come to see my shows and tell me what other people said, but never what she thought.'

Subconsciously Victoria may have been yearning for a show of love or pride from her mother, even an indication of approval would have done. But if anything, Helen seemed to harden, possibly through the pressure of coping with Stanley, who by that time had gone into decline with senile dementia and was having paranoid delusions about people surrounding Birtle Edge House. If Helen was not prepared to change then Victoria would have to learn to accept the reality that she would never have a 'normal' mother. The past could not be altered and without Helen softening in some way, it was highly unlikely mother and daughter would be able to develop a warm and loving bond in the future. Victoria needed to let go and acknowledge the situation was not salvageable and for this she needed expert help.

Talking uninhibitedly with a detached professional must have enabled Victoria to see the behavioural patterns that had permeated her life. She came out of therapy feeling more positive and more comfortable with herself, having realised what had been driving her all along: 'I discovered that I was worrying about some things that really weren't worth the bother, so I just let go.' Apparently reconciled to the fact that the relationship with Helen was irrevocable, she was free to fully devote herself to her children, her husband and herself without feeling guilty any longer.

For Victoria therapy was a practical solution to her problems. 'To me, it was like getting a car mended. I went to the expert and then when it was mended I left,' she explained. 'Therapy is a very sensible way of dealing with things. You pay for 50 minutes of someone's time to listen to you and it's very releasing. It's not a personal relationship. When you leave that room, they forget you.' Despite advocating therapy, Victoria was careful not to become dependent on it and stopped going once she had gone through everything she needed to, although she has not ruled out future sessions.

Victoria did not need to embark on another tour in 1993 but the full benefits of therapy had yet to take effect and she insisted on pushing herself on. Unfortunately this meant Geoffrey had to turn down work offers in order to maintain the domestic stability.

Right: The first floor rented flat in Oxford Street, Morecambe, where Victoria and Geoffrey made their home in 1977.

Below: Victoria in her trademark tie obliges the press on Morecambe Beach in August 1979. (Atlantic Syndication)

BUSH THEATRE

SHEPHERDS BUSH GREEN, LONDON W12 8QD

BOX OFFICE 743 3388

IN AT THE DEATH

BY

NIGEL BALDWIN, KEN CAMPBELL, RON HUTCHINSON, DUSTY HUGHES, SNOO WILSON, VICTORIA WOOD.

Cast

ALISON FISKE
JOHN FISKE
GODFREY JACKMAN
PHILIP JACKSON
CLIVE MERRISON
JULIE WALTERS
VICTORIA WOOD

Edited and Directed by	DUSTY HUGHES
Lighting and Sound by	CHRIS O'MAY
Costumes by	CAROLINE BEAVER and ANNA BARUMA
Music arranged by	JOHN FISKE
Stage Management by	RIK CARMICHAEL and CHRIS O'MAY
Production photographs by	NOBBY CLARK

IN AT THE DEATH is a new musical show written for the Bush and the Company. Work began on June 4th when the writers were commissioned to write their impressions of the week as seen through the newspapers, although not necessarily through the main headlines. The show we have evolved is based on the familiar obsessions of English popular newspapers — suicide, abortion, disaster and (mostly) death — and the stories that the writers have imagined from their readings of recent news. The show includes songs, sketches and short plays.

Left: The playbill for *In At The Death*, the 1978 Bush Theatre revue in which Victoria claims she finally found her voice. (Bush Theatre)

Right: Victoria wrote six songs for the revue, but it was the sketch *Sex* which attracted critical praise. (Nobby Clark/Bush Theatre)

Above: Slumming it. Victoria strikes a working class pose for the camera in 1980. Despite the glum look she had just been named the *Evening Standard*'s Most Promising Playwright and was about to marry Geoffrey. (David Lavender/*Sunday Times Magazine*)

Right: The future looked so bright for 20-year-old Birmingham University student Victoria. She had got her first break performing for local television and was about to be seen by a national audience on *New Faces*. But she had no idea of the rejections, frustrations and disappointments that lay ahead. (News Team International)

Above: Going solo – Victoria pictured in 1983 when she began her one woman stand-up act in earnest. (Denis Thorpe/the *Guardian*)

Below: In the swim. Victoria swam to lose weight for the television sequel to *Talent* which Granada made in 1980. (Ray Green/Popperfoto)

Above: The sprawling Cove Lea in the village of Silverdale which was Victoria's final Northern home before she made the move to London.

Right: Victoria worked the early morning canteen shift at Halstead's. Her secret 1997 visits to the factory in Whitefield, Manchester, were research for her situation comedy, *dinnerladies*. She is pictured with canteen manager Adam Ellis.

Victoria Wood OBE. A proud moment for Victoria pictured with Geoffrey, Grace and Henry outside Buckingham Palace in December 1997, but the real highlight of her day came afterwards when she attended her daughter's school carol service. (Universal Pictorial Press

Beginning in April, the 104-date tour would sprawl over six months with residencies at fourteen venues across the country. It would culminate with a record breaking fifteen nights at the Royal Albert Hall.

Likening it to working on an oil rig Victoria did four shows a week. Much as she loved touring, her devotion to her children came first. She made a point of taking the summer off to be with them and travelled home each night from any venue within two-and-a-half hours drive of London so that she could be home when Grace and Henry awoke. When returning home was impractical she took Henry with her, even when he had chicken pox. Grace had accompanied her on her 1990 tour and the only reason she remained in London with Geoffrey and cousin Rebecca was because she had started school.

The tour was the first time Victoria had faced a live audience since elevating herself to Highgate life and, while acknowledging the fact, she was at pains to stress that she did not belong there ('I don't fit in, I feel very out of it . . . It's too posh for me'). She almost implied she was living in her mansion under duress. She mocked the locale, saying that Kiri Te Kanawa was the lollipop lady, and that even the homeless slept on futons. At the bottle bank she was the odd one out amongst all the glamour; while others were depositing champagne and Perrier bottles she was dropping in marmite and pickle jars.

Onstage Victoria mocked a neighbour for having a nanny and instructing her to give the children raw carrot puree and creative play. In actual fact Victoria's life mirrored those she mocked. She had a nanny for her own children, Grace attended contemporary dance classes and Victoria gave permission for Henry to be photographed for a charity calendar, and he appeared in *Tatler* before he was even one. As she said in an interview with the *Daily Mail*, 'I don't do anything in the stage show that's akin to my life. You don't know much more about me at the end of it.'

Part of the routine involved Victoria listing the differences between real mothers and celebrity mothers – not surprisingly Victoria identified herself with the former (she says she was not surprised at being snubbed in a *Hello!* mother-and-child photo spread as she is not glamorous and Henry looks like something out of *The Beano*).

Besides encouraging the audience to identify with her, the

comparison between celebrity and real mothers also showed Victoria's preoccupation with 'real life'. Celebrity mothers get their figures back in two weeks while real mums carry their stomachs up to bed over one arm; celebrity mothers take their children for long walks on Caribbean beaches, real mothers stand on a tarmac car park with shopping shouting 'Well don't step in it again!'

It was not the only example of Victoria's double standards. 'I am 40 now,' she said at one point in the act. '25 years is long enough to go round sucking your cheeks in every time you go past a shop window . . . you see I just don't think it matters anymore.' Whether she would have been as upfront about her figure if she still weighed 13 stones and did not look so sleek is doubtful. Disturbingly, in light of her own experiences, Victoria used the plight of fat and friendless teenaged girls to get laughs. On wedding photographs, she said, there are always three 'normal' bridesmaids and a 'great whopping one' at the end in a kaftan. The use of the word 'normal' was telling as it indicated Victoria now regarded overweight girls as abnormal and objects for derision.

The onstage mateyness with her audience was all part of Victoria's act and those that assumed she was every bit as approachable offstage often got a surprise. 'On the stage I'm happy to be their best friend,' she said, but admitted: 'Once I've done the show I've got nothing else to give.' While not exactly on a par with royal frigidity, Victoria's stagedoor meetings with fans are characterised by a polite coolness and awkwardness. Those women she meets who have similar hairstyles to her own make her feel 'uncomfortable' and she deems their enthusiasm 'inappropriate'. She is far happier controlling them from the distance of the stage and is happy to trade on their misconceptions in order to do so: 'They're not scared to come and see me so it means once they're in the theatre I can go as far as I feel is right. Once they're in and the doors are locked.'

Explaining her act, Victoria said: 'There's hardly any situation in life that doesn't have humour. Everything I do is based on truth, and truth is usually serious, but my job is to turn it on its head. I like annoying people. I don't mind saying things you're not supposed to.' This was exemplified in her 1993 stage show when she incorporated another joke about the IRA. This time the gag concerned the bomb in the City which had killed a man. Victoria joked that it was not a bomb that had caused the explosion but the collective rage of twenty women with PMT when they discovered the chocolate machine was broken.

'People say that I'm cosy and domestic but I'm not really, I'm quite subversive really. But I keep smiling,' Victoria once said. 'I'm very anti-authority. My material is as spiky as someone like Alexei Sayle but I just do it in a jollier way.' This was evident in her treatment of royalty. Rather than a caustic attack on privilege Victoria made her point by cleverly deconstructing the royals' claim that they were just doing a job, and imagined the unlikelihood of ladies-in-waiting telling 'Liz' her horoscope over a fag. Similarly, the idea that the Windsors were just the same as 'us' was ridiculed by the image of a Lancastrian Queen Mother preparing to put Charles up by taking her knitting machine out of the back bedroom and putting a Farrah Fawcett Majors poster over the damp patch.

In her 1990 act Victoria did a routine about discovering she was pregnant and so a routine about the birth was a natural progression for the 1993 show. She started with the ante-natal class, which perfectly suited her central theme of reality being different to what we are told to expect. The audience was not spared the graphic detail of the agony of childbirth: the haemorrhoids that weigh more than the baby, vaginal stitches, pelvic floor exercises and the way in which babies completely change the life of a mother.

Elsewhere in the show there was the familiar multi-charactered routine which this time saw Victoria juggling characters and events at a wedding. There was also the usual attack on political correctness, with the anti-sexist and anti-circus lobby being the target when Victoria describes a visit to 'Wilhelmina Smart's Equal Opportunities Politically Correct Big Top', the highlight of which was two women in pinafore dresses; one said she was going to jump through a hoop, the other said she didn't have to if she didn't feel up to it.

Once again Victoria entered the political arena from a suburban perspective. Norma Major was described as 'the sort of woman who has a separate J-cloth for each bath tap' and Victoria remarked of male MPs: 'Never mind the balance of trade figures, a bit of Head & Shoulders wouldn't come amiss.'

Monologue-wise there were two new characters. Madeline was a Northern hairdresser and Madge was an aerobics instructor giving a low impact class for Fatties with Attitude ('Fattitude'). Visually arresting in clinging pink shorts and a vibrant floral leotard with excessive padding, Victoria used the physical humour of the aerobic routine for maximum effect. It was the character's lack of self-awareness that was most amusing ('I was quite hippy at one point'; 'There is a point with skinny when it can tip over onto scrawny. And I should know because I am dangerously near it myself.') Brilliantly observed, Victoria captured the cod scientific qualifications of such instructors – the 'glutonius maxitive', we are told, is the largest muscle and is connected directly to the brain; the hormone produced by an aerobic workout is 'phenophonabibametamorphonal'.

Victoria has never felt any allegiance with her fellow comedians and to her, the fact that the profession had become so high profile and attractive meant unwelcome competition. More and more comics had become stars, selling out stadiums and referring to comedy as the new rock 'n' roll. Victoria detested such aggrandisement and used the song 'Feeling In The Mood Tonight' to register her distaste. Musically very similar to 'Don't Get Cocky Baby' in *Nearly A Happy Ending*, it was a blisteringly savage, ego-puncturing attack. Comedy, Victoria sang with mock gravity, was rough and raw, it exposed pain. Witheringly, the boasts were juxtaposed with blunt reality.

> *Comedians are tough and hard*
> *We've all been hurt, we've all been scarred*
> *We all do ads for Barclaycard*

she deadpanned and continued to put things into perspective with the lines:

> *We're so brave at what we do*
> *Bomb disposal's tricky too.*

'Go With It' followed in the tradition of 'Bored With This', 'Don't Do It', 'Live For Now' and 'Bastards'. It was another song about self-determination, dream-chasing, ambition, effort and the importance of not settling for less. Underlying it was a seam of melancholy, a poignant reminder of Victoria's early days when it seemed she might not realise her own dreams.

'Isn't it a pity life was planned by a committee while the clever ones had popped out to the lav,' sang Victoria in the final song of the show. The lyric shared a sense of disappointment with 'Liz's Song' in *Good Fun* ('a body like a drawing by a student in a life class/Who was sitting at the back without his specs'). It was a comical song about the madness of existence ('We're only here cos an egg meets a sperm and then grows blobs on'). Birth, breathing, eating and dying were all 'barmy' to Victoria, who quoted Sartre along the way. Faced with such weighty issues her 'reasoned, sane, thought-out response is Bum! Bum! Bum!'

Stanley Wood had always made a point of seeing each of his daughter's new shows and had intended to witness her proudest moment when she played the Royal Albert Hall. But by the time the show arrived in the capital his mental condition had deteriorated to such an extent that it was impossible for him to make the trip. Victoria sold out the prestigious venue for fifteen nights during September and October, breaking Eric Clapton's previous record-breaking run as a solo performer.

The praise that had been heaped on Victoria in recent years had started to make even her realise she was good at her job. She was respected in her profession, admired by the critics and loved by the public, so when LWT withdrew their offer to make her film it was a humiliating – and very public – blow to her pride and ambition. They felt it was not commercial enough and Victoria was furious. Piqued, she went public with her anger and complained: 'The people at LWT were so rude. They told my agent they didn't want my film, but didn't have the decency to send me a letter. I won't be doing any more *Audiences With Victoria Wood* or anything else for them, unless I'm desperate.'

So personal was the project to her that rather than simply abandoning it, as she had with previous screenplays, Victoria bought it back and took it to the BBC. It was purchased by Margaret Matheson, the executive producer for Screen One. The last time she had been at the BBC was in 1978 when, as producer of the *Play for Today* series, she had been responsible for *Scum*, Roy Minton's controversial play. Matheson was also the co-founder of Zenith Productions which had been behind such films as *Wish You Were Here*, *Personal Services* and *Prick Up Your Ears*.

The BBC could only afford to make a £1 million production and Victoria took a pay cut and resigned herself to a more modest film. But although the corporation had helped her save face, Victoria was not afraid of criticising it. 'The BBC doesn't know anything about programmes any more,' she said. 'They treat it like a branch of Woolworth's. You can't do that with comedy and drama.' Ironically for someone whose act is so dependent on brand names, one of the main reasons why Victoria remained loyal to the BBC was the absence of commercial breaks.

Trauma of a different kind occurred on 13 November 1993 when Victoria's father died. Stanley passed away in Bury General Hospital of bronchopneumonia and coronary heart disease. Victoria was not there and her tour continued. It was left to the 74-year-old Helen, who had had to cope with her husband during his illness, to register the death three days later. 'I think the heart attack was lucky, because at some point he would have had to go in a home,' said Victoria.

The death of her father was the first time she had encountered mortality on such a close personal level and it may have caused Victoria to consider the effect of the death of their father on her own children. Victoria had often proclaimed that weight was irrelevant, but at more than 20 stones Geoffrey's health was in danger. Unlike the children, he had resisted Victoria's vegetarian diet, but he did pay attention when his worried wife urged him to attend the Weigh Ahead course run by Glasgow doctor Cherie Martin, who believed that dieting made people fat, not thin. It was certainly the case for Geoffrey who had attempted diets since the age of seven. Each time he tried a new diet he lost weight for a while, then piled it back on.

Victoria and Geoffrey had an agreement whereby they would work alternate years, allowing them to advance their individual careers and enjoy a satisfying domestic life with the children. Although 1994 had been designated as Geoffrey's year, the filming of *Pat and Margaret* meant Victoria once again took precedence. 'You cannot be sure when you will fall out of favour', was how she justified it.

Filming commenced in May and took up most of the summer. The casting, as always, included Victoria's repertory company of Julie, Celia, Duncan and Anne Reid. There were also parts for the loyal Deborah Grant, Frances Cox, Sue Wallace and Roger Brierley. It was Victoria's first serious acting role for fourteen years and she obviously relished it because she publicly expressed a desire to play more straight roles, something that she deemed herself to be incapable of in the past.

The film starts with motorway services cafeteria worker Margaret Mottershead and her colleagues embarking on a coach trip to Peacock Studios in London for the filming of *Magic Moments*, a *Surprise Surprise*-style show. The show's special guest is Pat Bedford (Julie Walters), a Joan Collins-type actress who is queen of the American soap, *Glamor*.

The surprise is that Pat and Margaret are sisters who have been separated for 27 years. They are reunited on air, much to the interest of journalist Stella Kincaid (Deborah Grant) who is writing a book about Pat. Vera, a pensioner in a Northern old folks' home is also watching and she tells a member of staff that she is Pat's mother.

Pat quickly makes it clear to Margaret that she wants nothing to do with her and tells her to leave. Wandering the studio corridors, Margaret meets Pat's personal assistant, Claire (Celia Imrie), who, not knowing Pat's mood, jollily bundles Margaret along to the hospitality suite. Because Margaret misses her coach home she is put up at the swanky Regent Hotel with Pat. She attempts to make conversation and reveals that she too is not exactly overjoyed by the reunion. Pat can barely bring herself to speak to her sister. The following morning Margaret phones her boyfriend, Jim (Duncan Preston), to explain what had happened but his dominating mother takes the call and does not pass on the message.

Margaret makes another attempt to bond with Pat but is appalled when Pat offers her a cheque to sign a document denying kinship. Margaret is about to leave when the crew arrives to make the *Magic Moments* follow-up film and cover the press conference.

Stella meanwhile, has a phone call which informs her that their mother is in an old folks' home and she heads up North to investigate.

Margaret's boss, Bella (Lynda Rooke), tells Stella she is unhappy with Margaret for leaving her in the lurch and Jim's mother is also interviewed and uses the opportunity to try and put Jim off Margaret. Stella also meets up with a news stringer who tells her the story of a local couple who built a Spanish apartment complex over a chemical dump which resulted in local people losing their life savings.

Back in London Pat realises the positive public relations opportunities the reunion offers. When the newspapers come out Margaret and Bella are disgusted at the way their words have been twisted. Jim is also upset about what Margaret has purportedly said and decides to drive down to London to see his girlfriend. Margaret's reaction is similar and she decides to drive up North to explain. Pat is horrified when she spots a small article about her mother, Vera. Fearing that Vera will ruin her reputation, she joins Margaret on the trip North, determined to find Vera before Stella does. They find the nursing home but the Vera there is not their mother; she is a senile fantasist.

Jim arrives in London and meets Claire who explains that he has missed Margaret, and they both travel up North together.

Stella tracks down the woman responsible for the Spanish apartments fiasco, while Pat and Margaret attempt to find accommodation for the night. They end up at Margaret's bed-sit. We learn that Pat was thrown out of the house when she became pregnant at fifteen and Vera lied to Margaret that she had run away. Pat did return but there was no one at the house. Vera's prostitution had got her into serious trouble with the law and Margaret was fostered out.

Jim arrives at the wrong moment and tired, confused and emotionally mixed-up, Margaret snaps at him and ends the relationship.

Pat and Margaret go for a meal at the cafe of their youth where they meet up with Claire who passes on a note from 'a fan' (Stella). The note directs them to the home of the property developer, who is in actual fact their mother. Vera (Shirley Stelfox) is unrepentant about her treatment of them and during a verbal confrontation she makes it clear that she never loved them. Stella arrives on cue with her photographer and Pat anticipates it will be her downfall – until it dawns on her and Stella that far from destroying her career, it has all the makings of a bestseller and mini-series, providing Vera can be tied down to an exclusive contract. Margaret makes it up with Bella and Jim, who finally stands up to his mother.

At the airport Pat is preparing to fly back to LA. Margaret cannot be persuaded to join her even though Pat says she needs her. In the VIP lounge Pat is sitting with Vera and it emerges that she will be staying with Pat in Hollywood. Reading a magazine article Pat casually remarks that mothers of celebrities are currently very popular. She winces when she realises the implications.

The film ends with Margaret and Jim tidying up Margaret's childhood cafe, which Pat has bought them.

'Margaret's all the people who don't have a voice, who don't have money, who don't have any way of getting themselves up the ladder,' explained Victoria. 'My sympathies lie naturally with people like Margaret, people without money or wonderful gifts, the general mass of people who spend their lives swimming desperately just to keep afloat. And I suppose that, if I'm honest, there is a part of me that feels, or rather felt, very vulnerable and patronised and this is my way of showing that side of myself.'

Always keen to engender public affection and maintain her image as Everywoman, it was inevitable that she would play the part herself. Victoria had always been interested in exploring the lives of those who, through circumstance, were unable to move very far from the world into which they were born. This was particularly evident in Bren, the character she would later play in the situation comedy *dinnerladies*, and in the many songs where she inhabited the lives of the less fortunate. She was evasive when I asked her whether she felt relief or regret at never having experienced such lives first hand. Indeed, through her work, and despite the image she projects, there is a sense that she has somehow missed out on 'real life'. It is the ultimate irony that the woman who is deemed a representative of the masses has only once had a 'normal' job, and that was a brief spell as a barmaid at university.

Victoria has been famous for almost as many years as she was anonymous and she was honest enough to admit that she shared some of Pat's personality. In essence the film illustrated the two sides of herself. 'It was both me. It was that battle between the one who can never get on, a sort of impotent person, and the one who's so determined to get on there's no room for anything else.'

Refusing to stay in a certain hotel because it 'looked like a brothel', attempting to suppress the publication of unflattering school photographs, reacting haughtily and humourlessly to a doorstep prank by *Punch*, ignoring her personal driver ('She doesn't expect to be spoken to') is typical Pat behaviour. Perhaps because Victoria was occasionally guilty of such behaviour herself, she could easily make these traits part of Pat.

Like Pat, Victoria used the unhappy past as a receptacle for the negativity in her life. Pat buried it, whereas Victoria took an almost perverse delight in referring to her young self as a dirty, smelly liar and thief. The steely twosome were both determined never to experience such a life again and used their personal histories to remind themselves how successful and removed from such misery their present was.

Identity and maternalism are the two central themes of the film. Pat cannot function without the trappings of fame. She sees herself not as a person, but as an icon and a business ('Pat Bedford Inc'). She can exist only through the media and her identity is dependent on the press ('I, sexy yet vulnerable, and I'm quoting from *Harper's* here'), a worshipping public and superficial externalities ('I'm Knightsbridge, I'm grooming, I'm camisoles'). In Pat's language it is possible to see how the image has run away with the reality. She tries to use a sophisticated vocabulary to match her image, but it does not come naturally and she ends up speaking unintelligible nonsense ('there's been somewhat of a virago', 'thanks to your umbilical incompetence', 'the sooner you get a grip on that factum, the more likely you'll do so').

Because Pat lives in a world of exteriors, physicality is of utmost importance to her. Her spirits are raised by a flattering photograph of her legs and depressed by worries about a sagging chin. Her horror at being linked to a Northern waitress is matched by worries about how Margaret's appearance ('a woman whose buttocks practically skim the carpet') may reflect on her. The importance of the physical to Pat is further demonstrated in her journey to her original self. So strongly has she blocked her past that she actually has to *see* the unmarried mothers' home and her childhood home in order to further the 'healing' process.

Physicality of place is also important. A motorway services kitchen is contrasted with the International Arrivals Hall of Heathrow; a small bed-sit with the presidential suite of the Regent Hotel; the North with the South. And as well as the internal journeys which the characters have to make, the film abounds with frantic cross-country dashes. The soulless television studio, devoid of an audience, appropriates Pat's cold-heartedness when she first tells Margaret to get out of her life. And the scene where Margaret is trapped in the studio building, frantically banging on the window to her unseeing friends, is a symbol of how Margaret, like Pat, is trapped in an unnatural situation that removes her from her world.

To maintain her image Pat has to be in total control, irrespective of the truth. She pretends that Margaret is not her sister, that her mother is dead and that she never had a child. Canute-like, she tries to have a live television programme edited. At one point Margaret tells her: 'It's a pity I live in real life and not your imagination.' Real Life is a recurrent concept in Victoria's work.

In Hollywood Pat had disguised her background in order to assimilate, and when she travels back to her origins she has to disguise herself in order to fit in. The denial of her self leaves her with no secure identity and no 'home' and to regain this she has to be stripped of the falseness. This is achieved by the various humiliations she is subjected to which bring her closer and closer to her real self. It starts in London with the embarrassing public revelation that Margaret is her sister. Pat, who is first seen being fêted at Heathrow Airport, soon finds herself waiting by the Ladies' at a motorway service station, drenched with a hose, forced to wear a shell suit and denied access to a Northern hotel. She has to physically return to her humiliating family home and the degradation of the unmarried mothers' home to fully complete her 'cure'.

The theme of identity is also reflected in the part food plays in the film. Pat the Star's diet includes organic grape juice, herb tea, champagne, skinless chicken and mango. Margaret, who is 'in chips' doesn't like croissants. Victoria, who used to gorge on junk food and praised the merits of chip butties, now names wholemeal bread with avocado, tomato, cucumber and Alfalfa sprouts as her favourite sandwich. She eats organic food, sips peppermint tea and raves about the potassium-giving benefits of banana.

Food also represents identity in the bed-sit scene where Pat offers to rustle up her favourite meal. All she needs is pasta, virgin olive oil, beef tomatoes, herbs and an avocado. Margaret has a tin of spaghetti, a jar of pickle and some powdered milk. Food is also used to show the shades of grey in the characters. Revisiting the Swiss Cottage Cafe where she worked as a teenage waitress, Pat devours her pre-famous favourite meal of egg, chips, peas and double fried bread with relish. And in the Regent Hotel Margaret discovers a liking for champagne. On an additional note Stella refers to Pat and Margaret's home town as being in 'black pudding country'. Victoria's own home town, Bury, is famous for its black pudding, a dish that would be every bit as unpalatable to the vegetarian Victoria as a return to her roots is for Pat.

The other big theme of the film is maternalism. Negligent and damaging mothers occur frequently in Victoria's work and, in this work particularly, Victoria was afforded the opportunity to examine the relationship she had with her mother.

One example of a bad mother in the film is Jim's. In this lying smothering creature (a more caustic version of Maureen's unseen parents in *Talent*), Victoria showed how dominant mothers are every bit as damaging as negligent mothers. They are utterly selfish and controlling and disguise manipulation as love. The dyslexic Jim cannot read the situation until Claire points out that his mother was thinking of herself, not him.

A fuller examination of a bad mother and the consequences comes in Vera. It is sometimes overlooked that Pat and Margaret are only half-sisters. The half they have in common is Vera, their respective fathers disappeared early in their lives. This set-up allowed Victoria to dissect the mother–child relationship by making the mother the sole influence on the girls' lives.

While Victoria's own mother was no sluttish Vera, Helen Wood was just as 'absent' in Victoria's childhood, locking herself away with her wool and work. Pat blasts Vera for what she did to Margaret, the little girl she left at eleven because she could not be bothered giving her the love and care of a mother. It was when Victoria reached eleven that Helen could concentrate fully on her academic career. Margaret also mirrors Victoria in the way she yearns to have a baby with Jim, perhaps to cancel out her own miserable early years and replace them with the 'right' sort of mother–child relationship.

There is anger at their mother's treatment of them, but also an unspoken trauma in both Pat and Margaret concerning lost motherhood. Vera had children she did not want, Pat and Margaret wanted children they could not have; Pat lost her son through adoption and Margaret lost her child through miscarriage. The presence of the heavily pregnant Claire, proudly showing scans of her baby and delighting in each little kick serves as a constant reminder of their loss, but this was more accident than intention as Victoria was forced to incorporate Celia Imrie's real-life pregnancy into the script at the last minute.

In the film it is the star journalist Stella Kincaid who powers the plot by stirring up the sediment in the characters' lives. She threatens to expose Pat and thus forces her into a race back to her Northern roots. In doing so a chain reaction is activated which makes Margaret, Pat and Jim re-examine their lives.

Stella has echoes of Pat, her own publicity is pinned to her office wall and there is a hint that the glamorous star journalist has equally humble roots, thanks to a passing mention of her time on the *Leicester Mercury*. Victoria's cautious relationship with the press is mirrored in Pat's paranoia. The prospect of a journalist interviewing her mother would have delighted Victoria about as much as it did Pat.

The idea of the fractured family (like the Woods) plays a significant part in the film. Initially, there appears to be a vast gulf between Pat, Margaret and Vera, who do not even have a surname in common (Pat's reeked of the Home Counties, Vera's belonged to a different nation and Margaret's clanged with Northernness). Yet the underlying similarities between the three give an added dimension to the characters.

As blood relatives Pat and Margaret are bound to share characteristics. Outwardly they seem to enjoy their lives, but they have had to convince themselves of this and it is a very brittle existence. Both know they are utterly dispensable; falling ratings of *Glamor* mean Pat's contract might not be renewed, and Margaret's contract at the motorway services means she can be disposed of without any notice. The sisters are united in their unhappiness.

The half the half-sisters have in common is Vera, and if Pat has inherited her mother's determination, ruthlessness and resilience, it follows that Margaret too must have absorbed some of her mother's qualities. The common link is denial; Vera and Pat deny their past and Margaret denies her present. As she admits to Pat at one point: 'I know I spent all yesterday saying I wasn't jealous and I was just glad to see you and I was happy living the way I do – well I'm not. I don't want to be like this.'

A symbolic device that also unites the mother and daughters is the Spanish apartment complex. It was built over a chemical dump in much the same way that the characters have built their lives on insecure and polluted foundations. Like a time-bomb, the dump has consequences for the future just as the buried feelings of Vera, Pat and Margaret have.

The three all share a strong desire for a glamorous lifestyle. It is Vera who ends up looking forward to a life in Hollywood with Pat and sharing equal billing with the likes of Jackie Stallone as a celebrity mother, but Margaret too has yearned for the same thing ('I want what you've got!'). Although Margaret ultimately decides to 'give it a go' and remain in England with Jim, she is not averse to benefiting from Hollywood. It is Hollywood money that buys her the cafe; she fully intends to make visits to LA and she stands to become something of a celebrity through her link with Pat. A mini-series of her family life is on the cards and she is already imagining Meryl Streep portraying her.

The idea of the separated siblings leading vastly different lives and then being reunited was not unique dramatically. And the convenience of a well-timed pools win and a property development scandal to further the plot did border on cliché. But Victoria's genius shone through in her treatment of her characters and her decision to make Pat, Margaret and Vera neither exclusively good or bad, wrong or right.

Pat operates in a profession full of hypocrisy and viciousness. At first she is presented as a Queen Bitch, but through Victoria's depiction of the celebrity landscape, the audience can, however reluctantly, sympathise with her. Pat is despicable but if she is to survive in such a backbiting profession can she really be blamed for adopting its customs? Even Victim Margaret is able to defend her sister.

Despite being an obviously sympathetic character, Margaret is not some blameless saint. She has settled for less and existed in a state of frustration, bemoaning her lowly lot in life but not acknowledging that she is partly responsible for it. She indulges herself with her unhappy childhood and harbours a 27-year-old grudge against Pat ('You should have helped me'). But Pat, who had it far harder than Margaret, was brave and pro-active enough to take a risk and head for London, rather than settling for a familiar rut. She is justified in telling the envious Margaret 'Then work for it! You've no idea what I had to do to get where I am now – do something!' One could easily imagine today's Victoria telling her 22-year-old self this same thing.

Victoria even managed to elicit some sympathy for Vera who, it must be said, had not had an easy life. She had been a prostitute with 'two kids in a rotten council house, nosy neighbours, useless bloody husband smoking himself to death'. And it cannot be ignored that Vera, who was fully aware of Pat's celebrity, never once tried to exploit her for financial gain until Stella appears on the scene.

In the climactic showdown Vera fully acknowledges that she is hard, cold, unkind and emotionally closed. But she has a very strong point when she says to Pat: 'Would you have got out if I hadn't shoved you out? . . . You should be thanking me for making you hard inside, because that's what pushed you on.' This overlapped into Victoria's personal life and begged the question, if Helen Wood had not been so remote and disinterested as a mother would Victoria have felt such a compulsion to make her mark?

'What we really need is a happy ending,' says Stella, but it was to Victoria's credit that she avoided a neat conclusion. Unresolved issues were left hanging in the air. Vera has still not shown any remorse, Pat (albeit involuntarily) is prepared to collaborate with the dreaded Stella and prostitute her family for a book, and Margaret chooses to remain in the locale of her unhappiness, even though she admits: 'there's nowt doing here'. The airport farewell between the two sisters, with its painfully awkward 'hug', suggests that all has not been solved.

By the time Victoria wrote *Pat and Margaret* she was extremely wealthy but she could also draw on her penny-pinching days in the Morecambe flat. Her own changed financial circumstances enabled her to empathise with both of the film's leading characters. She knew that money matters, and its jingle could be heard throughout the film. The many outstanding debts of responsibility between the characters, apologies owed, paybacks, prices to be paid and costs to be counted were all explored. The transactions also extended to the value the characters place on themselves.

The script crackled with pithy lines. 'You couldn't get abortions round here then. We didn't get muesli till last year,' says a Northern housewife. 'I don't think I knew what love was till I bred my first Afghan,' remarks Vera. It was a measure of Victoria's generosity that she gave many of the film's most memorable lines to Thora Hird. It had been an ambition of Victoria to work with the actress who, like Patricia Routledge and Julie Walters, she shares custody of with Alan Bennett. Victoria had first attempted to work with Thora back in 1985 for *As Seen On TV* but the actress was not free until 1989. When Victoria tried to get her for her playlets in 1989 she missed the opportunity by a matter of days. As Jim's mother 'She's playing you for a giddy kipper' was one of Thora's most widely quoted lines, but her most celebrated remark came in the indignant reaction to the news that Jim and Margaret had sex on her bed: 'Not on the eiderdown.'

Recognisable Woodisms in the script included a raffia reference and the quirky career boast formula (a woman is described as being 'very high up in gum hygiene').

Pat and Margaret was broadcast on 11 September and was as popular with the critics as it was with the public. 'A masterful piece of work' said Thomas Sutcliffe in the *Independent*, while in the *Observer* John Naughton described it as 'a morality tale with great style and much class'. Writing in the *Daily Telegraph*, Max Davidson praised Victoria's 'splendid performance' and the *Independent on Sunday's* Allison Pearson described her as 'one of our finest writers, with a brain like a razor and an ear finely tuned to every emotional wavelength'. The dichotomy of the public figure and the private figure and the nature of fame had resonances which not even Victoria could predict, and the BBC repeated it on 6 September 1997 as part of its rescheduled programming to mark the funeral of Diana, Princess of Wales.

It said something about Victoria's pulling power that 9 million viewers watched the film, compared with the 2.4 million Screen One audience the previous week. The film showed a new maturity and sophistication in Victoria and for the first time in thirteen years she was able to show she was capable of writing a sustained piece of drama. It also demonstrated that Victoria, who used to mock her own acting abilities, was an accomplished actress, particularly when it came to scenes of pathos. Her performance earned her a BAFTA Best Actress nomination and the film itself received a BAFTA Best Single Drama nomination, an award it won at the British Press Guild Awards. But most satisfying of all for Victoria was the way in which she had proved LWT wrong so spectacularly.

No sooner had the film been broadcast than the script was published, by Methuen. As always, there was no dedication to either her parents or siblings; instead Victoria thanked the cast and crew. Further income was generated by her voicing a talking book of *The Princess and the Frog* and recording a shortened version of her 1993 stage show for the BBC. As with her *All Day Breakfast*, the Geoff Posner-produced and directed *Victoria Wood – Live In Your Own Home* was given a prime-time slot on BBC1 on Christmas Day, attracting 13.38 million viewers and making it the sixth most popular programme in the country.

Despite such viewing figures, it prompted a backlash by some critics, who had grown tired of Victoria's habit of recycling material. 'I'm as big a sucker for nostalgia as anybody, but this was déjà vu,' remarked A.A. Gill in the *Sunday Times*, before adding: 'Victoria Wood has become a cross between Pam Ayres and Joyce Grenfell . . . . The crooning and the mugging and the nudge-nudging were very predictable. It ceased to be anything more than tired grinworthy stuff about a decade ago.' The *Daily Express*'s Compton Miller complained that he felt like he had blundered into a Christmas party while sober.

Victoria's performance was, however, nominated for a BAFTA,

but when she lost out to Rory Bremner cameras at the televised ceremony captured her indignation, giving the public a rare glimpse of the spontaneous Victoria. Undoubtedly disappointed, she could at least console herself with the money generated by video sales of the show.

CHAPTER 13

THERAPY had finally freed Victoria from the compulsion to inflict a punishing schedule upon herself and, reflecting on her 1994 workload, she decided to prioritise. 'I thought, hang on, you don't actually have to work this hard . . . I was running too fast,' she said. Having lived through a miserable childhood herself, Victoria was determined that her own children would not suffer: 'Awards and fame are so fleeting. They don't bear comparison with having a relationship with two little children.'

Defying public expectation by undergoing therapy seemed to free Victoria to explore other areas that did not necessarily match her public image. One of these was Quakerism. She and Geoffrey started going to meetings to improve their lives together. Analysis had certainly helped the relationship ('We used to fight and try to change each other but since we've both had therapy, life has become more peaceful') but they needed spiritual assurance. They had always believed in God and had experimented with churchgoing in the past but it 'just didn't do it' for Victoria. Clearly there was another hole in her life which needed filling.

The movement, which today has 18,000 followers in Britain and Ireland, began in the seventeenth century when people came together to revive what they saw as 'primitive Christianity'. It was particularly strong in the Midlands, Yorkshire and the North West. Quakers believe that everyone may have direct experience of God and they search for His love and power in the everyday world. The simplicity of Quakerism undoubtedly appealed to Victoria. Free of dogma, there is no church calendar to obey. The emphasis is on daily life and experience rather than festivals and creeds. Meeting houses have no ornaments or religious symbols and meetings are held on Sundays only because it is the most convenient day. Quakerism is also a very democratic religion with no appointed minister or pastor; anyone may speak when they feel inspired to and the responsibility for the meeting belongs to all. The act of worship involves a group silence where those present meditate on God.

'As I've got older, I am more interested in having a belief,' said Victoria. 'I think that when you are in your twenties and thirties you have so many other things going on in your head that there's not much space for anything spiritual. But it does help to have a belief. If you don't, it makes everything else seem pointless. To only think "you're alive, you have acne and then you die" makes you wonder what it's all for.'

While this more relaxed attitude allowed Victoria to reduce the pressure on herself, her idea of taking things easy was completely at odds with most other people's. A new edition of *Good Fun* and *Talent* helped keep her profile up and she performed a number of typical celebrity activities. These included supporting a campaign to give public libraries access to National Lottery money, unveiling a blue plaque at Eric Morecambe's former home in North Finchley, and being the first recipient of the Eric Morecambe Award, the first major award from Comic Heritage, the society dedicated to honouring Britain's great comedians. Victoria had briefly met the comedian in a Manchester lift. 'You're that girl,' Morecambe had said. 'Yes, I am,' replied Victoria, who was chuffed to be recognised by him.

Geoffrey was no doubt grateful for Victoria's new laid back attitude as it enabled him to do a show of his own. Admittedly a short run of *Shattering Illusions* ('one man's intrepid journey up his own sleeve') at the King's Head could not compare with Victoria's nationwide tours, but combined with a growing number of appearances on television quiz and game shows, it allowed him to establish himself as someone other than The Great Soprendo. However, it was not too long before renewed demands on Victoria started to interfere.

Victoria had travelled to Ethiopia in 1990 to make a documentary showing how Comic Relief money had been spent, and in 1995 the charity persuaded her to return to Africa. The trip had been arranged for Lenny Henry but he had to pull out and Victoria was his reluctant replacement. 'I didn't want to go at all,' she said. 'I only volunteered as a joke. I said, "if you want me to be patronising in Africa, I'm quite happy to do that".' She spent her week living with the Masara family in the tiny farming community of Chivi, Zimbabwe, milking cows, weeding vegetable plots, making clay drainpipes and digging troughs.

As someone whose offstage interaction with the public is characterised by a cold awkwardness and barely concealed impatience, it came as no surprise that Victoria declined the villagers' greeting offer of a dance. Living with 'strange people', she said, was not really her thing.

Refreshingly unsentimental, she was at pains to avoid condescension and refused to apologise for her own life of privilege. 'I was anxious it wouldn't come over the wrong way. I didn't want to say "these people have a worse life than we do". They don't have a horrible, violent, crime-ridden society like us. They just don't have any water – that's why there is so little food . . . I didn't feel bad. I think that would be patronising to pity them. They are not wounded pigeons, they are just people. I don't feel guilty for being born into this country and having enough money.'

The sketch which Victoria had been invited to write for Comic Relief 1995 saw her in more comfortable territory. It also demonstrated her more relaxed relationship with her rival Dawn French, for whom she wrote a Vanessa Feltz people-show parody. Victoria was happy to be a supporting character, alongside the likes of Lynda Bellingham and Jim Broadbent, while Dawn played the 'star'. The sketch was, as Victoria would say, completely barmy. Victoria's Birmingham housewife, Carrie, was married to a man who loved ping-pong more than her; Lill Roughley played a woman whose marriage lasted all of three minutes until her husband burped; Anne Reid's character lived next door to a man who thought his penis told him to order large portions of coleslaw from Kentucky Fried Chicken; Duncan Preston's character had undergone seventeen operations to make him look like his hero, Duncan Preston. But amidst this barminess Victoria's acute observation of daytime television was once again clearly evident. There was the affected indignance of presenter Dawn, the stiltedness of the contributors and the empty and meaningless 'audience' statements piped up at inopportune moments ('If love's on the table, who needs gravy?').

Victoria's African experiences for Comic Relief may have been largely responsible for her choice of journey when she was asked to film a Great Railway Journeys documentary for the BBC in the summer of 1995. While other presenters in the series travelled across places like

Canada and South America, Victoria turned down journeys in Paraguay and Vietnam in favour of a trip from Crewe to Crewe via the west and east coasts. It was an extremely intelligent decision in that it allowed her to examine the familiar – the everyday that was overlooked. It was a similar approach to her state-of-the-nation themed stage acts and it also had the advantage of setting her apart from the other presenters and maintaining her down-to-earth credentials with the public.

A reluctance to spend too long away from Grace and Henry also influenced her choice of journey. She filmed it in two-day bursts over six weeks, rather than in one block, so that she could spend as much time as possible at home.

The nature of the documentary called for a certain amount of spontaneity, which has never been one of Victoria's strong points. She radiated awkwardness when a drunken Scotsman gave her money for Comic Relief, and her encounters and interviews with a trainspotter, an extra from *Brief Encounter*, a Barbara Cartland-worshipping cafe owner and a woman with bits of the Forth Bridge falling into her back garden were rather stilted, uncomfortable, forced and patronising. It was only while recording the well-thought-out commentary back in the studio that Victoria added her faintly sarcastic comments and shafts of wit.

From the outset ('One of my biggest worries has come true. Under the new-style BBC if you're a comedian once you hit 40 you have to stop telling jokes and just be in documentaries') it was clear that this was a darker, more peevish Victoria Wood than the public was used to. In fact, throughout the documentary there was a sense of anger, despondency, gloom and pessimism. At Carnforth she sounded like a Northern matron bemoaning the state of the station, and at Barrow there was lazy outrage ('I have a huge prejudice against nuclear power – totally ill-informed, but deep rooted'). Cold sarcasm was used on several occasions, from the £125 wage of a rail worker ('I don't think you get much more than that for running the railways do you? Oh no, I'm probably thinking of £1.25 million') to Princess Diana's involvement with Relate ('Did I read Lady Di works for it now? I should think she's in there every morning, wouldn't you? Opening up and dusting the photocopier, in an overall'). In one of a number of digs against the Government she remarked: 'Now there's no jobs for young people I wonder if the government will decide it's not worth educating them and they might as well just start hanging around aged five, just to get used to it.' Even an eraser purchased from a Christian bookshop and made in Taiwan set her off ('Probably [made] by a four-year-old manacled to a workbench').

'What a filthy old world it is' exclaimed Victoria, who found York dirty, cold and so full of traffic fumes she could hardly breathe. Then, assuming the role of Everywoman, she cut through the flannel to state: 'We need to stop using our cars. We need good, fast trains that connect with other trains that are affordable, reliable, safe with proper food on them with clean toilets. There's no point calling us customers and smiling at us with walkie talkies if we can't even buy a ticket at our local station or book over the phone for a journey that involves two different railway companies . . . We've given up on travelling hopefully, but we do expect to arrive.'

'It has never been proved that being overweight is bad for your health' Victoria protested in 1991. When *Slimmer Magazine* used her as its cover star she raged: 'I think the whole slimming industry could do with a great big bomb shoved under it – I hate it.' Five years later, however, when Geoffrey had shed seven stones through a combination of healthy eating, Canadian Airforce Exercises, an exercise bike and a rowing machine, her opinion on the whole weight issue changed. 'I don't know a single fat person – well, perhaps one – who actually *enjoys* being fat,' she told the *Daily Telegraph*. The new slimline Geoffrey was pictured grinning in the tabloids, proudly disclosing that his waistline had shrunk from 46 inches to 34. 'He is a shining example' said Victoria in the *News of the World*.

Her own figure remained trim and toned thanks to the aerobics and healthy eating. It was important that she kept in shape for her tours, another of which was scheduled for 1996. Victoria spent the first few months writing the show and trying it out at venues in Watford and High Wycombe on Sunday evenings. Publicity posters for the show showed her hunching her shoulders with her jumper pulled up to her nose. It was an interesting image, suggesting a shyness that was curiously at odds with the scope of the very tour it advertised.

The 68-date tour kicked off in Leicester on 3 May and would take in Sheffield, Ipswich, Blackpool, Wolverhampton, Bradford, Newcastle, Bournemouth, Brighton, Nottingham, Oxford, Southend, Manchester, Cambridge and London. It was the first time Victoria had left the children at home, reluctantly conceding that it would not be fair to disturb their routines by dragging them all over the country. To ensure she would not be away from home for too long, she tried to work four out of every seven nights and took the whole of August off.

Photographs of Grace and Henry were the first things that came out of Victoria's bag whenever she entered a new dressing room, and home-made good luck cards adorned the walls.

July 1996 marked the 20th anniversary of Geoffrey and Victoria getting together, and to commemorate the occasion they bought each other wedding rings at last, engraved with the date of their first meeting. Victoria regards the day as of far more significance than her actual wedding day, and every year, she and Geoffrey arrange to do something special on the day. That year Geoffrey had wanted to celebrate by going windsurfing with Victoria in Majorca, but she forgot the plans and found herself working in Southend, so they booked into a hotel there instead.

For the tour Victoria performed an average of three dates at each venue, apart from Manchester where she has always received the most affectionate responses from fans who regard her as one of their own. The twelve nights she played at the city's Palace Theatre were topped only by another sell-out fifteen nights at the Royal Albert Hall. The tour was heavy going in itself, but there was the additional pressure of being accompanied by a *South Bank Show* film crew who followed the tour from Blackpool to Manchester. Her tantrum with London Weekend Television over the way it handled *Pat and Margaret*, and her vow that she would never work with the company again, was forgotten when the opportunity of being the subject of a prestigious and intelligent documentary arose.

Some of the topics the stage show targeted were rather dated. *Crossroads*, for instance, had not been on television for eight years, and savaging *Mr Men* books or discussing cellulite and trips to the supermarket was hardly cutting edge. But as Victoria said: 'I have no aspirations to push back the barriers of comedy.'

By now she had polished her technique. This involved taking a shared everyday experience, such as moving house, and using it to explore the English character with all its stubbornness, inhibition, cowardice and hypocrisy. As with her 1993 show, Victoria again explained how she was so out of place in Highgate, but again she did not risk incurring audience alienation by actually mentioning the place by name.

In her two previous tours she had covered, respectively, conception and birth, so she now naturally progressed to the pitfalls of caring for toddlers and how she had become an 'old bag mother' since having a second child. What was surprising was the way in which she incorporated her mother, siblings and miserable youth into a routine, which at one time would have been totally out of bounds. Discussing Christmas family get-togethers – a subject she had briefly touched upon in *Happy Since I Met You* and previously discussed in her 1987 stage show – Victoria asked:

'What is this invisible signal that goes out to normal intelligent people in their 20s, 30s, 40s, this signal that says "You must leave the place where you live, where you have a life, where you have fun, and where people respect you, you must leave that place, you must go back to the place where you spent some of the most miserable years of your life." ' The only thing worse, she reasoned, was spending Christmas with someone else's family. This routine once again allowed her to 'play' multiple characters and juggle their various exploits to increasingly hysterical effect.

It was apparent, though seemingly not to her laughing audience, that Victoria felt a certain distaste for the sort of lives lived and attitudes of those living in an avenue of semis, surely Victoria Wood heartland.

A balance was struck between her belief in the irrelevance of weight ('Every woman I know, of whatever size, has got a little roll of fat concealed somewhere') and her old habit of self-deprecation ('I've got a huge roll of fat round here which I don't worry about, except sometimes I think if I fell into a canal would anyone bother to throw me a life belt'). She told the *Independent's* James Rampton: 'I'm working on not being self-deprecating. But it's a British thing, I was born with it. I couldn't come on stage and tell them how marvellous I am.'

Victoria continued to build on her growing taste for mime, giving the audience a child's dazed reaction to its panicking mother; a patient of colonic irrigation; a facelifted dry cleaner; a woman trying to look alluring in lingerie; and a woman having an orgasm.

Disillusionment and dissatisfaction with sex featured once more ('It's never got any better. Sex. There's just something so stressful about it. I keep thinking in the end they will just have to faze it out altogether'). Victoria also continued to treat weighty contemporary issues with a deftly humorous touch. In the past she had looked at Aids and global warming and now she turned her attention to drugs. 'I can't see the point of Ecstasy,' she said. 'I think if I wanted to get dehydrated and jump around with a load of people I've never met before I could go to a Methodist barn dance.'

Friend of Kimberley made a welcome return, demonstrating a nice line in bathos ('I'm going to my evening class, it's a new one. Awareness of Self it's called. We use, like, Jungian techniques and confrontational therapies to bring about a profound change in our inner being. Well it was that or basic pastry'). The other two character monologues featured in the show were familiar types: Hayley Bailey the Step class instructor was a variant of 'Fattitude's' Madge, and there was yet another crass Northern woman giving yet another tour around yet another unappealing cosmetic surgery.

In her early stage shows the songs far outnumbered the stand-up (or rather sit-down) routines, but as Victoria's confidence grew the songs featured less and less. In *Lucky Bag* for example, there were eleven songs, but the number had been more than halved by her 1996 show. She opened with 'Baby Boom', an autobiographical overview of her past, present and future alongside the periods she lived through. Musically similar to 'Northerners', it featured familiar preoccupations with unsatisfactory sex, garments (tie-dyed granddad vests, elasticated slacks), brand names (Ex-lax, Doctor Scholl) and celebrity namedropping (Sue Lawley, Elton John). She also continued to portray herself as disorganised and off-kilter; a 'barmy sod' who feels like a thirteen-year-old. There was an unusual shaft of honesty, however, when she sang: 'Can't win, I never fitted in/never was a Sixties child' and asked 'Why am I so insecure?'

'Alternative Tango' was Victoria's most robust attack on political correctness. She gleefully used the word 'wanker', enjoying the effect it had on her surprised audience, and she delighted in coming up with graphic euphemisms for masturbation. By including terms like 'arsehole', 'Paki' and 'nig-nog' it was as if she was deliberately trying to shock the public out of regarding her as safe and cosy, but her indulgent fans would accept most anything from her and, anyway, the effect was diluted by mentions of IKEA, Rolo and polyester ties.

It was only fitting that a name used over and over again by Victoria should be honoured eponymously in song, 'Pam' (whose middle name is Pat – another of Victoria's most-used monikers) is an archetypal Wood character. She is anti sling backs but pro gardening trews; she calls the toilet 'the smallest room' and is totally nonplussed by whatever life throws at her. She prefers a game of rummy, an Ovaltine, a cup of cocoa, a Ruth Rendell, a bit of ironing or a slice of toast to sex. After Pam's divorce, lesbian Joan moves into her maisonette and disinterested Pam only agrees to a sapphic liaison if it finishes before an Alan Bennett television play starts. Mussolini got a mention in the course of this song, as did Babycham, Custard Cream, a golfing hat, a mauve string vest and a rainhood.

Despite denying any autobiographical elements, 'Andrea' was a song that perfectly captured the essence of the seventeen-year-old Victoria. Factually it does not correspond: Andrea in the song lives in a terraced house, works in a deadend job and goes out regularly with a big group of teenage mates. But the sense of her yearning; the urge to escape to 'a better day' was very Victoria. The driving, relentless rhythm of the song (whose message was similar to 'Go With It') echoed the pursuit of ambition. 'I'm really looking forward to when I won't be here/when I fly, fly away' sang Victoria/Andrea. 'The day I break away . . . will be the start of a better day'. Of course Victoria did not reach her better day as soon as she left Bury – or Birmingham for that matter – but like Andrea, she was kept going by a central belief that her ship would come in. The shows ended with the by now traditional 'Barry and Freda'.

The souvenir programme produced for the tour included a set of photographs of Victoria that captured her beauty. Typically, she did not take it seriously and on the back there was a mock advert for Suzy and Janey's makeover photos ('Don't just be ugly, be a liar as well'). In the 'before' photograph we see a lumpen Victoria with greasy hair, a triple chin and unflattering expression. The 'after' photograph showed a soft focus Victoria bearing an uncanny resemblance to Princess Diana. Even a back-cover joke in a theatre programme was used by Victoria to illustrate a recurrent point; the discrepancy between appearance and reality.

The critical opinion of the show was mixed. Reviewing the show in the *Observer* Sam Taylor described Victoria – the 'voice of Middle England' – as a 'clever, sweetly savage critic of British society' beneath her veneer of smugness and conventionality. But he added that the material was 'more like a career reprise than a new show'. In the *Mail on Sunday* William Cook wrote: 'The tension between her nationwide fame and her don't-mind-me stage persona stretches her provincial observations into taut stand-up routines', and said Victoria described the suburban hinterland 'with the acute ear and eye of a world champion gossip'. And the *Independent's* Mark Wareham compared Victoria's 'dazzling wordplay' to that of Alan Bennett in its pacing and dryness (not the best way of winning favour with Victoria, who resents being regarded as Bennett's 'Siamese twin').

The *Independent on Sunday's* Ben Thompson was one of the few dissenters. He wrote: 'There is an uncomfortable suspicion that Wood's much-vaunted flair for the everyday might actually be rooted in contempt rather than sympathy. And the objects of her scorn . . . are easier targets than she pretends . . . there can be an unsavoury hint of small-mindedness about her, and it would be refreshing if, just occasionally, her comic standpoint could be other than one of aggressive common sense.'

Victoria would have loomed large in the public consciousness even without the show, which won her the Top Female Comedy Performer title at the 1996 British Comedy Awards. In September her *Great Railway Journey* was broadcast ('One of the best on record. Every minute was full of real wit and original observation,' wrote the *Daily Telegraph's* Stephen Pile), and later that month she was the subject of a revealing one hour *South Bank Show* documentary. The following month she appeared on cinema screens for the first time in Terry Jones's version of *The Wind In The Willows*, which, despite being crammed with such British comic talent as Steve Coogan, Michael Palin, Stephen Fry and John Cleese, was not a success. Unimaginative and low budget it still managed to limp into ninth position in the cinema charts, but that was mainly due to its opening coinciding with school half term. In light of its dismal performance it was fortunate for Victoria that she should have had such a tiny cameo in the venture. She played The Tea Lady as a comic Northerner.

She went from working with the Pythons to competing against them in November when the BBC celebrated its 60th birthday with a televised awards ceremony, *Auntie's All Time Greats*. *As Seen On TV* beat *Monty Python's Flying Circus* as the favourite comedy series, and Victoria herself defeated John Cleese as the favourite comedy performer. A highlight of the occasion was a special one-off episode of *Acorn Antiques* in which Mrs Overall came out as a lesbian and the show, now sponsored by a stairlift company, was clumsily updated for the 1990s with an Internet Sushi bar backdrop.

A short break in Victoria's packed schedule allowed Geoffrey to take a turn at working and he appeared in pantomime at Bradford. But it was not long before Victoria was back in action, making a documentary on carers for Comic Relief and recommencing the tour in April. It took her to Wolverhampton, Nottingham, Halifax, Scarborough, Portsmouth, Birmingham, Cardiff, Bristol and Reading. By the time she played her last show at the Liverpool Empire she had been seen by more than half a million people.

Although she loved performing live Victoria was looking to explore other areas and for all her complaints about the arduousness of life on the road she set in motion a chain of events that very nearly exhausted her mentally.

Easter 1997

The middle-aged woman in her regulation white overalls doles out another ladle of baked beans in the factory canteen. She started her shift at 6 a.m. but still seems strangely alert. The hungry queue of employees of Halstead's, manufacturers of slip resistant vinyl safety floorcovering, eye her with a mixture of curiosity, suspicion and timidity.

'Do you know the difference between a dick and a chicken leg?' braves one of them. The canteen worker, with her dyed blonde fringe peeping out from beneath her white trilby, doesn't.

'Well we're 'avin' a barbecue tomorrow, d'you want to come?'

She laughs, unfazed. Strangers often feel compelled to tell her jokes. We are in Whitefield, a Northern town within the borough of Bury. Its unloveliness made it a perfect location for the gritty 1962 kitchen sink drama, A Kind of Loving, and John Schlesinger filmed scenes in Coronation Park just across the road from the factory.

She is from round here, but as she serves up another rasher of bacon the thought does not depress her. A sudden burst of laughter from a bunch of gossiping women at one of the tables attracts her attention. She strains to eavesdrop and add to the many mental notes already stored. Later she will photograph the kitchen and canteen.

On 23 October 1998, the canteen overalls were replaced with an expensively tailored deep-blue corduroy suit for the press launch of *dinnerladies*, the situation comedy that sprang from Victoria's research at the Whitefield factory.

Virtually all 60 seats in Screen Three of the Leicester Square Odeon were filled with journalists, eager to see Victoria's first television series in nine years.

She had first considered writing a situation comedy as far back as 1979 when her own particular favourites were *Oh No It's Selwyn Froggitt*, *Last of the Summer Wine* and *Fawlty Towers*. But, ever the perfectionist, she had bided her time until she knew she was capable of producing something that met her own high standards.

'I wanted to do something in television again after quite a long break and I also wanted it to be something where I could concentrate on the characters, which you just can't do in a sketch show . . . I was very interested in what I could do with the format. It was complicated but really exciting,' she said. Victoria added: 'Sitcom is such a horrible phrase now. It's almost synonymous with crap . . . Often writers are constructing a group of people who don't have any reality. They're writing without passion . . . Those shows never say anything. You have to really want to write a sitcom and have something to say that can only be said in that form.'

The solitary nature of writing and touring her one-woman shows during those intervening years had also begun to take its toll and, despite the plaudits and adulation, Victoria discovered it was lonely at the top. 'I was just concentrating on the theatre and then suddenly thought: "I'm just getting so lonely standing on stage on my own and going into the office on my own. I want to go in a room where there's other people",' she said at the Little Havana Restaurant after the press screening.

Situation comedy is the most lucrative form of television writing, but also the most demanding. Characters need to be established and sustained, plots have to be developed and carefully structured and in the increasingly accountant-led BBC, success has to be immediate. For Victoria, who happily admitted she didn't need the 'dosh', it was a chance to exercise her comedy muscles. She had already explored virtually every format of television, from the talent shows, variety shows, magazine programmes, quiz shows and plays of her younger days to the sketch shows, chat shows, commercials, screenplays and documentaries of the 1980s and 1990s. Apart from hosting *Question Time* or reading the news, situation comedy was the only unchartered territory left.

Her one-time female rivals, Dawn French and Jennifer Saunders, had already tested the water with *The Vicar of Dibley* and *Absolutely Fabulous*. Their success suggested that the transition could be smooth and something that audiences would readily accept.

'I'm interested in the emotions of small things,' said Victoria. 'I tend to look at life from the chip pan level. Finding the universal truth from the mundane.' It was not surprising therefore that she should choose to set her situation comedy in a factory canteen. The idea had first entered her mind in 1995, but her punishing tour schedule meant she had to put it on hold. Expounding on her choice of location she said:

'I wanted it set where I would have no outside filming, it would just be in that setting so it had to be flexible enough so that people could come in and out, that they could interact with customers and could also interact amongst themselves, they could be working or not working, they could be having a tea break.'

The public still regard Victoria as a down-to-earth Northern woman and it is an image that she does not go out of her way to dispel. The affection with which she is held and the belief that she is 'one of us' is still very important to her. She knows from her own youth how damaging exclusion can be to her own psyche, and commercial considerations mean she cannot afford to alienate her fan base by being ostentatious about her now wealthier lifestyle. But it is largely overlooked that Victoria has never had any real experience of working-class life. This posed a problem when it came to writing about life in a factory canteen. As she herself said: 'Good sitcoms . . . show you a world that you didn't previously know existed.' To gain an understanding of it she despatched her personal assistant, Amy Whittaker, on a recce to Halstead's and another factory near Manchester, but it was the Whitefield firm's canteen that suited Victoria's needs. 'It had the right number of women and was the right size of factory,' she explained.

The then canteen manager, Adam Ellis, got something of a surprise when Victoria phoned him herself to see if he minded her visiting. A date was fixed for early March 1997 and besides Adam, only personnel manager Jim Falcus and the chef knew about the visit in advance.

'It was very low key and that's the way she wanted to keep it,' says Adam. 'If we'd have announced it there would have been people queuing up to get in. She stayed for a couple of hours the first time, just to get a feel for the place. She took a load of notes and photographs and asked me a lot of questions regarding how typical the canteen was. She's a bit of a perfectionist and she said there's nothing worse than seeing something on the television that people who are involved in the industry know is wrong.'

Victoria warned him that if word got out about her visit she would abandon the planned series, even if it meant losing out financially. A few weeks later she left her plush suite at Manchester's Midland Hotel for the 30-minute drive to Halstead's in time to start work on the 6 a.m. shift.

'She wasn't so shy that time. She didn't speak to the customers that much but she spoke to my girls. She was mainly after characters and did a lot of watching,' recalls Adam. 'People were pretty shocked to find a star serving them breakfast. Quite a few of them felt embarrassed.'

Victoria, who operated the till and served at the counter, as opposed to doing any actual cooking, clocked off at 1 p.m. and sat eating her lunch in the canteen with Amy and Adam.

'She was watching and listening to what was going on around her. She took note of the ones that were loud or outspoken, what they were saying and why they were saying it,' says Adam.

'I'm very glad my many years as a lollipop lady have finally been recognised,' was Victoria's sardonic response to the announcement in June 1997 that she had been awarded an OBE in the Queen's Birthday Honours. It was a statement which neatly displayed her perceptive wit – there had been a push for unsung heroes to be honoured – and at the same time the self-deprecation reassured fans that she was still 'one of them' despite the honour. When she received the award from Prince Charles that December she took Geoffrey and the children with her, and even wore a short skirt for the occasion. Buckingham Palace was a world away from the supermarket aisles and semis her public associated her with and, perhaps mindful of this, Victoria stressed that the real highlight of the day was going to Grace's school carol service later that afternoon and tucking into cheese sandwiches afterwards.

The end of her UK tour saw the end of Victoria's relationship with the Richard Stone Partnership, the agency that had represented her for 21 years. More than two decades in the business had given Victoria enough experience of how to conduct her own affairs and she no longer required the agency's services. She had her own successful production company for her television work, and the Phil McIntyre organisation looked after her live tours.

Her departure from Stone coincided with Victoria's biggest

gamble yet; a test to see if she could cut it abroad. For someone so used to being lauded it was a brave decision, but also a necessary one if she was to continue to fulfil her ambition. Her television shows had been shown in Australia and New Zealand but she had never performed there live. The Antipodean tour lasted from 22 July to 8 August and Geoffrey, Grace and Henry travelled with her for an unconventional family 'holiday'.

'It was so odd because no one knew who the hell I was at all . . . and you think, "Right, well this is where I earn my money,"' said Victoria. She need not have worried. Her material was only slightly adapted and travelled well, ensuring the tour was a complete sell-out.

When she was not touring, writing, filming or promoting (a video of her latest tour and a CD collection of ten of her old songs and four from the 1996 show were both released in 1997), Victoria supplemented her income by working the after-dinner speaking circuit. By 1998 she was the second highest earning female speaker after Margaret Thatcher. Along with personal appearances at £16,000 a time, video sales and corporate work, this took her yearly income up to £750,000. The video of the two-year-old stage act brought more money in when it was sold to ITV and re-titled *Still Standing*.

CHAPTER 14

A week after *Still Standing* was broadcast Victoria was back up North for a final visit to the Halstead's factory canteen. This time she was accompanied by a designer and during her three-hour stay many more photographs were taken which would form the basis for the canteen in her situation comedy.

The lessons she learned from writing *Wood & Walters* still influenced her approach to script writing and for *dinnerladies*, as she named the series, she followed her usual practice of over-writing. The scripts were written in a 200-page refill pad over a period of six months, with each draft taking two days to write. 'I was just working it out as I went along,' she explained. 'And I had to write a few episodes to see what the hell it was all about and after I'd written three I thought "Oh, now I understand what it's all about" and I threw those three away and started again.' The attention to detail was minute. In episode one Dolly expresses distaste for Tom Jones because he was once pictured on the front cover of the *TV Times* squatting in his swimming trunks. This had indeed been an actual cover shot more than twelve years previously.

'I had the idea. I had the setting. But who was I going to people it with?' pondered Victoria. 'I knew what I wanted to achieve, but it was a complicated journey to get there. I knew it was about a group of women in a factory canteen so I asked myself who are they? And how many? At first I thought there were about seven but I couldn't manoeuvre seven people's stories in half an hour. Once I got it down to five it was a lot simpler.'

Most of the roles were written with specific actors in mind, but when it came to the other parts Victoria was determined to have a say. She sat in on auditions and her opinions carried as much weight, if not more, as those of Geoff Posner and casting director Susie Bruffin. Naturally there were parts for Duncan Preston, Julie Walters, Anne Reid and Celia Imrie, and smaller parts for those who had worked with her previously and shown loyalty (Bernard Wrigley, Sue Wallace, Andrew

Livingston, Peter Lorenzelli and Graham Seed). David Firman once again arranged the music.

'When I got the call from Victoria asking me if I wanted to be in her sitcom it was like music to my ears,' said Duncan Preston. 'I hesitate to say there's a lot of me in Stan, but I am a very orderly guy naturally, and that's what he is. I don't think I'm as earnest as him and whereas I like a laugh, Stan doesn't know how to laugh. If the world were full of people like Stan it would be a chaotic disaster, but it would be a lovely place to live because there'd be no malice – there's no malice in him. In 1954 his mum ran off with a piano tuner and all he's had is his dad, who plays the ukulele. Stan has never married because he likes to keep all his tools in the living room.'

Julie Walters was only too happy to be appearing with Victoria again, this time playing her crazed mother, Petula Gordeno. It was the first time she had appeared in a situation comedy apart from two lines in *The Liver Birds* in 1978.

'When I first came up with the idea, I was determined not to use Julie,' said Victoria. 'People must think I can't work with anyone else. But as I was writing it, I knew it was inevitable she would be Petula. I genuinely couldn't think of anyone else who could do the part better. I just had to give in.'

Julie described Petula, another in a long line of grotesque old crones, as: 'One of those people who are always boosting her image. She is not a liar, but she embellishes absolutely everything . . . She fantasises and makes things bigger than they are, but some things she says are true, so you don't always know if she's telling the truth or not, she is someone who lives on the edge of society.'

Like Petula, Celia Imrie's Philippa was a character who popped in and out of the series. A Surrey refugee, Philippa was eager to please and anxious to be accepted by the girls. As Head of Human Resources and the only Southern character, Philippa was a useful contrast and point of dramatic conflict.

The casting of Thelma Barlow as Dolly attracted most media attention. It was the actress's first television role since leaving *Coronation Street*; once again Victoria had given a boost to the career of another former resident of Weatherfield.

The two had already met socially on a number of occasions through their mutual friend, Anne Reid. 'I don't know whether it was something Victoria saw in us, she had seen us together as friends and we do josh one another around a lot,' said Thelma. Victoria had been keeping an eye on the actress ever since Anne had hinted that Thelma was thinking of leaving the soap opera.

'My ears went "Ping!" . . . I thought Thelma and Annie would be a really good twosome, I just had a good feeling about them . . . I just think her comedy performances on *The Street* were absolutely fantastic,' said Victoria, who wrote to Thelma as soon as she announced she was quitting the soap.

'I was thrilled,' said the actress. 'I was particularly pleased that she had such faith in me and I really didn't want to let her down.'

Anne Reid, who played Jean ('down to earth, quite dry, in marriage guidance because her sex life has gone wrong') was another fan of Victoria. 'She's a very good writer, that's why I like doing it. She writes wonderful parts for women,' she said. 'Victoria writes the best parts, her stuff is so funny, it's very, very real and the characters are wonderful.'

The characters of Twinkle and Anita were the only main roles that required new actresses. 'They were sort of floating parts, as I was waiting to see who would get the tone,' explained Victoria. By creating two young characters Victoria was aiming to attract a younger, and therefore wider, audience.

Bolton actress Maxine Peake was given the part of the inappropriately named Twinkle, who was a version of *Good Fun's* Lynne. Although Maxine had eventually won a scholarship for RADA she had been rejected by every amateur dramatic group in Bolton and had been turned down by the Manchester Youth Theatre and the National Youth Theatre. She applied to Manchester Polytechnic three times but, like Victoria, failed to get into its theatre school.

'I went to the audition, and to be quite honest I didn't think I would get it, it was just great to meet Victoria Wood,' said Maxine. 'Two days later I got a recall and after I'd done it I really thought, "Oh no, that was terrible, I haven't got it." I then got a phone call from my agent to say I had got the job! I was thrilled and excited.'

dinnerladies was only her second part after graduating. She had previously had a small role in the Julie Walters' film *Girls Night*, part of which was filmed in Bury's Art cinema, once frequented by the young Victoria.

'Twinkle reminded me of people I went to school with,' said Maxine. 'She is seventeen, she's not the brightest penny in the jar, but she's good fun, she likes to have a laugh and she's a lovely girl underneath. I used to have friends like that at school, who were quite hard on the outside and then you found out underneath, they are quite soft. She is funny, has no dress sense whatsoever, and she doesn't care, she's not hung up about herself.'

Oldham's Shobna Gulati also benefited from Victoria's Midas touch. 'It's an extraordinary part,' said the former linguist and accomplished dancer, choreographer, comedian and singer. 'Although Anita is Asian, she is not Asian. She is very British. That was exciting because I normally work using culture traditions from India and this has drawn on my skills as an actor. She is just extremely well written and it's really easy to find her.'

Victoria's take on the show's dimmest and only Asian character was more succinct: 'They can't all be brain surgeons can they?'

Completing the *dinnerladies* cast was Andrew Dunn. Apart from Duncan Preston as the pedant and borderline retard, Stan, he was the only other male performer in the show of any significance. A member of the Hull Truck Theatre Company, Andrew had previously worked with John Godber and had come to acting late after originally training to be a teacher.

'I auditioned with Victoria in Manchester and read the entire six scripts. A few weeks later I was recalled down to London and read the part of Tony in front of all the regular cast. It was nerve-wracking! All of these famous people I'd just seen on television. They told me the same day I'd got the part, I was driving on the motorway and my agent rang me. I had to stop for a cup of tea as a celebration, it was fantastic.

'Tony is in his early forties, his wife has left him, the job is probably the only part of his life that is going right,' he explained. 'Working with the ladies he has a laugh with them and good rapport. He's a flirt but if anybody came on to him he'd probably run a mile. He is completely harmless, however. He and Bren like each other but they haven't got it together yet.'

Victoria based the sexually suggestive manager on a few people from her university days who talked about sex non-stop. 'He's not seedy,' she said. 'I did want to do realistic people.'

Through the situation comedy, Victoria decided to take another pop at her pet hate: political correctness. In the character of Tony, she was able to create an unreconstructed man who was overtly sexual without being sexist, offensive or threatening. 'Abuse and harassment are disgusting but when people go to work they do talk about sex – it's part of life. They say these things when they're intimate,' explained Victoria.

In the same way that Anita and Twinkle were partly created to appeal to a teenage audience, it seemed that part of Tony's role was to attract an adult male audience. Generally speaking this group had never made up a huge contingent of Victoria's audience, deterred by the idea that her act was dominated by gynaecology. As in most of her work, gynaecological matters did crop up in *dinnerladies*, with mention made of water retention, yeast infection, thrush, cystitis and PMT. But rather than demystify the mysterious world of women's issues for her male audience Victoria reinforced the sense of bewilderment. 'Lost in the land of No-Speakee-Ladytalk,' remarks Tony when the women are discussing bras. In this capacity he is acting as a navigator for men watching the show and if they do not understand the women's jokes, they can still laugh in recognition at Tony's reaction.

Tony's likeability meant he could articulate the frustration and confusion of men everywhere without becoming a sexist bigot. 'I'm not a dinosaur,' he explains. 'I quite like women in a sad, baffled sort of way, but can we please get a grip? Out of a workforce of five, at any given moment, one'll have pre-menstrual tension, one's panicking cos she's not, someone's having a hot flush, and someone else is having a nervous breakdown cos their HRT patch has fallen in the minestrone.'

For all his breezy sexuality ('Anyone for a gang bang?'), which was refreshing in an era of political correctness, Tony could be sensitive to women, which was no great surprise as he spent every working day surrounded by them. One tiny exchange with the veg man showed his awareness of traditional gender expectations while at the same time revealing that this Northern canteen manager was, in his own quiet way, a New Man. The veg man prattles on about the intricacies of a football match in much the same way as Brenda and Jean might discuss a vaginal prolapse. Tony falls in with the veg man, making the right noises and expressing the expected opinion on the match and then tells Brenda he had no idea what the exchange was about.

Victoria played Brenda Furlong – her unusual surname inspired by that of an old schoolmate. 'The character I wrote first of all was very bland and ordinary, she just had lines to help the story along. Then I thought I'd make her a bit more vulnerable, so her main interest in life is work, it's centred within that kitchen. A lot of her information comes from the television so she's articulate, but not in a clever way,' said Victoria. She said she identified with Brenda because she shared her enthusiasm and had experienced her lack of confidence.

There is genuine pathos in Brenda's low self-esteem, limited expectations and resignation to disappointment. 'I know I look stupid,' she says when reluctantly revealing her Christmas party dress. She is perfectly happy to catch the night bus home, where her idea of excitement is removing the labels off food tins so she can surprise herself with what's for tea. The understated romance that develops between Brenda and Tony across the series is touching. He flirts while she responds with diffidence. When he offers to take her to the Christmas party and when it finally looks like they are about to get it together it is inevitable that Brenda will end up disappointed but put a brave face on it.

'It just removes it from Sitcomland and roots it in a world I know,' said Victoria about the importance of tragi-comedy. 'Most interesting things – whether they're drama or comedy – contain both elements. The best drama has always got funny bits in it, and the best sitcoms have a truth and, if not pathos, then something underneath that isn't just happy and jolly. Otherwise, it's meaningless.'

To ensure Brenda was the most sympathetic character in the series, Victoria made her something of a martyr who radiates niceness. When Stan comes onto her she lets him down with the utmost kindness ('Blimey, Stan, I think I'm going a bit deaf or something. I didn't hear what you said then, and I won't embarrass you – telling you what it sounded like'). It is Bren who agrees to break the news to Twinkle's mother that her daughter might be pregnant; it is Bren who is prepared to sacrifice the others' good opinion of her by preventing the docu-soap in order to protect Tony; and it is Bren who makes Stan's day by ensuring Prince James pretends to remember him.

There was also a more technical reason for the existence of Brenda. 'There's got to be a sane centre in an ensemble piece and Bren is it,' said Victoria. 'You've got the two girls and the two older women and she's in the middle holding it all together. But within that there's leeway for her to do various different things. Her mother is completely mad, and that's Bren's story, what will happen with the mother? Every time she comes in, she upsets the equilibrium and spoils Bren's little world.' In fact the relationship between Petula and Bren seemed to be yet another commentary on Victoria's own relationship with Helen Wood. She certainly seemed to share Bren's enforced stoicism towards a neglectful mother. 'I've had post-natal disinterest for thirty years,' says Petula who put Bren in an orphanage as a child and then forgot the address.

Victoria wanted her characters to sound realistic and Northern. 'I don't know if it's an attitude or a form of speech that makes things sound funny. It's a very deflating, dismissive way of talking,' she once said. Consequently sentences were punctuated with 'like', 'me' was used instead of 'my' and abbreviations were omitted in favour of 'would you not', 'is it not', 'are they not' and 'did you not'.

It may have been situation comedy but Victoria applied her playwright's grasp of dialogue to the scripts. Conversations rattled with speculation, confusion, non-sequiturs ('I didn't realise every topic had to link up,' complains Jean. 'I didn't realise I was on *Blockbusters*'), surrealism, prattle, innuendo and banalities. Because there were many scenes where the characters, naturalistically, spoke at cross purposes, it required precision timing from the actors. 'Her choice of words is very funny and the order in which they're written. And they're not if you make a mistake,' said Celia Imrie.

'You have to be very sharp, you have to stay alert, because Victoria likes you to be very quick,' added Anne Reid.

The humour in some of the lines took some getting used to and Shobna in particular found it difficult. 'My instinct was to impart the funny bit at the end of the line, rather like the punchline of a joke, until Victoria said "Look, the humour is in the line itself. Just speak it." Of course she was right and once the penny had dropped, we were up and running.'

Rehearsals took place at the BBC rehearsal rooms in North Acton. 'It would be ridiculous to claim that we all felt comfortable at the beginning,' admitted Shobna. But Victoria's quest for authenticity helped relax the cast. A woman was brought in to teach them how to chop vegetables properly, but she took her task rather too seriously. 'That pretty much broke the ice because we were all put down to the same level and most of us just fell about laughing,' said Victoria. 'I was aware that Maxine and Shobna, in particular, might be a bit wary of me, but I was in a daze most of the time. I was writing through the night as well as working in the day, so I was forever locking myself out of my dressing room and forgetting my wallet and having to borrow fivers off everyone. I was less of an awesome person and more of a ridiculous specimen.' Victoria also helped lighten the atmosphere by being humorously blunt and verbally sparring with Celia, the only Southerner in the main cast.

'It was an interesting cast because, although we are all very different, everyone really wanted it to work,' said Thelma Barlow. 'The young ones were anxious because it was their first big show; it was Victoria's first television sitcom and I was nervous because it was the first thing I'd done since *Coronation Street*.'

For Victoria the opportunity to work with other people again after extensive touring was a joy. 'It was just brilliant. I've never worked so hard and laughed so much in my life.'

Rehearsals took up most of the summer and were followed by the filming at Television Centre. It was a measure of the corporation's respect for Victoria that she and every member of the cast had a fresh bouquet of flowers in their room every day.

Victoria gladly embraced a shooting technique for *dinnerladies* that was revolutionary for British television. Normally rehearsals take place from Mondays to Thursdays with one recording on a Friday evening. For *dinnerladies* a version of each episode was recorded on Friday night, but the following day Victoria and Geoff Posner analysed the show, deciding what needed to be cut for length and what needed to be removed because it had not worked. Re-rehearsals took place on the Saturday afternoon and the whole show was recorded again that night.

'It meant things like all your props changes and camera moves were all done much slicker, so you tighten the whole thing up,' said a delighted Victoria. 'It's like doing it in a theatre: you do it on a Monday night but by the Tuesday night it's always much better, everybody's relaxed. You never get that in television, it's always "Ah! We've done it. Oh God! I wish we could do it again!".'

The only drawback of the new method came from some of the editing decisions. 'You did have this rather painful process of saying to people, "You know that big line you've got? You haven't got it",' said Victoria.

Strongly disciplined, she expected the utmost professionalism from her colleagues and was very strict on set. Corpsing and mistakes were frowned upon and paraphrasing was the ultimate taboo. If anyone did make a mistake, Victoria was usually the first person they apologised to.

After her unhappiness with the 1989 BBC series of plays, Victoria was determined to make sure the mistakes would not be repeated with *dinnerladies*. She wanted control and achieved this by following the independent route: *dinnerladies* was co-produced by her own production company, Good Fun, and Pozzitive, Geoff Posner's company. For the first time she was credited as co-producer, as well as star and writer: her childhood fantasy of living *The Swish of The Curtain* had finally been achieved.

'I just wanted to make sure with this I had official recognition of what I was doing because always with my work I had an input, but if you call yourself a producer you've got an official input and people have to come and say "What do you think of this?" and you can then say "Actually, that's not what I want",' said Victoria. 'It was more relaxing to have that recognition because you knew things couldn't slip by you by accident. I wanted to be in on my own programme and have a good say.' The power this gave to Victoria (she insisted on a lower case title and even chose the colour of the costumes) made her regard the series as the first piece of work that truly belonged to her.

dinnerladies abounded with that staple of traditional situation comedy: the double entendre. The lines ('I could do with an unusual knob'; 'Where's my Clint?'; 'He's adjusting his nuts') would not have been out of place in any 1970s' situation comedy.

Victoria also gave a nod to the traditional situation comedy with attempts at catchphrases, although it is hard to imagine playgrounds and offices up and down the country echoing with 'Let's feed the faces of folk' and 'Shutter's going up'.

Parts of *dinnerladies* also shared the lack of realism that traditional situation comedies had. However sexually charged Tony was feeling, would he *really* have sex with Petula? Would Philippa *really* have an affair with the aged boss, Mr Michael? Would problems *really* be solved so neatly and conveniently? Standard situation comedy plots were used but only after they had passed through Victoria's barmy filter.

Central to each episode was the effect that different interlopers had on the core cast members and their working day. In episode one ('Monday') Jean is panicking about her daughter's wedding arrangements while Philippa impacts as the new Human Resources officer; in episode two ('Scandal') Petula shacks up in the factory with sixteen-year-old Clint. The interlopers are his angry mother, a docu-soap crew and a local television news reporter; in 'Royals', the canteen is visited by Prince James and his wife; in episode four ('Moods') the canteen is invaded by the mothers of the main characters; in episode five ('Party') the Christmas party saw Jean and Dolly's husbands and the comically misnamed Babs, Petula's strange friend, who was not the bubbly vivacious being her moniker implied, enter into events. The final episode ('Nightshift') saw the team pulling together to save the factory and at odds with the battle-axe of a temporary canteen supervisor.

Conventional though much of *dinnerladies* was as a situation comedy, it did contain elements of realism that helped elevate it. The characters talk about what is on the television and one has a period in the canteen toilet. They utter lines whose purpose is to promote naturalism rather than induce laughter. 'I can't remember what I was going to say' states Petula mid-utterance, and Brenda's thought process

('What are them things like cucumbers? Suffragettes!') shows an internal life rare in situation comedy characters. Even Tony's throwaway line that it takes two fives to dial out on the canteen phone serves to make the canteen seem like a real place.

Perhaps the most unusual way in which Victoria added realism was to have one of the central characters suffering from cancer. Tony's illness was totally unexpected in a situation comedy and thanks to Victoria's skilful handling, it seemed neither crass nor cynical. There was no shock announcement, melodramatic wait or neat conclusion at the end of an episode, instead the cancer hovered in the background throughout the entire series with occasional references made to his treatment, his checks and his condition. One might have expected the series to end on an optimistic note but Tony was absent for most of episode six because of his treatment, and when he did appear he was pale and in a fragile state.

The subject of television itself was interwoven into the episodes, with Victoria comically defining the necessary components of costume dramas and examining the phenomenon of the docu-soap. She also commented on the predictability of television movies, the rise of the Jerry Springer-style show, and once again mocked the nature of regional news ('She only normally gets to interview people who make furniture out of conkers'). She reflected on the nature of contemporary celebrity, where a person becomes famous after tripping up on television, and used television to differentiate the generations: Twinkle and Anita are baffled by references to *Rag, Tag and Bobtail* and Tony describes Petula as 'a woman old enough to remember *Maigret*'.

Weight was clearly no longer a personal problem for Victoria but the series included a familiar contempt for the diet industry. The double act of Dolly and Jean was used to show where Victoria's loyalties lay. The diet-obsessed Dolly was spiky and unsympathetic and her bitchy put-downs of Jean concentrated on her ample figure. To Dolly, 12 stone 2 is 'clinically obese' and while her constant weighing of herself, use of a mini-stepper, dietary requirements and facial exercises created laughter, they also implied a neurosis of character. Jean on the other hand is not hung up about her figure ('It's all a load of codswash dieting. All that misery for what?') and is portrayed as a much more honest, generous and likeable person.

Either out of mischief or as a further attempt to escape her safe and cosy image, Victoria used some near-the-knuckle gags. Romanian orphans were employed for comic effect; cancer sufferer Tony compared a salad bowl full of pulverised lettuce to a hospice; there is a crack about war atrocities; after Tony tells Enid his cancer's looking good she remarks cynically 'that's what they told you'; Babs is made a figure of fun because of her mental illness.

Victoria always refused to name Halstead's as the inspiration for the series, because 'they might not like it'. But the clues were there; the factory in *dinnerladies* was called HWD Components (Halstead's Whitefield?) and Enid tells Dolly: 'You must have had the biggest bottom in Whitefield.'

In the weeks prior to *dinnerladies* being broadcast it became apparent that the BBC was touting it as the revival of the Great British Situation Comedy. It was not a view shared by Victoria. 'I don't feel anything is riding on it except I want people to like it,' she said. 'I want it to be half an hour of television that people like, that's all.'

Because it had been nine years since her last television series, the press were naturally excited about *dinnerladies* and Victoria and the cast were the cover stars of most magazines and supplements. A nicely timed *Best of British* documentary about Victoria was screened on 11 November 1998, the day before the first episode of *dinnerladies*, raising Victoria's profile even higher (unlike later subjects Lenny Henry and Cliff Richard, no Wood relatives appeared in Victoria's programme). The level of expectation on Victoria would have been unfair if she had not set such exacting standards herself and she was prepared to take full responsibility. 'If it doesn't go down well it's only down to me,' she said. 'I can't say the producer did it wrong or the cast weren't up to it. Everything's gone as well as it could go.'

The first episode was broadcast at 9.30 p.m. on BBC1 and received a mixed reaction. After viewing it the *Mirror's* Tony Purnell confidently predicted a hit series, and the *Observer's* Kathryn Flett praised 'writing that is not a million miles from brilliant'. However, the *Daily Mail's* Jaci

Stephen criticised the playground humour of bodily functions for being 'as tedious as it is unfunny', and the *Mail on Sunday*'s Brian Viner felt it 'had the air of a sketch that wasn't sure when to stop'. In the *Independent* Serena Mackesy elaborated on such a point and wrote: 'Had it been in sketch format it would have been pretty good, as a sitcom, it left one staring at the screen in blank amazement . . . it's as if the plot had been surgically removed . . . a mystifying mess'. The *Daily Telegraph*'s James Walton criticised the 'resolutely old fashioned' show for having insufficiently differentiated characters and a weak performance by Victoria. '*dinnerladies*,' he stated, 'unlike the best sitcoms, is not a show to make you think.' *The Times*'s Paul Hoggart got it about right when he wrote: 'There were a few dud lines, but since Wood's script packed more inventive, original and funny gags into one episode than most British sitcoms manage in a whole series it seems churlish to complain.'

Part of the problem was *The Royle Family*. The groundbreaking situation comedy by Caroline Aherne – who had been inspired to turn to a career in comedy after seeing the television version of *Talent* – and Craig Cash, had preceded *dinnerladies*, and its unique realism changed the concept of situation comedy entirely.

The public were obviously disappointed with Victoria's new creation. A total of 12.24 million watched the first show, which made it BBC1's fourth most popular show and the twelfth most watched programme in the country. However, by the second week the figure had fallen to 10.59 million and the remaining episodes got an average of 9.45 million. *dinnerladies* was not even nominated in the Most Popular Comedy category at the 1999 National Television Awards, and although Victoria was nominated for Most Popular Comedy Performer for the show, she lost.

Perhaps fortunately, *dinnerladies* was shown too late to be nominated for the 1998 British Comedy Awards, where *The Royle Family* was named Best New Comedy. Victoria was, however, invited to the ceremony to present Thora Hird with a Lifetime Achievement Award. Her trademark dourness was evident ('Quite a thrill [to be here] cos I only usually go out of a Tuesday'), but there was also a rare glimpse of genuine sentiment. It would be going too far to say that

Victoria regarded Thora as a substitute mother figure, but at the ceremony Victoria was almost overcome with emotion. It was reciprocated by Thora, who referred to her in her acceptance speech as 'Our love', 'Clever Clogs' and 'the cleverest woman in Britain re entertainment'.

CHAPTER 15

VICTORIA commenced writing the second series of *dinnerladies* in January 1999. The mixed reception to the first series made a second inevitable as Victoria's professional and personal pride would not allow her to end a project on a lacklustre note. 'I don't normally do anything twice. But I felt for this to give it its best benefit I had to do more,' she explained. 'The first six were like an experiment. You don't know what you've done till you've had it out on the television.'

The scraps of paper on the floor she once relied on to plan a series had been replaced by magnetic wall charts to navigate the new, more intricate storylines. These gave an added cohesiveness to the new series, making it more of a comedy drama than a collection of self-contained programmes. As with the writing of the first series Victoria seriously considered abandoning the show half-way through. The loneliness was getting to her and she began doubting her comedic abilities. But as always, when things were difficult she seemed to deliberately make them harder, a habit that therapy had not cured. Consequently she decided to write ten rather than the usual six episodes, which, with rewrites, meant she wrote 70 half-hour scripts.

'I painted myself into a corner because I said from the start that I wanted to write it on my own,' she admitted. 'I thought if I write a sitcom at least I'll go into a room where there's other people but actually it would have been easier to have contacted the social services and get taken to a day centre,' she later commented. 'I just wished I had one other person that knew everything I was doing that I could talk to about it,' she said.

A trip up North in February gave Victoria a welcome break from her self-imposed isolation when she attended the Bolton Octagon's stage adaptation of *Pat and Margaret*. Christine Moore, who played Pat, would be rewarded for her performance with a small part in *dinnerladies* 2. Sue Cleaver, who had played Maureen in a 1996 run of *Talent* at the Octagon, was also rewarded with the more high profile role of Glen. After *dinnerladies* 2 she became a *Coronation Street* regular.

That March's Comic Relief provided Victoria with another distraction from the writing. An offer to revisit Africa was politely turned down and she instead involved herself with projects she felt more comfortable with. One of these was agreeing to be the guest editor of the special issue *Radio Times*. Victoria approached the task with her usual thoroughness and the magazine's editor Sue Robinson may not have been altogether joking when she said Victoria had 'terrified' staff into doing what they were told. She replaced columnists John Peel, Polly Toynbee and Alan Hanson with, respectively, Dawn French, Richard Curtis and Nick Hancock, and for the My Kind of Day feature she recruited Esther Mujawayo, a Rwandan widow. Victoria, in her role as editor, graced the front cover, power dressed and wearing an expression of paranoid smugness ('which I think covers most media jobs').

Inside she contributed a humorously scathing review of *The Archers* for the Soaps page, and also wrote a piece about On Digital and a letter to the medical page, which allowed her to mention bunions, peep-toe sandals and tartan slippers. In her Editor's Letter she discussed the scandal of recruiting actors to play talk show guests and pondered how much more interesting it would be if the likes of Judi Dench and 'the woman who plays the receptionist in Peak Practice' had been used instead.

It was Victoria's idea to interview Gordon Brown for the Questionnaire. Her questions were a mixture of the pertinent ('Don't you think that cancelling Third World debts would at least save a lot of paperwork?') to the mischievous ('With the recent spate of resignations, do you worry that you may buy incorrect garden furniture and have to resign?').

In the guise of 'Andrea Duncan' she interviewed Julie Walters in the clumsy style that borrowed from her 1990 creation, *Ooh Hello!*'s Debora Klepper. We learn that Julie is a gin-swilling nymphomaniac, whose seven husbands have included Bobby Crush and Larry Adler. Hated by film crews and famously infertile after a netballing accident, she has adopted the Harlem Globetrotters ('I had always been very admiring of Mia Farrow and the way she had adopted children at the least opportunity, some even differently abled, and with varying skin tones and eye shapes').

Apart from her editorial duties Victoria wrote and starred in a parody of *Hetty Wainthropp Investigates*. The thirteen-minute skit was crammed with cameos by Julie Walters, Duncan Preston, Judith Chalmers, Bobby Crush, Matthew Kelly, Celia Imrie, Shobna Gulati and Gary Wilmot.

Victoria, as Wetty Hainthropp, captured the mannerisms and delivery of Patricia Routledge perfectly. Once again she had turned to television itself for her inspiration and the programme was a brilliant satire of formulaic programming. Sending up the reliance on stereotype, Wetty gives directions: 'It's a terraced house, that's right, in the North. There'll be a brass band playing. You can't miss it.'

The improbability of the plot with its bizarre coincidences involved Alan Titchmarsh's evil twin brother, Adam, kidnapping Delia Smith and Rolf Harris, stealing Matthew Kelly's greasepaint and practising his maths so he could take over from Carol Vorderman. He was ready to kidnap any celebrity who threatened his chance of a successful television career but, as Wetty pointed out, he made the 'classic mistake' of stealing fishfingers from the bag of the very woman he tried to kill.

Filming the skit allowed Victoria to fulfil a personal ambition. After almost twenty years of including them in her act, she finally appeared on screen on the cobbles of Weatherfield with *Coronation Street's* Ken and Deirdre.

Another welcome break from writing *dinnerladies 2* came in April when Victoria flew to the 39th Golden Rose Festival of Montreux. The *dinnerladies* episode, 'Party', was awarded the International Press Prize, beating 99 other programmes submitted by 26 countries. The French were particularly impressed with it but, more significantly, it was the first real time Victoria's work had been tested on the international stage. That it triumphed showed Victoria that she could appeal to overseas audiences, something that many British comedians, however celebrated in this country, often failed at. She returned to London and writing with a new vigour.

In the early days of Victoria's career, when her insecurity was at its height and she was still quite naive, she tended to let herself be buffeted along by the press. Greater success and confidence led to her adopting a more businesslike and controlled approach. Interviews were only usually given if she had something to promote and she often dictated the areas to be discussed. Her rather cool personality did not exactly endear her to reporters, but they appreciated her professionalism. She was careful to obey the rules, never flaunting herself for the paparazzi, never getting drunk and definitely no messy adulterous affairs. She was therefore justified in expecting a degree of respect from the press and started to believe she was almost untouchable.

In the mid-1990s she said: 'I've had a soft ride . . . I used to worry that they'd [the press] just get their knives out for no reason, but now I don't think that's very realistic. Why would they pick me out as a target?' The answer came on Sunday, 5 September 1999, when Victoria learned she was no exception to any other celebrity.

She was working through the night on a *dinnerladies 2* script when a *News of the World* reporter arrived on her doorstep in the early hours. Through the intercom he informed her that the *Sunday People* was running a front page story about Geoffrey's eating disorder. Neither Victoria nor Geoffrey were prepared to give a comment, and they spent an anxious few hours waiting for the newsagent to open.

VICTORIA WOOD'S SECRET AGONY screamed the headline, *Hubby fears death from food addiction*.

The story revealed that Geoffrey had joined a local group of Overeaters Anonymous, an organisation that, but for the personal link, Victoria might have got some mileage out of in her act. Meetings involved group confessionals and it was these that reporter Rachel Bletchly had sat in on incognito.

We were told that 'tormented' Geoffrey had joined the group 'in a desperate bid to end his nightmare'. His terrifying food addiction meant he could literally eat himself to death, and Geoffrey reportedly said: 'I am a food addict and compulsive overeater and if I ever overeat as a way of life again, I will be dead. I have got to beat this.'

The story revealed how Geoffrey, who at one point had ballooned to 28 stones, had suffered dangerous breathing problems and fully expected to have a heart attack or fall asleep at the wheel of his car.

He said: 'I started overeating when I was three because I felt ashamed and humiliated. For the next 47 years, I never believed that I was going to live a year longer than I was already. But I am 50 now and not dead yet. I am frightened. All sorts of things scare me. But here I am in recovery, feeling great, with so many opportunities open to me. It is up to me to make the most of it.'

Victoria, who sometimes attended sessions to give support to Geoffrey, was convinced that the paper was trying to get some filth on her, the true star of the couple. If that was the case then Bletchly was disappointed as all Geoffrey had to say on his domestic life was: 'The things that are important to me are that I am the father of two children, I am married to a lovely woman and I believe in God.'

It was ironic that the subject of food and weight which had so dogged Victoria should return to bite her, even though she had overcome her own difficulties. To have a Sunday tabloid fill its first three pages with intimate details about personal matters would have been bad enough for any celebrity, but for Victoria, who believed she was in control and organised and somehow excluded from the hunt, it was devastating. She adopted an it's-only-tomorrow's-chip-paper attitude to the story but was deeply upset. There was no immediate public response, and a little later all Victoria would remark was: 'He's dealing with it on a daily basis, and I'm supporting him. We are both well and, apart from that, it's nobody else's business.'

Rehearsals of *dinnerladies* 2 began in the late summer of 1999. Just as Victoria had had to change some of Celia Imrie's lines in *Pat and Margaret* when the actress fell pregnant, she had to alter some of Maxine Peake's fat-dependent lines for the series when she turned up for rehearsals. Maxine had joined a slimming club and by the time rehearsals started she had lost nearly five stones. Another change was the replacement of Andrew Livingston by Adrian Hood as Norman the breadman.

Filming of *dinnerladies* 2 began in the autumn of 1999 in Studio 8 of BBC TV Centre and the last episode was recorded on 11 December. Before each session Geoff Posner gave a pre-amble to the studio audience – which consisted of such disparate groups as the Gloucester WI and Kent Police – before introducing Victoria. Standing on a wooden box in Bren's costume and wig she treated them to five minutes of old stand-up and filled them in on the series' plot developments.

The second series of *dinnerladies* was shown from 25 November 1999 to 27 January 2000, each episode averaging an audience of around 13.02 million, making it the eleventh most popular television show of 2000. The figure might have been even higher if it had been easier to keep track of the programme and its schedule. Confusingly, some weeks it was repeated on a Saturday evening while on other weeks it was not. Consecutive episodes were shown on 23 and 24 December and one episode was simply put back a week to make way for the football. Viewers who were unable to navigate such odd scheduling ended up confused if they missed an episode because the strands of plot ran through the whole series.

dinnerladies 2 had much greater depth than the first series, with many of the major characters having to adapt to some kind of fundamental change: Bren's mother dies; Anita has a baby; Stan's father dies; Jean's husband leaves her and she undergoes a mini-nervous breakdown; Bren and Tony have to decide on their future.

Victoria's plotting was highly intricate. Casual references in one episode would have much greater significance in later shows. In episode three for instance, we learn the recovering Jean fills her days watching the daytime television quiz *Totally Trivial* and in episode nine she confesses she entered on Bren's behalf and Bren's appearance on the show is a pivotal moment. In episode six Bren tells Anita that she would have liked a baby, which encourages Anita to leave her own baby for Bren in episode seven. In episode five Tony invites Bren to his friend's pub in Scotland and in episode ten that is where they plan to start a new life together.

But the plotting was not confined to *dinnerladies 2*. In the first series there were hints that all was not going well with the factory through talk of a merger with a Japanese company, the closure of one of the sheds and a lost contract. Consequently the announcement that the canteen is to close in episode ten of series two is believable, as opposed to being a convenient plot device. But perhaps the best example of Victoria's long range view can be seen in the resolution of Tony and Bren's financial worries. In episode one, series one, Petula asks Bren to dispose of a mobile phone. In episode ten of series two we learn it belonged to a criminal, since murdered, and his loot goes to Bren and Tony.

Each episode was given a specific date, which was sometimes relevant to the script (the last day to conceive a millennium baby, Christmas Eve, New Year's Eve and 29 February in a Leap Year). The series' time frame spanned from March 1999 to February 2000 meaning that episode six was actually broadcast on the same date that the programme was set. The decision to date each episode was partly influenced by *Dad's Army*, one of Victoria's favourite situation comedies. She observed that the show had timeless appeal because it was already set in the past and so could not date. Consequently, if there are any future repeats of *dinnerladies* the date captions will excuse it from criticism because it is effectively a time capsule.

Once again Victoria ensured Brenda attracted audience sympathy through her humble and saintly ways. But Victoria allowed Bren to undergo the same transformation she herself had gone through. The once easygoing Bren blasts Philippa for treating them as if they do not matter and she stands up for herself when the social worker puts pressure on her to provide a home for Petula. The parallels between Petula and Helen Wood continued; at one point Petula says: 'I had a baby once before but I never really got involved.'

For close on 20 years New Age beliefs and the whole healthfood movement had been a source of irritation for Victoria, who addressed the subjects in plays, sketches, film and stand-up. This reached its apogee in episode eight of *dinnerladies 2* when Kay Adshead (an actress used by Victoria on numerous previous occasions) was introduced into the canteen. As the New Age Christine she seemed to be a distillation of everything Victoria hated and was very nearly lynched by all the major characters.

The naturalism of speech and conversation in the series ('What's that word? Not unicorn – dilemma!'; the awkwardness in the immediate aftermath of a row) and the realism of Tony's continued cancer worries was offset by plot contrivances and an overkill of pathos and jokes. Although there were surprises in the series – Bren's secret husband, Anita's pregnancy – and incidents that defied audience expectation – Victoria overdosing on drugs, a verbal gag hanging on the word 'cunt' – all Victoria's usual trademarks were included, from date specification to High Street/brand names.

The audience heard the theme song as opposed to the instrumental in the second series. It was of the same lineage as the earlier songs 'Go Away', 'Go With It' and 'Andrea' in that it followed Victoria's pre-occupation with unfulfilled dreams and hopes crushed by everyday living.

The general consensus amongst the critics was that the show had improved considerably. 'A cracking script, brilliant ensemble acting and simple yet imaginative direction,' wrote Christopher Matthew in the *Daily Mail*. In the *Daily Express* Simon Edge said: 'The tired and bedraggled *dinnerladies* we used to know has re-emerged, transformed into a brilliant and sparkling piece of comic writing. The dialogue raced along at three times the pace of the first series.' And the *Daily Telegraph*'s Matthew Bond wrote: 'Its unashamedly antique feel has become part of its charm, its use of a single set . . . almost a gesture of defiance.'

Sir Christopher Bland, the Chairman of the BBC, cited *dinnerladies* as a potential long-running hit. But Victoria, finally satisfied that she had got it right, determined that there would be no more, stating: 'I've done what I wanted to do now.'

Rather less satisfaction was derived from how *dinnerladies* fared against other comedies. The first series competed against *The Royle Family* at the 1999 BAFTA awards in the Best Comedy Programme category. Julie Walters was also up against Caroline Aherne for the Best Comedy Performance. However, any judgement between Victoria and Caroline was avoided when the awards went to *Father Ted* and its star Dermot Morgan, who had unexpectedly died shortly after completing the series. The priestly comedy set on the eccentrically peopled Craggy Island may have won irrespective of Morgan's death, but there was always the suggestion of sentimentality which Victoria could use to defend *dinnerladies*' failure.

At the British Comedy Awards later that year Victoria may have been irked that *The Royle Family* beat *dinnerladies* as the Best British Sitcom and that Aherne was judged Best Comedy Actress while no one from *dinnerladies* was even nominated, but she could take solace that *dinnerladies* was named Best New Television Comedy. It was a category that was not applicable to *The Royle Family* and the distinction meant Victoria did not leave empty-handed.

A showdown of sorts finally came at the BAFTA awards in May 2000 where *The Royle Family* beat *dinnerladies* as the Best Sitcom. There was no way of avoiding the fact that Victoria had been eclipsed on the night by a younger talent. To confirm this, Caroline Aherne took the Best Comedy Performance title (three of the four nominees were *The Royle Family* cast members, the other was Dawn French for *The Vicar of Dibley*. No one from *dinnerladies* was nominated).

The *Radio Times*/Lew Grade Audience Award, voted for by *Radio Times* readers, Radio 2 listeners and GMTV viewers, gave Victoria a chance to show that she might no longer be a hit with the Academy, but she was still the viewers' favourite. However, *dinnerladies* came third behind *A Touch of Frost* and the gardening programme, *Ground Force*. It was time to go away and think up something new.

CHAPTER 16

VICTORIA began the new millennium by satiating one ambition and very nearly achieving her ultimate career goal of making a film. As part of the millennium celebrations the BBC screened *The Nearly Complete and Utter History of Everything*, a two-part sketch show with a cast made up of the cream of British comedians. It presented the ideal opportunity for Victoria to at last write and perform in a two-handed sketch with Thora Hird. Set in her Northern home ground of Radcliffe, Victoria used a favourite location; a hairdressing salon. She played the talkative stylist, and Thora the optimistic customer.

A little later in the year a much grander scheme of Victoria's ended in failure, as had all her earlier cinematic ambitions. The Women's Institute and Joyce Grenfell are intrinsically linked in the public consciousness, and if Victoria is a Grenfell of the modern age, then the Rylstone and District WI in North Yorkshire was her counterpart. In 1998 eleven of them, aged between 45 and 65, came up with the idea of posing naked for a charity calendar after the husband of one of them, Angela Baker, died of leukaemia. When the calendar appeared it gripped the nation, not so much out of prurience – the women were photographed behind strategically placed copper kettles and apple presses – but because of its quirkiness. A total of 90,000 copies of the calendar were printed making £350,000.

Their story contained elements that were so vital to Victoria's work: poignancy, friendship, humour and Northernness. *dinnerladies* had left her exhausted, but Victoria was astute enough to recognise an opportunity when it presented itself. Successful though *Pat and Margaret* had been, it still narked Victoria that she had missed out on breaking into cinema. *The Full Monty*, which also saw a resourceful bunch of friends stripping, had been a global hit and the story of the WI calendar had the potential to be a similar cinematic success.

Victoria entered into negotiations with the women to turn their story into a film, but she had not reckoned on a rival that even she could not compete with. Five of the eleven women wanted Victoria to do the film, but the remainder, including Angela Baker, signed up with Buena Vista, part of the Walt Disney Corporation.

One of the pro-Victoria brigade, Moyra Livesey, explained that Victoria's offer was financially far superior and would have resulted in a quintessentially English film. Expressing her disappointment at Disney's triumph, she said: 'People's feelings about how they are going to be portrayed come into it. Also Disney is not as "altruistic", shall we say, as Victoria Wood was going to be. Victoria was interested in the fact that all the money for the rights was going to charity. She had never come across that before. We had long talks with her and although there was no script we really liked what she was suggesting.'

Defending the decision to opt for Disney, Tricia Stewart said: 'The film is not so much about how much money we get upfront, but about how widely it is distributed, it has to be a success . . . and although we thought hard about Victoria Wood you have to go with you instincts.' Rather than risk being publicly beaten, Victoria withdrew her offer.

Obviously it was the missed opportunity to extend her fame internationally that disappointed her, not the lost financial rewards. Even without the film deal she earned £1.32 million in 2000, making her the eleventh highest earner in television. The money was made from *dinnerladies*, video sales, the £25,000 she charges for each 45-minute corporate performance (expenses and hotel fees are extra) and the commercial voice-over work she began accepting for such products as McVitie's Chocolate Digestives and Dyson cleaners.

Years of practice have enabled Victoria to skilfully bridge the dichotomy between being a private person and a public performer and nowhere is this more evident than in television interviews. In print journalism, where there is no live audience for her to play to, determined and patient interviewers have elicited glimpses into her private life. But once she is in front of a camera, she is extremely careful. Put bluntly, she uses her television appearances to promote her product. And when there is no new video, series or book to plug, she goes on automatic pilot and simply rehashes her stage act, employs an old song or trots out familiar anecdotes. Even when she was afforded the honour of having a whole *Parkinson* programme devoted to her in March 2000, she remained rigid. What could have been a revelatory *Face to Face*-style interview was disappointingly predictable. A glimmer of danger and moment of potential revelation – when Michael Parkinson asked for her mother's view on her success – was expertly side-stepped when Victoria gave the deadpan reply: 'I haven't told her'. The eruption of laughter from audience and interviewer created an effective diversion from any serious comment and the dismal relationship between Victoria and her mother remained unexamined.

In May 2000 Victoria presented *Don't Panic! The Dad's Army Story*, a 50-minute documentary about the situation comedy for the BBC to commemorate the 60th anniversary of the formation of the Home Guard. Thorough as ever, her research saw her watching forty episodes in one week, admiring the craftsmanship of writers Jimmy Perry and David Croft and sobbing at the sentimental scenes.

Later that year she enjoyed a double success at the British Comedy Awards. *dinnerladies* actually beat *The Royle Family* as the Best Comedy Programme, and although Victoria lost out to *The Royle Family*'s Sue Johnston in the Best Comedy Actress category, she did receive the Writer of the Year Award.

Jocularly acknowledging her troubled past she announced: 'I have been very lucky because when I was in my early twenties and I was very depressed and solitary and obsessive and overweight I met my husband who was exactly the same, so then there was two of us.' And, as if to prove that she could not be hurt or scarred by her history, she said: 'I'd like to thank my father cos he made sure I had the three things I needed as a child to become a writer: I was lonely, unpopular and bored.'

She continued to demonstrate her writing talents with a one-off sketch show which she co-produced. Victoria's reliance on television for inspiration reached its zenith with her Christmas Day 50-minute show for the BBC, *Victoria Wood With All The Trimmings*. Every sketch was either a parody of a television programme or a send-up of an oft-televised classic film such as *Brief Encounter* and *A Christmas Carol*. To present this she played a version of herself arriving at the BBC rehearsal studios to make her Christmas special. From the outset she firmly established her credentials as being Everywoman by arriving on a bus in a duffel coat.

Like her audience she is baffled by the bombardment of digital television programmes and adopted the persona of the down-to-earth, unspoiled, slightly bemused Northern woman surrounded by lunatics from an industry she seems to have accidentally stumbled into.

No sooner has she arrived than she discovers the making of her show will be filmed for the new digital channel, 'BBC Backstage'. She quickly learns of other new BBC digital channels (Upmarket, Downmarket, Newmarket, Makeover, Takeover, Good Old Days) and of the 'Mini-dig Viewer's Choice Micro Channels' (Wartime, Daytime, Tea-Time, Braindead and Knitwear). Along with digs at the BBC management's obsession for titles (we meet the 'Head of Christmas Decisions, Moral Dilemmas and Biscuit Supplies' and the 'Head of All-Weather Outdoor Seating') and mockery of television focus groups, the cumulative effect was one of Victoria, the embodiment of Common Sense, decrying the decline in television standards. As she says to a CCTV camera in the toilet:

'If I trip I'll be on *Auntie's Bloomers*, if I break a leg I'll be on *Hospital Watch*. If I come in here for a wee I'll be on Channel 4. If I don't have a wee I'll sneeze and wet myself and that will be part of BBC2's Incontinence Night!'

The entire show was a series of parodies exemplifying the fictitious digital channels which Victoria found out about at the beginning. There was a puzzlingly dated parody of the 1996 film *Brassed Off* under the 'BBC Upmarket' banner, which satirised all things Northern and in which Victoria indulged herself by jemmying in a silver band to perform with.

'BBC Wartime' was represented by a Second World War morale-boosting newsreel in which Victoria and Julie Walters played indomitable Cockneys in The Blitz. It was followed by 'BBC Knitwear', which applied the sensibilities, style and syntax of *ER* to the Women's Institute – perhaps a mildly sarcastic commentary by Victoria on the WI's business saviness in light of the failed film project.

'BBC Tea-Time' was a parody of *Brief Encounter* with a lesbian resolution, and 'BBC Braindead' allowed for a blisteringly cruel and extremely funny attack on docu-soaps in general and *The Cruise* in particular. The channel also saw Hannah Gordon mocking her own *Watercolour Challenge* show.

'BBC Good Old Days' sent up the Billy Cotton Band Show with Victoria and Anne Reid playing pianists Hilary and Valerie Mallory. Speaking in posh Received Pronunciation for the cameras, they bicker in Northern accents when the audience cannot hear.

Typifying 'BBC Upmarket' was a parody of a period costume drama. *Plots and Proposals* was tired, unoriginal and smacked of indulgence. The finale of the show was a would-be satirical song about Ann Widdecombe with Victoria playing the politician. Bland and banal, it seemed the only humour Victoria could mine from it was to make fun of Widdecombe's oversized figure.

Acknowledging the ghosts of Christmas TV past, Victoria included a skit on 1970s, right-wing comedians and a high-kicking Angela Rippon.

For once there was no need for the usual high density celebrity namedropping as the show was physically peopled by the famous.

Disappointingly for Victoria, her show failed to make the Christmas top ten. With ratings of less than 9.72 million it was a sobering lesson for her, especially as Caroline Aherne's 30-minute Christmas episode of *The Royle Family*, which immediately followed *All The Trimmings*, was the eighth most watched programme that Christmas.

More bad news came three days after the show was broadcast, when an embittered Bob Mason returned to haunt Victoria by going public about their relationship for the first time. The *Mirror* was the chosen mouthpiece through which he criticised Victoria for talking about what a rat he had been in interviews and in her act.

'The backlash seemed to start when she started to become very famous. It was like: "Right, now I've got the power – I can use it",' he said.

'I feel sorry for her to have carried that pain for all these years. It's been hard for me, too, because she's never forgotten it and nobody likes to be reminded with so much vitriol of their mistakes.

'I know I hurt her, but it must be hard to be nearly 50 years old and still not be able to forgive.'

CHAPTER 17

FORGIVENESS was not something that mattered in Victoria's relationship with her mother. Helen's lack of interest in her was all Victoria had ever known; it was just the way things were. It was not the ideal mother–daughter relationship but Victoria had grown immune to the situation.

Helen died in 2001. 'She faded away quite peacefully,' Victoria explained. 'She suffered from osteoporosis and had a hip replacement, but her femur kept snapping. She was so worried about it she didn't want to get out of bed. So she decided to stay there and gradually she stopped taking an interest in the outside world. She stopped reading. She just dropped off, really.'

The death of a parent naturally leads to reflection and Victoria came to partly understand why Helen was the way she was. 'I realised she was hugely clever and creative and she should not have been a housewife. If she'd only gone out to work, we would all have been a lot happier. Being in the house drove her mad. She hated housework . . . She was full of energy and batting against the walls with it. And this gave me a real sense that you had to have your own life.'

Once again Victoria put this philosophy into practice and announced another huge stage tour. It was scheduled to begin in May 2001 but had to be postponed when she had an emergency hysterectomy necessitated by painful fibroid growths in her womb. 'I wanted to delay the operation until after the tour, but they said if I did I'd spend most of my time back in casualty,' she said. After seeing three different specialists to gauge her options, the highly controlled Victoria had to concede defeat and the tour did not actually begin until July.

The 62-date stage tour, which began in 2001 and continued with a further 23 shows in 2002, served to remind the nation of just how good a live performer Victoria is, though one suspects selling out venues no longer represented much of a challenge or held the same thrill for her.

'I just thought I'd give it one more crack, thinking I might really enjoy it if I didn't have to do it any more, instead of just getting through it,' she said.

At It Again – a title that hinted at the new smuttier onstage Victoria – was a wake-up call to those who had forgotten the saltiness of her early material. The bawdy jokes and routines were something of a surprise to her newer fans.

'I think everything has moved on,' explained Victoria of her decision. 'If I did what I was doing five years ago it would seem quite mild. I'm just responding to the climate.'

Gynaecology, which had been a staple part of Victoria's act since the beginning, featured heavily. Almost the entire first half of the show was devoted to the saga of her hysterectomy. If anything, she went into too much detail, but it displayed a remarkably open approach to matters she would have once considered private and off-limits.

'This [the show] is very based on what actually happened to me. I wasn't scared to do it any more. I wasn't trying to hide behind something. I've got nothing to prove and I wanted to grant myself the freedom to talk about what I wanted to talk about.'

She was equally upfront about her eating disorder, which she once treated as a guilty secret. Even her 'strange relationship' with her mother, whom Victoria partly blamed for her problems, was referred to. 'I don't think I've ever revealed this much about myself on stage,' she said. 'But there's a fine line between being honest about things that have happened to you and letting people into your personal life.'

After the interval, when fans could buy such *Acorn Antiques* merchandise as teapots and Mrs Overall rubber gloves, the second half opened with Victoria in the guise of Stacey Leanne Paige, the Jane McDonald parody she first introduced in her Christmas 2000 television special.

Sluttish, shameless, untalented, egotistical and Northern (Stacey is from Radcliffe and proud of it), it was a viciously funny send-up. However, there was an uncomfortable feeling that as with her mockery of Debbie McGee, Victoria was setting her sights on easy and rather safe targets.

Back in Victoria Wood mode, she went into a lengthy routine about physical decline and the frustrations of middle age. Amidst this densely structured and expertly delivered piece there was an amusing detour into her failed attempt to be a perfect mother (on a day trip to East Anglia she ends up taking her children to the Tungsten and Ball-bearing Experience).

The show, which earned her the 2001 British Comedy Award Best Stand-up title, ended with a character monologue by the predictably named Pat. She was Victoria's third incarnation as a keep fit instructor, following in the steps of Madge and Hayley Bailey. Like so many of Victoria's creations, Pat was Northern, vulgar and an unprepared public performer.

Perhaps the most significant feature of the show was the way Victoria jettisoned the security of songs. Musical numbers had always punctuated her live act and in the early days they formed the main body of it, but now there were just two musical numbers. Neither of these was performed in her 'Victoria Wood' persona; instead it was Stacey Leanne who belted out the torturous power ballad 'Filling My Hole' and the singalong 'Shagarama'. It was a sign of Victoria's total confidence that she abdicated from the piano stool for the first time in her career and handed over keyboard duties to Nicholas Skilbeck.

The show resulted in some of Victoria's best ever reviews. 'A wonderful evening of shared humanity and joy in the company of the funniest woman in Britain' said the *Daily Mail*. In the *Observer* Stephanie Merritt described the show as 'a sustained two hours of brilliant material and unflagging energy'. And the *Daily Telegraph's* Charles Spencer praised material 'that is as humane as it is hilarious'. The *Guardian's* Brian Logan, on the other hand, was disappointed that Victoria relied as heavily on 'cheap scatology' as she did on perceptiveness.

'I admired the comic construction while feeling deflated by the low-horizoned world view that the routine propagates,' he wrote. 'There's nothing here to challenge anyone's cosy sense of England as a place of eccentricity, self-deprecation and mild social ineptitude. This is well-worn – too well-worn – Wood territory. It's time for something new.'

Industrious as ever, Victoria managed to fit in more television work despite touring commitments and, in October 2001, she presented two one-hour BBC documentaries charting the history of the sketch show from its origin in music hall to the present day.

The *Dad's Army* documentary she had presented a year earlier had received a favourable response from the critics, but their reaction to *Victoria Wood's Sketch Show Story* was much different. 'A deeply unsatisfying programme', 'Just another easy-on-the-brain, easy-on-the-budget anthology of comedy favourites' they wrote.

The documentaries were rather superficial canters through the development of the sketch show with contributions from such talking heads as John Cleese and Julie Walters. Victoria penned and performed in a couple of sketches in which she deftly deconstructed the comedy sketch, but the real treat was a new episode of *Acorn Antiques* in which Mrs Overall was shot by armed robbers.

Victoria was credited with presenting duties only and the programme suffered from such a limited input by her, prompting Christopher Matthew to remark in the *Daily Mail*: 'Her comic genius was imperceptible and the script could as easily have been delivered by a speak-your-weight machine.'

Victoria's operation and tour meant that her most ambitious project to date had to be postponed. The previous year, while travelling through the West End in a taxi, Victoria was amused by the thought of a poster advertising *Acorn Antiques: The Musical!* Aside from private amusement she was aware of the commercial potential of such a venture, reasoning 'it was the strongest brand in my back catalogue.'

Sir Trevor Nunn, who had previously written a 'very encouraging' letter to her, was enthusiastic when she went to the National Theatre to pitch her idea and there was a tentative plan to stage it at the National for Christmas 2001.

Victoria's 26-year relationship with Geoffrey came to an end in the autumn of 2002. Since Victoria admitted she had not seen it coming, it can be assumed that Geoffrey instigated the separation. Indeed, within four months of him moving out he was photographed kissing his tour manager, Helen Morris-Brown.

For Victoria, who had always believed they would go on 'until we were 99', the end of the marriage forced her to re-assess her celebrated powers of perception.

'You look back at the good bits and the bad bits and you think, were the good bits that good?' she said. 'You churn the whole thing over and oh, it's exhausting, trying to make sense of something that, in the end, you can't make sense of. But it shakes your perception of yourself on a really basic level. You think of yourself as part of a couple, and then you're not. It takes getting used to. . . . And what's odd is, the person that you are most intimate with is the person you cannot discuss this terrible situation with.'

Failure had become an alien concept to Victoria and experience had shown her that *her* way was the right way. However, the break-up saw her expressing a rare humility.

'I take a lot of responsibility. If I fucked up, then I bear the consequences,' she said. 'I don't feel hard done by. I've felt very guilty about my part in it. I felt a failure, completely. That's quite hard to live with. If you're quite a punishing sort of person anyway, then: woah, you've suddenly got the biggest mallet to whack yourself over the head with.'

An overly analytical person at the best of times, Victoria examined and re-examined herself, eager to find a cause for the disintegration of the marriage. She had viewed their togetherness as a 'loyalty pact' but realised that the assumption had led to a degree of complacency, which enabled them to behave in a worse way than if they were less sure of the strength of the partnership.

She also faced the unwelcome fact that she had inherited certain negative traits from her mother. 'There was lots of yelling,' she said. 'I became a replica of my mother, acquiring her short temper. I started to put myself in the same situations and picked up her patterns of behaviour. I'm not happy about that. I shouted a great deal – not at the children – but I did argue a lot with Geoffrey. We set each other off.'

Therapy once again helped her to deal with the upset and she was assured that her grief was perfectly normal. 'Normally it's irritating not to be unique,' she said, 'but in this case it was a huge comfort to me.'

Victoria had always intended to retire when she reached 50 but embarking on a new life as a middle-aged single woman seemed to propel her career onwards. Her previous disappointments and unhappiness served as inspirations and motivations and the end of her marriage may have done the same. Shortly before the shock separation she was in danger of being content – the enemy of ambition. Over the years she had shed her insecurities and neuroses, changed her physical shape and cauterised any unwelcome emotional entanglements. She went from being a cuddly curiosity to a fiercely professional and polished performer. But along the way she lost some of the messy humanity that allowed her to empathise so well with all those other disorderly, frustrated and unfulfilled lives. The raw, chain-smoking overeater who often stayed in bed for fourteen hours at a time certainly made mistakes, but she also possessed an endearing clumsiness and a warmth that later became absent.

Her 50th birthday signalled the shift up a gear. Far from locking herself away and giving in to depression and doubt, she threw a large all-female party for friends. It was at this party that she first mentioned the *Acorn Antiques* musical to Julie Walters, who responded enthusiastically.

In her youth, Victoria dealt with disappointment, rejection and failure by comfort eating and retreating into a slothful mode. In early 2003 however, she chose physical exercise to help divert her focus from the end of her marriage and began a twelve-week training programme for a marathon walk with her friend, the actress Harriet Thorpe.

The Playtex Moonwalk appealed to Victoria's sense of the ridiculous and her zeal for fitness. The night-time 26-mile charity walk involves around 15,000 women wearing bras trekking through the streets of London to raise money for breast cancer charities.

She had successfully completed the walk the previous year and gladly threw herself into it again. Hoping to publicise the cause she wrote, presented and was the executive producer of a subsequent 30-minute ITV documentary. The documentary was notable for Victoria's first prime time use of the word 'fuck', representing a more relaxed attitude to her cosy public persona. 'We're doing this for our breasts,' she told the assembled walkers. 'It's doing fuck all for our bunions but never mind!'

Work had always been an outlet for the adult Victoria and by the summer of 2003 she had completed the book and the music for *Acorn Antiques: The Musical!* It was not yet public knowledge and when interviewed Victoria only revealed she was writing a musical about the lives of four women.

During the same year she also wrote and filmed a BBC documentary on a subject that was very personal to her. *Victoria's Big Fat Documentary* was a well-researched, intelligent and thought-provoking piece of television and the two-part, two-hour documentary shown in January 2004 was aptly timed to give food for thought to those embarking on a new year diet.

The project saw her investigating the dieting industry – 'If dieting works you'd only have to do it once, wouldn't you?' – exploring the reasons behind eating disorders and looking at how people can be exploited and shamed because of their weight. Victoria enlisted an eclectic mix of interviewees for the documentary, including Nigel Lawson, Anne Diamond, Rosemary Conley and Johnny Vegas. Although she gave the UK marketing manager of SlimFast a thorough grilling (perhaps to avenge all the years she had glugged the drinks), Victoria was excessively sympathetic in an interview with Sarah Ferguson, overlooking the fact that the former Royal is a highly-paid ambassador for WeightWatchers.

In the second of the two documentaries Victoria travelled to LA in the hope of finding a more radical and forward-thinking approach to the weight issue. In a scene reminiscent of an early *Wood and Walters* sketch she went in pursuit of a 34-inch waist pair of trousers from an upmarket boutique. She also took part in a workout with camp aerobics guru Richard Simmons, interviewed a Hollywood casting director, interviewed the singer Carnie Wilson about her gastric bypass and celebrated with a group of over-sized belly dancers.

Far from being cynical about her visit, Victoria reported that her preconceptions about American 'happy fatties' were blown out of the water. 'They're not happy because they're fat; they're fat because their lives have damaged them and they have taken a decision not to waste any more energy in changing their bodies but put it into enjoying themselves . . . that's what I would like to pass on, all that energy, all that confidence, that affirmation that we are okay, we do deserve to be here.'

She summed up with the advice: 'If life gives you a belly – go dancing!'

Victoria said she did not write *Acorn Antiques: The Musical!* with the intention of having Julie, Celia Imrie and Duncan Preston in the cast.

She claimed it did not occur to her that they would want to be in it and that she assumed she would have to recruit people from musical theatre.

Julie tends to turn down West End offers because they take her away from her family. She was offered the chance to reprise her Oscar-nominated role of the dance instructor for the stage musical version of *Billy Elliot* but rejected it so she could don Mrs Overall's pinny once more. There were conditions though. She insisted on a maximum of six shows a week. Victoria, who originally had no intention of appearing in the show ('It's not really what drives me, being on stage with a wig on') solved the problem by offering to play Mrs Overall on Monday nights and Wednesday matinees

Once Julie registered her interest, Celia and Duncan quickly signed-up. The three confirmed their commitment after a two-week workshop of the musical in the February of 2004, but the only problem was finding a time when both Julie and Sir Trevor Nunn would be available.

Victoria spent the spring and summer doing rewrites of the show, taking on board what had been learned from the workshops. She somehow found time to film a cameo as Queen Mary II for the film *The League of Gentlemen's Apocalypse*. Jokily comparing her screen time to Dame Judi Dench's in *Shakespeare In Love*, Victoria reasoned that she too could be up for an Oscar.

Up until November *Acorn Antiques: The Musical!* was still without a West End venue so there was much relief when word came through that the Theatre Royal Haymarket would be available. *Acorn Antiques* was open for business. And what a lucrative business it would turn out to be. The £2million show broke the record for the most expensive West End theatre tickets, but in doing so attracted negative publicity.

Group Line, Britain's largest independent supplier to bulk purchasers, and Lashmars, a founder member of the Society of Ticket Agents and Retailers, both refused to sell the tickets on the grounds that bulk-buying was too much of a financial risk. Agents claimed they were told they would be charged a £4.75 booking fee on every transaction if they did not buy tickets in advance.

Group Line managing director Simon Warwick complained that making ticket agents buy in bulk at high prices meant they took all the financial risks.

He said: 'It isn't so much the price – it's the concept of the partnership between producers and agents starting to break down, when they ask you to take the risk. An insurance broker doesn't underwrite the business. The insurance company does that. If we are buying the tickets, we are taking the risks. If Phil McIntyre thinks he can get that price, then good for him. But I think it is expensive.'

Warwick added: 'We've had very few requests for the show and, when we have, people have said "you must be joking" and walked away from it.'

Lashmars, a founder member of the Society of Ticket Agents and Retailers, also decided not to sell tickets for *Acorn Antiques: The Musical!*

Carol Lashmar said: 'We've been asked to pay an additional booking fee. That means that either we don't make any money on the tickets or, if we add our own booking fee, the ticket price becomes ludicrous for our customers.'

Defending the decision, Phil McIntyre spokesman Paul Roberts pointed out that the high ticket price was due to the fact that the 888-seat theatre was significantly smaller than many other West End venues.

He said: 'I think you have to look at the whole ticket range. Everything has been done to make it as accessible as possible. The cheapest price is in line with the rest of the West End. I think Victoria Wood and Trevor Nunn would have liked the ticket prices to be lower. I would have liked them to be higher but it's all about compromise.'

When asked her views about the frustrations of an audience that might want to see both herself and Julie in the show, Victoria simply suggested they could buy tickets to see both versions of Mrs Overall.

Mindful of accusations that she could be deemed to be exploiting the goodwill of original *Acorn Antiques* fans, Victoria stressed that the show would be so much more than a longer version of the television episodes and bridled at suggestions that it was a 'revival'.

'It's a completely different idea because *Acorn Antiques* was a series of sketches and this is a full-length show,' she said. 'You can't just rely on audiences knowing the original; you've got to engage them all over again.'

She added: 'It's useful to have such well-established material, but that guarantees nothing. I see a lot of musicals and some of them are real shockers. I know people's expectations are high; we've done everything in our power not to disappoint them.'

Sir Trevor Nunn, who had won praise for directing recent revivals of *Oklahoma!, South Pacific* and *Anything Goes*, attempted to give gravitas and legitimacy to the enterprise and stated: 'Satirising the second-rate has always gone down well with British audiences. Victoria is a clever satirist – she understands the awfulness that's at the heart of a lot of modern culture, and she knows how to make it funny. The concomitant of that is that she's also aware, in a melancholy way, of change. A lot of *Acorn Antiques* is about missing the old days, a nostalgic delight in the awfulness of those times. It's about fear of progress.'

Five years after the original idea for the musical, the cast and production team got together for the first time in the December of 2004 to begin rehearsals. The show, with a 20-strong cast playing 46 characters, was Victoria's most ambitious project yet. The three-hour-long musical was to preview from 31 January (almost 20 years to the day that the first episode aired on *As Seen On TV*) and then run from 9 February until 21 May. Despite the controversy over ticket prices, advance sales were good.

Victoria was on such a high that, on the advice of her therapist, she temporarily stopped her sessions and instead allowed herself to enjoy the experience of working with friends and colleagues. And having learned from the mistakes of her past she allowed herself time off during the ten day Christmas break and indulged herself by watching episode after episode of her beloved *Frasier*.

One of the reasons Victoria's career has endured is because of her resolute refusal to latch onto fashionable comedy trends. 'I don't know much about comedy, it doesn't interest me that much, I just like doing it,' she said. 'I care very much about what I do and I don't really care what other people do.'

The results of such single-mindedness have buoyed her self-belief and despite her indifference to the fashions and fads of British comedy over the past three decades she has remained firmly rooted in the public consciousness. In the first few years of the new millennium *As Seen On TV* was voted the best sketch show ever by *Radio Times* readers. The same publication also named her the best stand-up comedian of the last fifty years and the funniest woman on TV. And she and Julie Walters were awarded the Outstanding Achievement Award at the British Comedy Awards 2005.

Such popularity undoubtedly interests Victoria, but it is no longer something the actively strives for out of a desperate need for validation. She was philosophical when she was beaten by Billy Connolly in a MORI poll to find out Britain's favourite living comedian and was equally untroubled when she was placed 27th in a Channel 4 poll of more than 300 comedians, writers and producers to find 'The Comedians' Comedian'.

But she was genuinely moved when BAFTA honoured her with a tribute in February 2005. Friends and colleagues were out in force to celebrate her achievements with presenters Richard E. Grant and Julie Walters describing her as 'a living legend' and 'massively generous'. In addition to clips charting her career there were filmed tributes from Richard Curtis, Dawn French, Jennifer Saunders, Michael Parkinson and Eric Sykes.

Ted Robbins, one of the contributors, (and the warm-up man from her *Wood & Walters* days at Granada) described Victoria as a 'shy show-off' and this held true because Victoria was too shy and embarrassed to watch her tribute out front. Perhaps this was a hangover from having a mother who believed it was wrong to give praise. Instead, she watched it on a monitor backstage with only her make-up artist for company. When she did appear on stage to acknowledge the standing ovation and accept her award from Julie Walters in character as Mrs Overall, Victoria wittily avoided sentimentality by explaining: 'I did start watching it and then I couldn't watch it because somebody said that UK Gold were doing a back-to-back bumper *Bargain Hunt*.'

The BAFTA tribute cannily ended with the *Tip Top Tap* number from *Acorn Antiques: The Musical!* Victoria engineered a more blatant advertisement for the show by writing and presenting a 50-minute documentary on the making of the musical, which she sold to ITV. It was something of a luvvie fest with everyone singing each other's praises but, significantly, it was co-produced by Phil McIntyre Television and Blue Door Adventures Ltd. The latter was Victoria's new production company and its name was inspired by the Blue Door Theatre Company from *The Swish of the Curtain* – the book which had so influenced Victoria 45 years earlier.

Victoria said the musical was a completely different idea, not just an extended episode of *Acorn Antiques*. Presumably she was referring to Act 1 which saw the principals of the axed soap joining Sutton Coldfield Light Operatic Society in the Enoch Powell Arts Centre. Their pretentious and megalomaniacal director (Neil Morrissey) intends to turn the show into something 'incredibly subversive', a post-apocalyptic holocaust of a play.

In actual fact Victoria recycled some of her material – some a quarter-of-a-century old. Earnest, politically and socially aware theatre was satirized in both 1980's *Good Fun* and the *To Be An Actress* documentary insert in *As Seen On TV*. And the concept of a musical inspired by an unlikely source material had been done in *Whither The Arts?* another *As Seen On TV* spoof documentary which looked at the making of *Bessie!*, the Bessie Bunter story.

At one point in Act 1 Morrissey's character states: 'My vision is my scalpel'. The character is almost a direct lift of Jim Broadbent's pretentious playwright in *Staying In*, one of Victoria's 1989 playlets. He too believes he is a visionary who uses theatre to attack middle-class complacency and declares: 'My pen is my scalpel'.

A conveniently timed windfall (echoes of *dinnerladies*) allows Bo Beaumont (the 'actress' playing Mrs Overall) to sack the director and take *Acorn Antiques* in its original form into the West End.

Act 2 of the musical was what an expectant public paid for – the set of the shop drew applause. It was the familiar and well-loved *Acorn Antiques*, complete with missed cues, fluffed lines, injury, haemorrhoids, ludicrous plots and the added bonus of musical pastiches (even though Mrs Overall's hilarious song about the merits of macaroons and cups of tea over sex was strongly reminiscent of 'Handicrafts' from *Good Fun*). A more vampish Miss Babs was revealed, Duncan Preston as Mr Clifford was blatantly out of the closet and there was a new Miss Berta in the form of Sally Ann Triplett who, thanks to the shock revelation of a third sister, actually found herself playing a triplet.

The cast acquitted themselves well but Julie Walters was the undoubted star of the show. Whether she was urging the audience to say it believed in 'undemanding, middle-brow entertainment' a la Tinkerbell, or ruining the pace of a showstopping dance number with her contorted gait.

The idea of *Acorn Antiques* as a West End musical was amusingly surreal but once it got a hold, the surrealism snowballed. Royal photographer Lord Lichfield was soon photographing Mrs Overall for a *Radio Times* front cover and in the Laurence Olivier Awards 2006 the show received three nominations. It was nominated for Best New Musical, Julie Walters was nominated for Best Actress in a Musical and Celia Imrie was nominated – and won – for Best Supporting Performance in a Musical.

The show was a success with the public and while it garnered some hugely positive reviews, some critics were less enthused.

'Wood is as sprightly a lyricist as she is a dramatist, composer and everything else,' wrote Benedict Nightingale in *The Times*. 'The result is mischievous, good-natured, charming. But a comic masterpiece? Not really.'

Victoria's motives were questioned by Chris Bartlett in the *Stage* who wondered whether she was embracing the genre or simply attacking it. He described the show as: 'a two-hour skit based on a series of five-minute ones' but praised 'some wonderful set pieces'.

The BBC's Mark Shenton criticised the 'desperately over-extended' show for being 'Filled out with weak pastiches of musicals from *Les Mis* and *Company* to *A Chorus Line*'.

'In trying to be a backstage cross between *Crossroads* and *The Producers*,' he wrote, 'it unfortunately doesn't become about the making of bad theatre but a piece of bad theatre itself.'

The harshest critic was the *Guardian's* Michael Billington who described the show as: 'a load of slack, self-indulgent rubbish scandalously overpriced' and 'a pitiful waste' of Victoria's talents. 'Sending up the second-rate,' he wrote, 'always smacks of smug condescension and camp.'

Director Nunn did not escape censure: 'He has failed to ruthlessly cut and edit a sprawling, inchoate piece that doesn't know when to stop.'

Billington highlighted the unoriginality of the idea, pointing out that shows and plays such as *Noises Off*, *A Life In Theatre*, *Forbidden Broadway* and even *The Pirates of Penzance* had already mined all of the jokes. And done them better.

Despite the mixed critical reaction, the public loved the show and mindful of the financial opportunities, Victoria decided to take the musical on a seven-month nationwide tour taking in 24 cities and scheduled to begin in Salford, Greater Manchester, in December 2006. Confident of her abilities, she decided to extend the challenge and replaced Sir Trevor Nunn as director.

Although ticket prices for the touring show were more affordable than the West End show, it remains to be seen how the production will fare with the absence of the show's original principals. Without the pull of Julie Walters et al, the work will be judged purely on the quality of the writing and the staging, perhaps resulting in a truer evaluation.

During the West End run of *Acorn Antiques: The Musical!*, and despite the fact that she was performing twice-weekly in it herself, Victoria did not forget her more altruistic obligations. The musical meant she had to reduce her involvement in the 2005 Comic Relief fundraiser, but she still managed to pen special episodes of *The Archers*, which aired over five days. During that time celebrities Ewan McGregor, Liza Tarbuck, Sir Ian McKellan and Stephen Fry each had a slot to argue their case that they should be the celebrity chosen to appear in the Friday episode. Stephen Fry won the public vote and found himself in an Ambridge where a homicidal Jill Archer was worried about his request for some special marmalade. Stephen arrived with his entourage (which included McGregor as his aromatherpaist, Tarbuck as his bodyguard and McKellen as his cranial osteopath) and neatly solved all the villagers' problems.

Such commitment once again demonstrated that Victoria was never one to limit her talents. Indeed, her career has been marked by having more than one thing 'on the go'. She learned this from her father's example and it was also a reaction to the fallow earlier years of her career.

Victoria said the 2001 stage show would be her last. 'I've got things in me that can't necessarily be encapsulated in a stand-up show,' she explained. Her documentaries and the musical were evidence of this, but Victoria yearned to produce something that married creativity with depth. She had always gravitated towards writing about 'the little people', those who led quietly unspectacular lives, so the real-life war diary of a Cumbrian housewife was ideal material for her.

She had been given Nella Last's diary years before and had always thought it was a fantastic story. Nella, a Barrow-in Furness housewife, married to a shop-fitter and joiner, began her diary in 1939 as a volunteer for the Mass Observation Archive. This was set up to record the views of ordinary British people and recruited volunteers to observe British life, and diarists to record day-to-day account of their lives.

The diary expressed Nella's thwarted hopes and small frustrations about her lot in life. 'If I could choose,' she wrote in August 1940, 'I'd like to be a man when I "come again". Men do seem to get the best out of life. All the responsibility and effort, all the colour and romance.'

Such lives lived out of the spotlight are a gift to Victoria who not only wrote the ITV drama but also took the lead role. It is often forgotten that she is a trained actress, but her performances in *Talent* and *Pat and Margaret* showed that she can tap into a seam of understated melancholy and subtlety.

Filming of *Housewife 49* began in the summer of 2006. The story followed Nella as she struggled to come to terms with her difficult marriage and her sons growing up and no longer needing her.

Victoria said of the drama: 'This is not the war of the newsreels – it's about tiny domestic difficulties, chilly church halls, lumpy custard. And Nella is fighting her own war, one that she hopes will end in liberation.'

EPILOGUE

SEVEN years away from becoming a pensioner, Victoria shows no signs of slowing down. But career aside, it seems that at last she will be able to experience some of the enjoyment she missed out on as a teenager. Single, financially secure with a daughter, who is now a woman herself, and an adolescent son, a large circle of friends and living in the capital, Victoria has the opportunity to enjoy life. It has taken many years, but she has finally realised the importance of living for the moment.

'I was always planning ahead, saying "When I'm 50, I shall do this or that",' she said. 'I have learnt not to do that and I am much happier. Living in the present, you actually experience things, rather than always thinking or worrying about the next thing. I used to be perpetually anxious . . . I have been too perfectionist about lots and lots of things, too rigid. It doesn't work, it just rebounds on you. You are constantly fighting a losing battle if you say that life only works if I do this and this and this. Then the minute one piece falls away, you feel that you've failed. That's the terrible snare of perfectionism. You can never be perfect, so you are always struggling.'

Although she is hopeful she will find love and someone to share the remainder of her life with, the prospect of dating terrifies her. 'When I was at university, you just slept with each other. There was no dating involved. You just . . . had sex. Then I met Geoff, and that was that. I was in a big relationship, and it went wrong. And that's why I've not wanted to do anything about another relationship.'

Will she retire? It seems unlikely as there are still so many projects she wants to do. Ironically, she endures as England's Everywoman, articulating the thoughts of millions even though she herself admits: 'Sometimes I have to think: what would a normal person do? I don't always know.'

SOURCES AND ACKNOWLEDGEMENTS

Principal printed material cited and quoted:

BOOKS

Brown, Pamela. *The Swish of the Curtain* (Thomas Nelson and Sons Ltd, 1941).
Hind, John. *The Comic Inquisition, Conversations with Great Comedians* (Virgin Books, 1991).

PERIODICALS AND NEWSPAPERS

Anon. 'The "New Face" of stardom for Victoria'. *Evening Mail*, Birmingham, October 1974.
Anon. *Manchester Evening News*, June 2006.
Anon. 'Our love has taught me how to laugh'. The *Mirror*, July 1996.
Anon. *Rochdale Observer*, September 1968.

Appleyard, Bryan. 'Victoria Wood: leaving the one-liners behind'. *The Times*, January 1982.
Appleyard, Bryan. 'As seen over the digestives'. *The Times*, October 1986.
Bamigboye, Baz. 'Victoria's line to success'. *Daily Mail*, September 1990.
Bartlett, Chris. *The Stage*, February 2005
Billington, Michael. *The Guardian*, February 2005.
Bonner, Hilary. 'Funny Girl'. *Daily Mirror*, November 1986.
Bourke, Kevin. 'Send her Victoria!' *Manchester Evening News*, July 1996.
Bowyer, Alison. 'Star's jibes are no joke for Bob'. The *Mirror*, December 2000.
Briscoe, Michael. 'The girl who made a fat friend the most unlikely heroine'. *Daily Mail*, August 1979.
Brooks, Richard. 'Growing out of Acorn'. The *Observer*, November 1989.
Clarke, Steve. 'The light-hearted subversive'. *Daily Telegraph*, December 1994.
Clarke, Steve. 'Changing track on Victoria's lines'. *Evening Standard*, September 1994.
Connolly, Ray. 'A childhood: Victoria Wood'. *The Times*, October 1989.
Cunningham, John. 'Game for a laugh'. The *Guardian*, October 1983.
Dickson, E. Jane. *Radio Times*, February 2005.
Dickson, E. Jane. 'Victoria's plum role'. *Daily Telegraph*, September 1994.
Donnelly, Gabrielle. 'Let's face it, I just love showing off'. *Woman's World*, February 1987.
Duncan, Andrew. 'He's the man who makes Victoria laugh . . . and love'. *Woman's Own*, December 1989.

Edgecombe, Mervyn. 'I've practically given up the idea of a family'. *Woman's Own*, November 1986.

Etherington, Jan. 'The magical world of "The Soprendos" '. *TV Times*, January 1982.

Freeman, Carole. 'How it all went wrong for a New Faces hit'. The *Star*, Sheffield, November 1978.

Gannon, Louise. 'Victoria is not amused by slimming'. *Daily Express*, September 1991.

Gannon, Louise. 'Victoria's happy tale of babes in the Woods'. *Daily Express*, December 1992.

Glass, Susan. 'Life's pure magic keeping my Queen Victoria amused'. *Today*, June 1990.

Goodwin, Judi. 'A girl with talent'. *Manchester Evening News*, May 1980.

Grice, Elizabeth. *Daily Telegraph*, September 1996.

Hardy, Frances. 'There's no knocking Wood'. *Daily Mail*, January 2005.

Highfield, John. The *Star*, Sheffield, September 1990.

Jagasia, Mark. 'Victoria in a jam over calendar girls of W.I.'. *Daily Express*, March 2000.

James-Glover, Ian. *Sunday Mercury*, May 1974.

Jardine, Cassandra. 'I am much happier now I'mnear50'. *Daily Telegraph*, May 2003.

Kingsley, Hilary. *The Times*, September 1994.

Kon, Andrea. 'Babe and the Wood'. *TV Times*, December 1988.

Lane, Harriet. 'Victoria's Secrets'. *The Observer*, January 2005.

Levin, Angela. *YOU* magazine, June 1993.

Marks, Cordell. 'Hot shot Victoria is aiming for the top'. *TV Times*, August 1979.

Middlehurst, Lester. 'Learning to be a Quaker has given me a new outlook on life'. *Daily Mail*, November 1998.

Middlehurst, Lester. 'Victoria is still amused'. *Daily Mail* Weekend magazine, September 2001.

Nightingale, Benedict. *The Times*, February 2005

Paton, Maureen. 'Farewell Victoria'. *Daily Express*, October 1986.

Pearce, Garth. 'Pals who are helping Victoria to shine'. *Daily Express*, January 1985.

Pearson, Allison. 'Seriously funny'. *Daily Telegraph* magazine, November 1998.

Peregrine, Anthony. 'Victoria, Queen of humour'. *Lancashire Evening Post*, April 1986.

Picardie, Ruth. 'Comedy'. *Evening Standard*, September 1993.

Power, Eithne. 'Taking comfort in a bag of chips'. *Sunday Times* magazine, July 1985.

Pratt, Tony. 'Victoria queens it over the men'. *Daily Mirror*, May 1980.

Rampton, James. 'Victoria Wood: as not seen on TV'. *Independent on Sunday*, March 1996.

Reade, Brian. 'Victoria Hollywood'. The *Mirror*, June 1995.

Rees, Jasper. 'Victoria has the last laugh'. *Daily Telegraph*, September 2001.

Robson, David. 'Funny Girl'. *Sunday Times* magazine, March 1980.

Rouse, Rose. 'Mending her woes'. The *Guardian*, May 1996.

Search, Gay. 'Woodwork'. *Radio Times*, November 1986.
Simpson, Val. 'I'm tired of saying bye-bye to my babies'. *Daily Mail*, September 1994.
Shepherd, Rose. 'Touching Wood'. *Sunday Times* magazine, September 1990.
Sheridan, Peter. 'Educating Julie'. *Daily Mail*, January 1982.
Smith, Alistair. *The Stage*, December 2004.
Smith, Rupert. *The Guardian*, February 2005
Summers, Sue. *YOU* magazine, August 1994.
Sweeting, Adam. 'All joking apart'. The *Guardian*, August 1994.
Wallin, Pauline. 'It was a doddle milking the cows . . . just like breast-feeding really'. *Today*, March 1995.

The help and co-operation of the following institutions is gratefully acknowledged:

BAFTA
BBC
Birmingham Library
Birmingham University
British Film Institute
British Library
Bury Grammar School (Girls)
Bury Library & Archives
Bush Theatre, London

Central Library, Manchester
Crucible Theatre, Sheffield
Duke's Playhouse, Lancaster
King's Head, London
Newspaper Library, London
Octagon Theatre, Bolton
Phoenix Theatre, Leicester
Press Association
Theatre Museum, London

Although this is an unauthorised biography I have conducted two interviews with Victoria Wood in a journalistic capacity and have had several interviews with Christopher Foote Wood for the *Bury Times* newspaper.

I am also indebted to:

Billy Armstead
Clive Barker
Eric Bentley
Graham Bentley
Gail Branch
Joe Dawson

Adam Ellis
Cyril Farrer
Kevin German
Alan Haydock
Graham Howarth
Lindsay Ingram

Robert Jackson
Diane Leach
Annabel Leventon
Joan Lloyd
Gerry McCarthy
David Morton
Andy Roberts
Janet Robinson

Dave Roscoe
Norman Rushton
Peter Skellern
Graham Spencer
Chris Taylor
Hilary Wills
Joan Wood

Every effort has been made to trace, seek permission and acknowledge those holding the copyright to material used in this book. Any omissions will be corrected in future printings.

Neil Brandwood, September 2006

INDEX